VENI † VIDI † TRUCIDAVI

CAESAR
THE KILLER

Imagine a book about an unnecessary war written by the ruthless general of an occupying army—a vivid and dramatic propaganda piece that forces the reader to identify with the conquerors and that is designed, like the war itself, to fuel the limitless political ambitions of the author.

James O'Donnell
"Introduction", *The War for Gaul: A New Translation*

Master statesman or master demagogue, superman or supercharlatan, Caesar has fascinated twenty centuries of the European mind. I recall remarking casually to a well-known scholar that T. Rice Holmes had been bewitched by Caesar, and receiving the reply? *Wen hat er nicht bezaubert?* [Who hasn't he charmed?]

John H. Collins

In that man were combined genius, method, memory, literature, prudence, deliberation, and industry. He had performed exploits in war which, though calamitous for the republic, were nevertheless mighty deeds. Having for many years aimed at being a king, he had with great labor, and much personal danger, accomplished what he intended. He had conciliated the ignorant multitude by presents, by monuments, by largesses of food, and by banquets; he had bound his own party to him by rewards, his adversaries by the appearances of clemency. Why need I say much on such a subject? He had already brought a free city, partly by fear, partly by patience, into a habit of slavery.

Cicero (*Philippics* 2.116; Oct 24, 44 BC)

VENI † VIDI † TRUCIDAVI

CAESAR THE KILLER

A Man Who Destroyed Nations So He Might Be King

DENNIS SULLIVAN

VENI, VIDI, TRUCIDAVI: CAESAR THE KILLER, A Man Who Destroyed Nations So He Might Be King

Copyright © 2023 by Dennis Sullivan

All rights reserved. No part of this book may be used or reproduced in any form, electronic or mechanical, including photocopying, recording, or scanning into any information storage and retrieval system, without written permission from the author except in the case of brief quotation embodied in critical articles and reviews.

COVER ART — Swiss artist Charles Gleyre's 1858 painting "Les Romains passant sous le joug" ("Romans passing under the yoke") from the Musée cantonal des Beaux-Arts de Lausanne. Depicted is the humiliated Roman army of Consul Lucius Cassius after suffering defeat by the Helvetian (Tigurini) chief Divico in 107 BC at the Battle of Burdigala (modern-day Bordeaux).

BOOK DESIGN — Meradith Kill | The Troy Book Makers

Printed in the United States of America

The Troy Book Makers • Troy, New York • thetroybookmakers.com

To order additional copies of this title, contact your favorite local bookstore or visit www.shoptbmbooks.com

ISBN: 978-1-61468-796-2

DEDICATED TO

Professor Charles Anthony Giglio

and

All the great Latin and Greek Teachers

of

The Classical Association of the Empire State

Who labor in the vineyards

of

Liberalissimae Artes

CONTENTS

Dedication v
Preface ix

LIST OF ILLUSTRATIONS
Portrait of Julius Caesar viii
Map of tribes in Gaul during the first century BC xxiv
Roman soldier stabbing barbarian woman during war 20
Coin depicting temple of Clementia decreed for Caesar 74

1: CONVENING A GRAND JURY 1
2: BEGINNING IN MEDIAS RES: THE SLAUGHTER OF TWO NATIONS 9
3: IN PRINCIPIO: THE SHOT HEARD ROUND ALL OF GAUL 21
4: STANDARDS OF JUSTICE BY WHICH TO ADDRESS CAESAR'S CAMPAIGN
    OF TERROR 37
5: MANGO MAGNUS DECAPITATORQUE: THE GREAT SLAVE-TRADING
    DECAPITATOR 47
6: BEFORE GOING ON: WHAT DID CAESAR SAY HE WAS UP TO?
    THE COMMENTARII 59
7: HISTORY SAYS CAESAR WAS NOT NATURA LENISSIMUS 75
8: THROAT-SLITTING AS A SHOW OF MERCY? 83
9: TERRORIZING AN OLD MAN WITH A DEATH SENTENCE 91
10: THREATENING TO DELETE A PERSON FROM HISTORY 99
11: TRYING OUT MASSACRE AT AN OUT-OF-TOWN VENUE 109
12: POMPEY OFFERS A MODEL OF EFFECTIVE STRUCTURAL CHANGE 117
13: L'ÉTAT C'EST MOI 125
14: AFTERWORD 141
15: EPILOGUE 151

References 161
Bibliography 289
Acknowledgments 313
Author Bio 314

PORTRAIT OF CAESAR completed toward the end of his life. Known as the Tusculum portrait or Tusculum bust, it was discovered around 1825 but not determined to be Caesar until the Italian archaeologist, Maurizio Borda, confirmed the identity in 1940. The features are consistent with Caesar's image on the denarius struck in 44 BC by the Roman moneyer Marcus Mettius to commemorate the politician's fourth installation as Dictator. Paul Zanker (p. 302) Professor of Storia dell'Arte Antica at the Scuola Normale Superiore in Pisa, describes the dictator's features as: "We see a long neck with folds, an extremely projecting back to the head, a hollow and partly bald forehead, the spare hair combed forward over it." The Roman historian Velleius Paterculus (2.41) said, Caesar was, *"forma omnium civium excellentissimus,"* that is, "he surpassed all his fellow-citizens in beauty of person."

PREFACE

I MUST BEGIN THIS TOME WITH A SEEMINGLY OFFBEAT CONFESSION. After having spent several years living in the world of Julius Caesar, I came to the conclusion that the twenty-first century personage who reminds me most of Caesar is Donald Trump, the former President of the United States. Both were addicted to power and both sought to gain and keep that power as a political dictator. At least in Caesar's case, for now, that ambition was fulfilled.

There were vast differences between the two men—exit Trump stage right—in that Caesar was a man of intelligence, culture, class, and education, and otherwise a paradox of the greatest proportions. And a great part of that paradox had to do with a highly complex personality that at its core turned out to be no more than a "one-trick pony." How many times did the great Roman orator Cicero exclaim that the trick was to become a king and impose his vision of a good society on Rome and all her dominions? Indeed Plutarch says (*Caes* 4.8) that Cicero was "the first to see beneath the surface of Caesar's public policy and to fear it, as one might fear the smiling surface of the sea, and who comprehended the powerful character hidden beneath his kindly and cheerful exterior . . . [and] that in most of Caesar's political plans and projects he saw a tyrannical purpose." Thus, anyone who has spent time with

Gaius Julius Caesar knows, it is a highly challenging chore to assemble the pieces of the puzzle of how his personality came to manifest itself in his own, and in his nation's, destiny.

First of all, for a certain segment of Rome, Caesar was a man of immense popularity. Plutarch (*Caes* 4.4) says he "won a great and brilliant popularity by his eloquence as an advocate, and much good will from the common people for the friendliness of his manners in intercourse with them, since he was ingratiating beyond his years." The instances of such gratuities are multitudinous. He could move a crowd, he could shame an army into action, indeed a myth arose that he was clement by nature.

When Caesar became *curule aedile* in 65, he walked into a job that required insuring that Rome's streets were cleaned and kept in good repair, that grain and water were distributed regularly, that markets operated honestly, and that public festivals were celebrated in a way that pleased the man on the street. Every public aedile wanted to curry favor with the populace but Caesar was willing to go deep into hock to ingratiate himself, indeed shattered all norms of extravagance. With "theatrical performances, processions, and banquets," Plutarch (*Caes* 5.6) tells us, "he washed away all memory of the ambitious efforts of his predecessors in the office. By these means he put the people in such a humor that every man of them was seeking out new offices and new honors with which to requite him." Not only did he decorate, as Suetonius says (*Div* 10.1), "the *Comitium* and the Forum with its adjacent basilicas, but the Capitol as well, building temporary colonnades for display." Gradually "the people would be glad to have him triumph over all opposition and be the first man in the state." (Plutarch, *Caes* 6.7)[1]

What distinguished Gaius Julius Caesar from other aediles and fellow nobles working their way up the ladder of the *cursus honorum*,[2] was not simply his extravagance in the "bread and circuses" arena but that he engaged in intellectual pursuits that caught the attention of learned men like Cicero. Following in the footsteps of his live-in boyhood tutor, the grammarian Marcus Antonius Gnipho, he produced a two-volume grammatical work on the Latin language *De Analogia* which he dedicated to Cicero for reasons to be discussed elsewhere. What boggles the mind is not that he was able to accomplish such a feat but that, as Suetonius says (*Div* 56.5), he penned the work "while crossing the Alps and returning to his army from Hither Gaul, where he had held the assizes." Critics such as Marcus Cornelius Fronto (*De bello Parthico*, 9), himself a grammarian of note, thought such an assessment insane: how could a man pen such a work while "bullets" whizzed by his head?[3] It was and remains part of the aforementioned Caesarian paradox; with Caesar, one always has to look twice, at the very least, to discover the truth.

When Pliny the Elder looked, he saw a man (*HN* 7. 91) who had the most "innate mental vigor . . . [a] native vigor and quickness winged as it were with fire." He "used to write or read and dictate or listen simultaneously," Pliny says, "and to dictate to his secretaries four letters at once on his important affairs—or, if otherwise unoccupied, seven letters at once."[4] Plutarch reminds us (*Caes* 63.7) that on March 14, the day before his death, during dinner at Marcus Lepidus's house, "Caesar chanced to be signing letters."[5]

And this kind of dedication was not limited to administrative matters. On the battlefield, even as a young man not yet 20, a heroic act brought Caesar the much-respected *corona civica*, an honor bestowed on a soldier who had saved the life of a fellow citizen in the line of battle.[6] His heroics occurred during his very first tour of duty during the Siege of Mytilene in 81. The inquisitive mind begs for details.

Years later, when his army was engaged in a see-saw battle with the Nervii tribe he, as commanding general, took up a shield and headed to the front lines. He says in his own record of the event that, (*BG* 2.25.2), "The rest of the men were tiring, and some of the rearmost ranks, abandoning the fight, were retiring to avoid the missiles; the enemy were not ceasing to move upwards in front from the lower ground, and were pressing hard on either flank. The condition of affairs, as he saw, was critical indeed, and there was no support that could be sent up. Taking therefore a shield from a soldier of the rearmost ranks, as he himself was come thither without a shield, he went forward into the first line, and, calling on the centurions by name, and cheering on the rank and file, he bade them advance and extend the companies, that they might ply swords more easily." The goddess Fortune, his favorite, was looking down upon him as a guardian angel might.[7] Indeed, one can say his cup overflowed with luck until the fateful Ides of March.

Again, how paradoxical that a military giant in the order of the great Alexander was the first to envision a public library for the City of Rome. Although his friend and the consul of 40, Gaius Asinius Pollio, oversaw the construction of the cultural emporium years after Caesar's death (between 39 and 28 BC), the idea had been first broached by Caesar himself. Suetonius (*Div* 44.2) says he wanted "to open to the public the greatest possible libraries of Greek and Latin books, assigning to Marcus Varro the charge of procuring and classifying them."[8]

And because he was always looking for ways "to put the condition of the state in order" as Suetonius (*Div* 40.1) notes, he used his authority as *pontifex maximus* to bring the Roman calendar into harmony with the cycles of the sun. Plutarch (*Caes* 59.5) says he, "laid the problem before the best philosophers and mathematicians and out of methods of correction which were already at hand compounded on one which was more accurate than any." Among those he assembled were the esteemed Alexandrian Greek astronomer and peripatetic philosopher Sosigenes and the *scriba* Marcus Flavius who himself had written a text on astronomy.

Denis Feeney, a classics teacher at Princeton, suggests (p. 197) that the ideological underpinnings of Caesar's grammatical text and the calendar came from the same source, that is, it was the, "Caesarian regulating and ordering urge at work in the reform of the calendar as in the grammatical work On Analogy which argued for the same kind of systematizing appropriate to the Latin language: Caesar was seeking a kindred harmony between nature and grammar and between nature and the calendar."⁹

University of St. Andrews classics scholar Lindsay G. H. Hall (p. 28) goes a step further by suggesting that Caesar's rules for grammar were the ideo-linguistic counterpart to military warfare, the dictator seeking to produce a Latin that acted as "ringfences against contamination by obvious rhetorical baggage or alien artistic ornament... [thus the need for] "imposing linguistic order on the world against rebarbative tribesmen ... two sides of the same intellectual and ideological coin." And when Caesar started essentially Rome's first newspaper and gazette, the *Acta Diurna*, the proceedings of the Senate were published there to have senators' words written in stone and put before the public without duplicity. It was part of his long-considered populist agenda.¹⁰

Ringfences against contamination or not, even the anti-imperialist poet Lucan in his *"Pharsalia"* or *"De Bello Civili"* artistically projected Caesar as a thinker of merit. In lines 178-181 of Book 10 he portrays the general as an inquisitive ethnographer in love with truth (*amor veri*). And although he describes Caesar as a thunderbolt (*fulmen*) he envisions the dictator sitting at a banquet with the Egyptian sage Acoreus questioning him about Egypt's history and calendar. He desires to know about the country's geography, customs, rituals, the appearances of the gods and inscriptions on ancient shrines. He tells the priest that, if he could find all there was to know about the flow of the Nile, he would give up waging war on his fellow Romans. And yet, his desire for glory never allowed him to grasp the cultural genius of the nations he warred against; to have done so, he would have shot the apex of his *cursus honorum* in the proverbial foot.

And given what Plutarch said regarding Caesar's ability to "work a crowd," endearing himself to the populace, with or without bread and circus, one would think that such a quality translated into him having a cadre of supportive friends. But the reality was quite different in that Caesar had no real friends to speak of. He was successful in making alliances and opportunistic connections with individuals but those "friends" were never, as University of Glasgow's Catherine Steel notes, "part of a consistent or permanent group. He formed no lasting alliances, nor any documented close friendships, at least not with other men." Even his most trusted lieutenant, Titus Labienus, a tactical genius who had charge of the Roman army when the commander was absent (serving as the general's *legatus pro praetore*), broke with his superior in 49 when Caesar crossed the Rubicon. More than a few accused Labienus of being a deserter but William Tyrrell says (1970, p. 36) such was not the case, that Labienus "joined the legitimate government in its struggle against a revolutionary proconsul who placed his own *dignitas* above his country." Cicero labeled the defection (*Fam* 16.12.4) "a very severe blow in the fact that Titus Labienus ... declined to be a partner in his crime."[11]

But there are instances, however few, that show Caesar as a friend to a friend in need, especially in the case of his secretary and manager of his private affairs, Gaius Oppius.[12] Suetonius says, (*Div* 72.1) when Oppius, "was his companion on a journey through a wild, wood country and was suddenly taken ill, Caesar gave up to him the only shelter there was, while he himself slept on the ground out-of-doors."[13] A quite possible scenario for, as the late French historian Gérard Walter (p. 93) says, here was a man who once took a "taxi" everywhere he went throughout the City of Rome and now "rode for hours and hours through almost impassable roads on a spirited and restive charger which he managed with extraordinary ease. He, who felt ill at ease as soon as the buckle of his belt was fastened a little tighter than usual, now donned a superb and massive cuirass [breastplate] of which he readily bore the weight and pressure and which henceforth would be an integral part of his favorite dress. He, who never dared touch his hair for fear of disarranging its artful style, now exposed it all day long to the wind and sun and did not trouble to hide his ever-increasing baldness from the gaze of his soldiers ... [he] stripped himself of all the old habits which might hinder the unbridled race toward glory."

And for some associates, even Caesar's treasonous take-over of the government was not a cause for severing their relationship with him even in their memory. In a letter to Cicero (*Fam* 11.28.2) five months after Caesar's death (*August* 44), Gaius Matius declares his continuing love for the assassinated dictator saying, "I am well acquainted with the allegations made against me since Caesar's death. People blame me for showing grief at the death of a dear friend, and expressing my indignation that the man whom I loved had been killed. For they say that country should be preferred to friendship, as though they had actually proved that his death has been beneficial to the Republic. Well, I will speak frankly. I confess that I have not attained to that height of philosophy. For in the political controversy it was not Caesar that I followed, but it was a friend whom—though disapproving of what was being done—I yet refused to desert. Nor did I ever approve of a civil war, nor of the motive of the quarrel, which in fact I strove my utmost to have nipped in the bud."

And the esteemed historian, statesman, and overseer of the first library, Asinius Pollio, in a letter to Cicero in March 43 says (*Fam* 10.31.4), "To Caesar, indeed, who regarded me as one of his oldest friends, though he had not known me until he had reached his own splendid position, I was attached with the utmost devotion and fidelity. What I was permitted to do in harmony with my own opinion I did in such a manner as to procure the warmest approbation of all the best men."

It is amazing that, even in the twentieth century Caesar continued to have supporters who saw no fault in him or his stars though, even in their praise, point to the general's tragic flaw. The late British historian Thomas Rice Holmes in his legendary *Conquest of Gaul* (p. 59) recalls that, "Caesar was neither vindictive nor cruel" but then adds, "to those who defied him, and especially to those who broke faith, he was absolutely ruthless." Ruthless? Maybe that's what Sallust meant (*Cat* 54.4) when he said, "for himself he [Caesar] desired great power, the command of an army, and a new war in which his talents might be displayed." They were all part of Caesar's vision to create a well-oiled Caesarian world order; early on he had something in mind.

And, his modus operandi in displaying those talents, as Dio (38.11.5) suggests, "was not so much concerned about what had already happened as he was to prevent future attacks." Thus, he was a preventer-in-chief as well as a pretexter-in-chief. He sought to deter challenges to his authority in his very last days in Gaul with barbaric tactics. In 51, when leaders of the Carnutes prepared Uxellodunum as a fortification to fend off the Roman army, Caesar rushed to the site to take charge personally.

To force the occupants of the stronghold to surrender, he cut off the fortification's water supply. Then, when the enemy was finally captured, as Hirtius says in the final book of *De Bello Gallico* (8.32-44), he "cut off the hands of those who bore arms against him." The preventer-in-chief (8.44.1-2) believed "that there would be no end to his troubles if several states should attempt to rebel in like manner and in different places, [thus he] resolved to deter others by inflicting an exemplary punishment on these." And the handless souls had already surrendered!"[14]

The late social psychologist, Hans Toch (pp. 168-169) described such a person as a "norm enforcer." Toch had developed a typology of violent men ranging from "rep defenders" to "catharting bullies." He said the norm-enforcer was someone who sets himself up as a "one-man posse" and "undertakes the task of becoming the conscience of society." As a "slayer of dragons" he arranges situations "so that he will get in the first blow . . . he goes to extreme lengths to make this move so as to be referred to as an executioner." Norm-enforcers, Toch says, "attack any abuser of power or violator of decency they spot, often without much prior notification" exactly what Dio said about Caesar's tactics.

Cicero says the ideology that informed such acts was operative from the very first days Caesar was in public office. Suetonius (*Div* 9.2) picked up on it when he says, "Cicero too seems to hint at it in a letter to Axius, where he says that Caesar in his consulship established the despotism which he had had in mind when he was aedile."

Perhaps he had in mind Caesar's gathering together 320 pairs of gladiators, 640 warriors, (Plutarch *Caes* 5.9), a military contingent that caused fear in the Senate. But the number turned out to be "somewhat fewer pairs of combatants than he had purposed; for the huge band which he assembled from all quarters so terrified his opponents, that a bill was passed limiting the number of gladiators which anyone was to be allowed to keep in the city." (Suetonius, *Div* 10.2) As the old adage goes: some people love a parade, Caesar loved an army. He loved money, he loved fine things, and he loved an army.

And such fear with regard to this aspect of the future dictator's disposition did not arise without foundation. In 75, when still a private citizen (*privatus*), without legal authority, Caesar raised an army and pursued the pirate gang who had taken him hostage on the open sea; he found the culprits and executed them against the commands of the governor. (Suetonius, *Div* 4.3) The following year, when allies of Mithridates began harassing regions around Rhodes—even though the Senate had dispatched consuls Marcus Licinius Lucullus and Marcus Aurelius Cotta to deal with the Pontic threat—on his own authority Caesar "levied a band of auxiliaries," Suetonius (*Div* 4.2) says, "and drove the king's prefect from the province, thus holding the wavering and irresolute states to their allegiance." Velleius (2.42.2) tells us to keep in mind "he was but a private citizen without authority." And later, when he was preparing to start his campaigns among the barbarians, and felt that the Senate had not fully armed him for battle, "he added to the legions which he had received from the state others at his own cost," that is, he practiced a kind of alternate statecraft. He wanted things to be the way a king wanted them.

Cicero, in his famous Second Philippic speech, delivered seven months after Caesar's death (October 44) reminded Rome that the dictator (116) had, "for many years aimed at being king, he had with great labor and considerable personal danger, accomplished what he had intended."

Even the title of Caesar's book documenting his extended proconsular administration, *De Bello Gallico*, was not only about Gaul but also

Spain, Switzerland, Portugal, Germany, Britain, even parts of Belgium and the Netherlands. Caesar had set himself up as the savior of Rome which Cicero reified in his axial speech *De Provinciis Consularibus* in 56. The counselor argued that Rome needed to give the general carte blanche to continue wiping the barbarian off the face of the earth. Thence, Caesar was formally recognized by his triumvirate cohorts as Rome's official norm-enforcing punisher-in-chief.

Like a modern-day criminologist Dio in Chapter 11 of Book 38 of his history of Rome clarifies Caesar's theory and method of punishment. He says (38.11.3-4) the general "possessed in reality a rather mild nature and was not at all easily moved to anger." And yet, he adds, Caesar "nevertheless punished many . . . Yet in such wise that it was not done in anger nor always immediately. He did not indulge his wrath . . ." which means he did not go off like mad-man Nero "but watched for his opportunity," as Dio says, "his vengeance pursued the majority of his foes without their knowing it." Like a professional hit man with ice water running though his veins, he secured his vision of a just world order à la Caesar as if writ in an *Evangelium secundum Caesarem*.

By adhering to the mandates of such a gospel, to stay with Dio, "he visited his retribution secretly and in places where one would least have expected it, both for the sake of his reputation, in order to avoid seeming to be of a wrathful disposition, and also to the end that no one should learn of it beforehand and so be on his guard, or try to inflict some serious injury upon him before being injured." Underscore: to avoid seeming to be.

Thus, to repeat, throughout his decade-long campaign of terror in Gaul, Caesar remained not so much concerned about what had already occurred as he was to prevent future attacks. His punishment was not only retributive but designed to deter, he was always looking for a pretext to homogenize or neutralize peoples, nations, and dissident souls, defined as living on a lower-plane of cultural existence and demonized as "the barbarian."

Dio goes on, "he took vengeance even beyond what was fitting, with an eye to his own safety." And this had nothing to do with "What was once done [which] he could never make undone by any penalty, but because of the severity of the punishment he would for the future at least suffer no harm." His war on "Gaul" was an unrestrained and continuous act of punishment. He was the perfect storm Rome needed to handle problematic inter- and intra-tribal conflicts that had plagued the City of Rome for centuries. In retrospect one is inclined to conclude that the vicious dictator Sulla was small potatoes compared to his subsequent counterpart. As Appian (2.106.1) notes about the tenor of society after the civil war, Caesar was "feared as no one had ever been before."[15]

Thus, he not only made enemy nations bow down before him to preserve the nation's *dignitas* but bulldozed problematic individuals into groveling submission. Suetonius (*Div* 20.4) reminds us of Cato being "dragged from the House by a lictor at Caesar's command and taken off to prison. When Lucius Lucullus was somewhat outspoken in his opposition, he filled him with such fear of malicious prosecution, that Lucullus actually fell on his knees before him."[16]

Thus it was not Rome's *dignitas* for which Caesar fought but his own, he telling his fellow citizens often enough that, "For him *dignitas* had always been foremost, and more compelling than life" which required him to compel others into servitude and even slavery. When dictator, to protect that *dignitas*, as the late Bryn Mawr classicist, Lily Ross Taylor, notes (1949, p. 174), Caesar "attempted to bind to himself in a kind of superclientele all the senators and citizens alike." Appian (*BC* 2.106.1) reminds us that all "magistrates immediately upon their inauguration should take an oath not to oppose any of Caesar's decrees." And Antony, after Caesar's death, reminded the gathered throng about, Appian (*BC* 2.145.1) adds, "the oath by which all were pledged to guard Caesar and Caesar's body with all their strength, and all were devoted to perdition who should not avenge him against any conspiracy."[17]

Scholars of ancient history have noted that, despite Caesar's intellectual pursuits, he never took to philosophy which is not surprising. Two thousand years later, the great Zen philosopher D. T. Suzuki said, "That's why I love philosophy: no one wins." But Gaius Julius Caesar had to win; there was no room for "other." While "crossing the Alps," Plutarch says, "and passing by a barbarian village which had very few inhabitants and was a sorry sight, his companions asked with mirth and laughter, 'Can it be that here too there are ambitious strifes for office, struggles for primacy, and mutual jealousies of powerful men?'" Whoever the companions were, it is a most interesting musing. Was political conflict inherent in the smallest theatres of social life? Caesar's response to the query was, Plutarch continues, "in all seriousness, 'I would rather be first here than second at Rome.'" And all others, whether Gauls or Germans or Britons—split an ethnic hair if you like—were a threat to Roman stability as defined by Caesar in a special way, that is, toward a dictatorship that allowed the "first" man to impose a vision of social life upon the world that would rival, nay outdo, even the likes of Alexander the Great.

Thus, Caesar's war journal, his *Commentarii*, is filled from beginning to end with explosive catch-phrases that gnawed at the unconscious fears of the Romans. He was a successful propagandist beyond compare. At the very beginning of his campaign of aggression Caesar (*BG* 1.2.4-

5) warns Rome that the enemy could be on the steps of the Forum the following morning "*facile finitimis bellum inferre possunt*," that those barbarian hordes love to make war "*homines bellandi cupidi*," and do so with a chip on their shoulder "*magno dolore adficiebantur.*" In short, they were all (*BG* 1.31.5) "*homines feri ac barbari*," gruesome, ferocious unpredictable animals. And his task in "Gaul" was to fashion their heathen manners according to the dictates of the *ratio Romana* and, when non-cooperative, to neutralize them as he might knock wooden pieces off a chess board.[18] The *De Bello Gallico* says he thought the latter a more lasting solution.

Cicero, a great observer of Caesar up close and from afar, was well aware of the dictator's contradictions as mentioned at the outset. Plutarch (*Caes* 4.9) has him saying, "When I look at his hair, which is arranged with so much nicety, and see him scratching his head with one finger, I cannot think that this man would ever conceive of so great a crime as the overthrow of the Roman constitution."[19]

The fourth-century soldier and historian Ammianus Marcellinus (29.2.18) projected a view of Caesar examining his life when he got old. He begins by saying that in terms of power, "royal power—as the philosophers declare—is nothing else than the care for others' welfare; that it is the duty of a good ruler to restrain his power, to resist unbounded desire and implacable anger, and to know—as the dictator Caesar used to say—that the recollection of cruelty is a wretched support for old age. And therefore, if he is going to pass judgment affecting the life and breath of a human being, who forms a part of the world and completes the number of living things, he ought to hesitate long and greatly and not be carried away by headlong passion to a point where what is done cannot be undone; of which we have a very well-known instance in olden times."

The recollection of cruelty as a wretched support for old age? Was Ammianus suggesting that Caesar would experience a remorse-filled death bed conversion of sorts? When Casca struck the first blow on the fateful morning of March 15, 44 BC, Caesar did not utter, "I deserve this for my war crimes and all my crimes against humanity" but rather, as Plutarch (*Caes* 66.8) says, he shouted something like, "Vile Casca; what is this all about? Have you lost your mind?" Caesar did not see himself deserving a cell in Dante's hell like vile Casca and his band of assassins like Brutus and Cassius. There was no recollection of his cruelty as Rome's greatest, shall we say, Slaughterer-in-Chief. Hence the subtitle of this work: Caesar the Killer. He was indeed a man who massacred nations to see his dream of being a king fulfilled.

To find out what the nature of that cruelty was and how it affected the world of Rome and the tribes Caesar sought to obliterate in her name, *procedamus Galliam in pace*.

For details, see following page.

The map depicts the Roman provinces and tribal groups of the Gallic area in the late 1st century BC. Though the Suebi are not shown here, they were located to the east of the Chatti (shown). Pliny the Elder (NH 4.28) says the Suebi and Chatti were part of a "race" of Germans called the Hermiones. The "clan" or grouping also included the Hermunduri and Cherusci. Tacitus gives the name Suevia to the part of Germany that ran from the Danube to the Baltic; the Romans were familiar with the Suebi for some time having referred to the Baltic Sea as the Mare Suebicum. Describing the confederation, Tacitus (Germ 38) says, "We must now speak of the Suebi, who do not, like the Chatti or the Tencteri, constitute a single nation. They occupy more than half of Germany, and are divided into a number of separate tribes under different names, though all are called by the generic title of 'Suebi.'" As is recorded in the text, they were responsible for ousting the Usipetes, Tencteri, and Ubii from Germany. Strabo (7.1) describes the nation as being nomadic in nature compared to the Chatti and Cherusci in that they "easily change their abode, on account of the scantiness of provisions, and because they neither cultivate the land nor accumulate wealth."

CHAPTER 1

CONVENING A GRAND JURY

If I were to begin an essay on Julius Caesar by declaring that he was one of the great mass murderers in Western history, I suspect a goodly number of scholars of ancient Roman history would rain Zeusian bolts upon my head from the floor of their passing chariot.[20]

Therefore, I will move the declaration into the realm of a testable hypothesis and begin anew: Julius Caesar was one of the great mass murders in Western history and, to determine the truth or falsity of this allegation, I hereby convene a grand jury and summon every reader of this essay to serve as a juror to help render a verdict.[21]

In his relentless aggression against the tribes of Gaul from 58 to 50 BC, which will serve as the basis of the evidence to follow, Caesar engaged in a genocide or ethnic cleansing or war crimes—we will determine which later—of vast proportions to pad the résumé of his *cursus honorum* and secure a place in history like no other. And by vast I mean he slaughtered more than a million during his proconsular administration in Gaul. Ancient historians such as Suetonius say it was because of an Alexander the Great complex he could not shake.[22] The conquest of Gaul was a trophy to parade before the people.

In the twenty-fifth chapter of Book Seven of his *Natural History,* Pliny the Elder provides us with Caesar's corpse count during his provincial administration contending that, "I would not myself count it to his [Caesar's] glory that in addition to conquering his fellow-citizens he killed in his battles 1,192,000 human beings, a prodigious even if unavoidable wrong inflicted on the human race, as he himself confessed it to be by not publishing the casualties of the civil wars."[23] Those are the figures the great naturalist offers.

He also says that Caesar produced that level of ruin during 50 pitched battles, more than any general up to that point in Roman history. He outdid his third-century Roman counterpart, and distant mentor, Marcus Claudius Marcellus, whose résumé of slaughter shows a battle count of 39.

More than 150 years before Caesar achieved his feat, that five-times-elected-counsel, known as the "sword of Rome," had shown his progeny how to successfully thrust the *gladius* of the SPQR into the loins of barbarians, win accolades, and thereby conquer and destroy foreign powers who refused to "negotiate" with Rome on Rome's terms.[24] A sad irony is that historians have described Marcellus as possessing the virtue of *clementia,* as being a man of mercy—which reflects a twisted sense of mercy, a belief that the station and worth of another is equal to one's own.

How odd or contradictory or simply propagandistic that more than a century later, the dictator-to-be also came to be associated with *clementia* and *humanitas,* the Senate going so far as to decree a temple of *Clementia Caesaris* erected to honor his commitment to mercy and forgiveness. Suetonius (*Div* 74.1) says he was clement by nature, *natura lenissimus*: such an unfounded reality; he was not so. He was a politician who forgave when it counted and, when there was no political payoff, it was the way of the big sword of Rome.

Long before Caesar came to turn on Pompey in a civil war for control of the most powerful position in the ancient world, the Romans had created a culture that encouraged—required is truer—all of its officials to wage war as the most direct route to achieving standing in society, moving the *cursus* of their ego along and adding far more than a quid or two to their private coffers. Some give 10 years as the minimum amount of military service to count as anything.

The former Columbia University historian, William Harris, in his landmark study of war and imperialism in the Roman Republic, says war-making became an almost biological necessity for the aristocracy of the city.[25] It is a large claim to be sure but Polybius in a rather incriminating statement sheds light on Rome's drive to wage war on the Dalmatians in 156 BC. He says (32.13.6-8) "their chief motive for action was . . . they did not at all wish the Italians to become effeminate owing to the long peace, it being now twelve years since the war with Perseus and their campaign in Macedonia." By undertaking a new war they would "recreate, as it were, the spirit and zeal of their own troops."[26]

It seems force was the only means the Romans had to solve problems that entangled them, as we see in Caesar's campaign in Gaul and later in his contest with Pompey. With respect to the exercise of power, Polybius says (1.37.7) the Romans, "to speak generally, rely on force in all their enterprises, and think it incumbent on them to carry out their projects in spite of all, and that nothing is impossible when they have decided on it. They owe their success in many cases to this spirit . . ." An incredible indictment of a nation's governing ethic especially when it came to subduing the forever-dreaded bar-bar.[27]

It would be wonderful to have Julius Caesar before us today and force him, so to speak, to take stylus in hand and complete the Minnesota Multiphasic Personality Inventory (MMPI), or some other psychological measure of a person's natural propensities, so we might have an assessment of the psychological dimensions that drove him to compete with Alexander and his contemporary Pompey for the title of greatest conqueror in the ancient world, the heavyweight champion of earth.

The poet Lucan in his epic *Pharsalia* (2.657) offered a peek into Caesar's character when he described the dictator's work ethic, *Nil actum reputans si quid superesset agendum*. That is, "if he thought something remained to be done in a given situation, then he was not done until that was done." Hence, once he started with the slaughter of several hundred thousand Helvetians in 58, he was driven to subjugate every last tribe in Gaul and any other nation or tribe he defined as an imminent threat to Rome's sovereignty—and his personal *dignitas*—his worth in the marketplace.[28]

In Act III, Scene II of his eternally-lauded "Julius Caesar," William Shakespeare has Marc Antony standing in the forum addressing the citizens of Rome. He speaks the oft-quoted and well-known, "Friends, Romans, countrymen, lend me your ears;/ I come to bury Caesar, not to praise him./ The evil that men do lives after them;/ The good is oft interred with their bones . . ."

When a young student first reads these lines, he has to think twice, maybe three times. What does it say about a person's legacy, about how one person assesses another's history? Caesar might have refused the offer to become king or emperor, "the crown," three times but it was not out of concern for aiding the Republic but for enhancing his own political capital—as was the case with many of the offers of *clementia* he proffered to his enemies during the civil war. The complexity is daunting.

Thus, we are not here to re-bury Caesar but to resurrect his bones; we are here not to praise him but to impeach him the way citizens of any country might impeach its first-citizen and leader before a grand jury after they have left office—however retroactive or retrospective that might be. We have come to look at the evil Caesar did and left behind in fields so drenched in blood that, in similar circumstances, the fields of war Rome left behind were referred to as *magna copia*, that is, the flesh of so many bodies had become enriching compost that crops flourished with abundance for ages.[29] If there is good in Caesar with respect to his campaign in Gaul, and even in his early-life ventures, you, Dear Jurors, will find it in his resurrected bones.

When Shakespeare's Antony finishes his honored speech, a bold citizen among the gathered throng yells, "If thou consider rightly of the matter, Caesar has had great wrong." Such ideological nerve. He was saying that, if an honest conscience—like a sworn-in jury—were in charge of assessing Caesar's résumé—a propagandistic definition of "rightly"—we'd see that Caesar got a bum rap. The victimizer was victimized.

One of the other plebeians standing by offers a justification by saying Rome could have done worse, that Caesar was the lesser of two evils: "I fear there will a worse come in his place." We presume he is referring to Gnaeus Pompeius Magnus, Pompey the Great, whose enemies had dubbed him "*adulescentulus* carnifex," "the boy butcher."[30] Of course such a question is moot. Pompey, the loser in a contest of wills and armies, was assassinated four years before Caesar proclaimed himself dictator for life.

Thus, in our assessment of Caesar's acts, Ladies and Gentlemen of the Jury, we are called to fix our eyes upon not only his role as the "*carnifex Gallorum*" but his earlier life as well to see if there were hints about what was in store for Rome and the world at large. Hopefully your courage will supersede that of Caesar's contemporaries who raised not a word of objection as the death-count of the general's campaigns arrived in Rome year after year presumably to the sound of jubilant cheers. As the late Northern Illinois University classicist John Collins (1972, p. 21) says in his brilliant work on our defendant, "if there was a single Roman of the year 58 B. C. who felt morally outraged by the aggression of the proconsul of Gaul, his sensitive conscience has left no trace in the extant sources." And, in terms of Caesar's massacres, that includes his fiercest ideological opponent Cato the Stoic.

So we present our case to your sensitive consciences, dear members of our esteemed panel, so we might produce a bill of particulars detailing Caesar's crimes against humanity or whatever the law says they shall be called. Was he Western Civilization's first great genocidist or is there another more appropriate moniker for this systematic dealer in death? Is it too prejudicial to justice to refer to the defendant, against whom we seek an indictment, as *Imperator Carnifex*?

Plutarch says Cicero knew him best. He (*Caes* 4.8) says Cicero was "the first to see beneath the surface of Caesar's public policy and to fear it, as one might fear the smiling surface of the sea, and who comprehended the powerful character hidden beneath his kindly and cheerful exterior . . . ." Later in his biographical sketch of the dictator (28.3) he adds, "Caesar had from the outset formed this design, and like an athlete had removed himself to a great distance from his antagonists, and by exercising himself in the Gallic wars had practised his troops and increased his fame, lifting himself by his achievements to a height where he could vie with the résumé of Pompey." Indeed, as we shall see, vie even with the envied successes of Alexander the Great. Caesar had an ideal-self he needed to be and an ideal society he sought to create.

There is the old maxim "never say never" but I venture to say we never see the Rome of the Republic negotiate with a nation or tribe—though there were treaties—whose reality differed from its own imperialist principles and cultural standards, and Caesar was the Eternal City's poster boy for transforming that ideology into genocidal warfare. When all is said and done the poster boy's *De Bello Gallico* is actually a confession of guilt.

For now, to play on the words of Cicero (*Brut* 158), "*pergamus ergo ad reliqua et institutum ordinem persequamur in pace.*" Let us proceed then without further digression and pursue the plan we set upon.

CHAPTER 2

BEGINNING IN *MEDIAS RES*:
The Slaughter of Two Nations

THE MOST DIRECT WAY TO ASSESS the nature and extent of Caesar's atrocities during his proconsular administration in Gaul is to jump, as Virgil might say, *in medias res*, that is, into the middle of the story, after Caesar's engine of war was sufficiently oiled and in full operation. Thus, we find ourselves in the midst of the massacre of two German tribes—the Usipetes and Tencteri—by Caesar's legions in the spring of 55. It is not hard to imagine that a simple soul taking a morning stroll down the Via Sacra ever knew such nations existed.[31]

The two tribes ancient historians tell us—as does Caesar himself—had been on the move for three years looking for a new home. They had abandoned their digs on the east side of the Rhine in search of new lands to settle on after being evicted by the formidable and persistently aggressive Suebi tribe whom Caesar (*BG* 4.1-3, 19; 4.10) describes as "the largest and most warlike of all the Germans."[32] Of this eviction Dio (39. 47.1) says "the Tencteri and Usipetes, German tribes, partly because they were forced out from their homes by the Suebi and partly because they were invited over by the Gauls, crossed the Rhine and invaded the country of the Treveri."

As history has shown—and again Caesar joins in—when any foreign tribe crossed the Alps and was unsettled and on the move, especially when the numbers were large, the nerves of Rome were set on edge, some would say neared panic and, to allay their fears, engaged in cathartic pre-emptive strikes.[33] It's somewhat of a generality but, as William Harris has documented, the Romans were not beyond setting up pretexts for war. He says (p. 172) in "handling international relations . . . the Romans were always careful to offer a *pretext* for going to war; they took care not to appear to be the aggressors, but always to seem to be defending themselves and entering war under compulsion." Once the pretext was established, the Romans moved ahead bolstered with a justification that they were engaged in a *bellum justum,* warring for self-preservation. But the just war theory was absent from any of Caesar's considerations when deciding what enemy to create and pursue and eventually annihilate.[34]

Thus, when the Usipetes and Tencteri showed up en masse in Gaul—in the hundreds-of-thousands strong—Caesar says (*BG* 4.6) he felt compelled to take swift action, "for fear that otherwise he might have to face a more serious campaign." The Germans—as he began to refer to them generically—had received some encouragement from "some states . . . inviting them to leave the Rhine, and promising to furnish all things demanded of them." Such kindness Caesar claimed, "encouraged the Germans to range more widely, and they had already reached the borders of the Eburones and the Condrusi, dependents of the Treveri."[35] That is, they had moved too far inland for Rome's comfort.

We might call Caesar the master of the pre-emptive strike and the unbridled transgressor of any ethos that governed peaceful international relations. What Tacitus (*Ann* 13.57) said of German tribes can easily be said of him, that he had "a love of deciding everything by warfare."

Here, as in the study of all legal cases, the facts are critical so we need to take time to understand the events that led to the slaughter. In no way did Caesar meet the criteria that Roman law had established for engaging in a just war.

By 55 the Usipetes and Tencteri had failed to find a suitable place to settle in Germania and headed to the area of the Rhine where the Menapii "possessed lands, buildings, and villages on both sides of the river." As indicated, the German tribes had already wandered "for three years in many districts of Germany ... [until they] reached the Rhine."[36] The size of the caravan was said to be 430,000 strong but again we must always approach such numbers with caution.

When the wanderers reached the Menapii community living on the east bank [German side] of the river they laid siege to the settlement; the besieged tribe fled across the river and set up "garrisons at intervals on the near [west] side of the Rhine ... to prevent the Germans from crossing." Presumably they had moored their boats to docks on the western side of the river to prevent the marauders from using them.

The Usipetes and Tencteri then tried the hidden-ball trick; they picked up stakes and began to leave the area. Upon witnessing this reversal, however strange it seemed, the Menapii cautiously headed back across the river to retake their settlement on the east bank. But the interlopers, in hiding, came back with all due speed and took the Menapii by surprise. After killing many of them (*his interfectis*) they commandeered their boats, crossed the river and seized their dwellings and supplies on the western side of the river to sustain them through the coming winter. We do not know if the killing continued or whether some Menapii escaped but we do know that Caesar cared less for their well-being than for his authority, for he had had strategic encounters with them during his previous two years in Gaul.

Caesar was informed that "the Germans" had crossed the river and were now in Gaul, the territory he had been assigned to oversee for his proconsular administration. He determined it was a matter that required immediate attention. Therefore, in April he left his winter quarters earlier than was his custom "for fear that otherwise he might have to face a more serious campaign" (*BG* 4.6.1) in the future—acting as a savvy preventer-in-chief.[37]

In the meantime, having been encouraged by some Gallic tribes with offers of provisions, the migrant tribes pushed further into the interior having "reached the borders of the Eburones and the Condrusi, dependents of the Treveri." (*BG* 4.6.4) To stop their further advance, Caesar called together the chiefs of several Gallic nations—which ones he does not say—and after he "comforted and encouraged them" requisitioned horse soldiers because "*bellum cum Germanis gerere constituit*," he had made the decision to make war on the Germans. The die of a massacre-to-come had been cast.

With a select group of horse soldiers he headed in the direction where the two tribes were reported to be. The Germans, apprised of the movement of his troops toward them, sent ambassadors (*legatos*), that is, official envoys, to confer with him, informing him that "they had come [into Gaul] against their will, being driven out of their homes: if the Romans would have their goodwill, they might find their friendship useful." (*BG* 4.7.3-4) For a place to live, they were offering themselves as allies.

Fully acknowledging Rome's dominion, they asked if Caesar might consider assigning them sections of land on which they could settle or perhaps he would allow them to stay on the lands they had seized from the Menapii. They assured him that, "the Germans did not take the first step in making war on the Roman people," nor yet, "if provoked, did they refuse the conflict of arms, for it was the ancestral custom of the Germans to resist anyone who made war upon them, and not to beg off." (*BG* 4.7) And their prowess as warriors ought not to be minimized because, "They yielded to the Suebi alone, to whom even the immortal gods could not be equal; on earth at any rate there was no one else whom they could not conquer." (*BG* 4.7.5)

Caesar told the ambassadors that their tribes would never be on friendly terms with Rome as long as they remained in Gaul; they had to leave immediately; there was not enough room for so large a throng without them doing further harm to people and land alike. But he did give them the option of settling with the Ubii on the eastern side of the river, a tribe whose ambassadors happened to be at the moment in Caesar's camp. They too had been harassed by the Suebi and, as friends of Rome, had come seeking Caesar's help.[38] He said he would order the Ubii to find some lands for them to settle on.[39]

The German ambassadors said they would go back to their people and report on Caesar's offer and return in three days; they asked Caesar to not allow his forces to advance any closer to their camp. Caesar would not agree to such a proposal knowing that most of the cavalry of the Germans were out foraging and plundering, thus he considered the request for a three-day waiting period a ruse. It was the general's projection because it was the very same strategy he had used three years before with the Helvetii.

When Caesar's troops were about 10 miles from the German camp, the ambassadors of the Usipetes and Tencteri returned and asked Caesar that he not push ahead further and to send word to his vanguard not to engage in any fighting. They requested three additional days so they might send ambassadors to the Ubii to discuss how they might settle among or near them. Caesar continued to think the offer a ruse believing the enemy were still waiting for the return of their horsemen to bolster their ranks.

He said the best he could do was move three or four miles forward so his troops could have access to water and that they, the Germans, should send a contingent the next day to solidify plans. He says he sent word to his cavalry upfront to take no action until his full army had arrived.

But when the German army, comprised of 800 horsemen, saw a Roman contingent of 5,000 move forward, they—we surmise they believed they were being attacked—engaged Caesar's troops who, he says, were taken by surprise, they thinking a truce had been agreed upon. Caesar said that 74 cavalry—natives from the province—were killed in the skirmish. Among them were two Gallic-born soldiers whose deaths Caesar describes in a melodramatic nationalistic obituary in his commentary to win the hearts of the people back home.

Thus, he decided he was done talking with ambassadors whose army had engaged in the treachery of an ambush; he said any general worth his salt would be crazy to let things go further. The time had come for the Romans to teach the German barbarians a lesson in ambassadorial good manners.

However, "The next morning, as treacherous and hypocritical as ever," Caesar says, "a large company of Germans, which included all the principal and senior men, came to his quarters, with a double object—to clear themselves (so they alleged) for engaging in a battle the day before, contrary to the agreement and to their own request therein, and also by deceit to get what they could in respect of the truce. Caesar rejoiced that they were delivered into his hand, and ordered them to be detained; then in person he led all his troops out of camp, commanding the cavalry, which he judged to be shaken by the recent engagement, to follow in the rear." (*BG* 4.13. 4-6)

First of all, the German leadership had asked Caesar to keep his troops at a safe distance to avoid potentially-dangerous miscues. They were not interested in a fight; they just wanted to find a place to live. Secondly, they had requested time to meet with the Ubii to see if they might settle among or near them. Finally, with respect to adhering to an ethic of fair play (*fides*) in international negotiations, a Roman field general forcibly, and wrongly, imprisoned ambassadors of a sovereign nation during a truce. The *fides in colloquio* concept of Roman law required at a minimum that Romans respect the integrity of the other side especially during a truce. Indeed the Roman concept of *bona fides* did not even allow a tutor to purchase something from a *pupillus* and, if he did and the item came from a *non bona fide* sale, the sale was void.[40] Even at that level of everyday interpersonal exchanges, the principle of justice was stringent

As indicated, however, in Caesar's strategic thinking, the die of war had already been cast. He ordered his troops to set up in the traditional Roman triple-line formation (*triplex acies*) that signaled war was about to begin. With their usual speed, the battalions entered the travelers camp and caught them off guard. They were indeed caught off guard believing their elders were in Caesar's camp peacefully negotiating for lands to settle on.[41]

It was a wholesale slaughter. Caesar's account says only a few of his men were wounded while a goodly number of the enemy, 430,000, were destroyed.[42] That is the number he gives, among whom were the women and children of the two tribes. When the women and children tried to escape, the general ordered his horse soldiers to run them down and slaughter them on the spot.[43] The child-bearers and future warriors of the nations were slaughtered as if soldiers of war.

Victory or not, news of the attack made its way to Rome by courier with headlines shouting that Caesar has slaughtered nearly half a million barbarians and Rome was now a safer place for all to live—and the numbered dead were Germans no less. Again, the vast majority of Romans had never heard the names Usipetes and Tencteri uttered until then.

But, when it was revealed in the Senate that a field general had attacked two nations during a truce, a cadre of Senators considered the tactic to be a serious breach of *fides;* the commander had committed an act that was an affront to the gods and thereby made Rome subject to divine retribution and theoretically less safe.[44]

One group of senators, spearheaded by Marcus Porcius Cato (Cato the Younger),[45] Caesar's greatest political opponent in the Senate, claimed that Caesar's acts were indeed criminal, and evil deeds of that nature were sure to bring the wrath of the gods upon the city.[46] He argued before his colleagues that Caesar be turned over to the remaining members of those tribes and be tried according to their laws of justice.[47] The suggestion was laughed at; indeed the Roman Senate did the exact opposite, decreeing that Caesar be honored with a public thanksgiving, a *supplicatio*, for his success in ridding Rome of another threatening barbarian horde.[48]

And in his melodramatic account of the death of his two-Gallic-born soldiers the day before—Piso Aquitanus and his brother—and the massacre that followed, the wily propagandist delineates who was and who was not a worthy victim. His choice of words for his narrative declares that the lives of those two men were of greater worth than over 400,000 barbarians. By avenging the deaths of two heroes, he was protecting the civilizing force of Roman life. As the classicist Jonathan Barlow (p. 147) has noted, the Gallic-born Piso by being Romanized had "thrown in his lot with civilization." Roman values had heightened his sense of *virtus, fides,* and *pietas*.⁴⁹ Any assault on the civilizing process of Rome needed to be avenged as much as that of the two men he eulogized. His retributive *memoria tenebat* modus operandi, which he debuted three years earlier, was a warning to others not to act so as to put Roman civilization in jeopardy.

To make his account of the massacre more palatable to the Roman ear, Caesar no longer distinguished the tribes by name but referred to them generically as Germans, a people or peoples the Romans feared more than the Gauls, having sacked their city in 390 BC under the leadership of the Senones chief Brennus. No one of any political consequence was allowed to forget the outrage. The Romans nourished their fear and hatred of the barbaric Gauls in the phrase *metus Gallicus,* and their more heightened fear of the Germans in the proverbial *terror cimbricus*. Psychologically the Romans were always looking over their shoulders to see if some tribal version of the Cimbri were at the gates of the city ready to lay waste to Roman lives.

Involved in a mass migration—similar to that of the Helvetii three years earlier whose story is to follow—the Upisetes and Tencteri acceded to Caesar's demands in their effort to find a peaceful solution to the pressing problem of finding a new home (*BG* 4.7.2-5;11.1-3;13.5). No matter how one wishes to view Caesar's immediate assessment of the threat, he was letting Rome know that his response to the mendacious presence of those tribes had saved citizen lives from seeing the dreaded disease called "German" infect their homes and rape their wives and daughters. The picture the late classicist Anton Powell paints is: "Don't excuse the Tencteri and Usipetes: they may have effectively assailed the authority of your own body."

And, as just mentioned, when reports of Caesar's victory—slaughter is the operational word—finally reached Rome, a contingent of senators said Caesar had violated the *fides publica*, the solemn word of Rome. Handing him over, a *deditio*, a concept and practice long familiar to Roman administration of justice was what Rome in such a situation demanded.[50]

When we look at what the ancient historians have to say about the *deditio*, we see Plutarch (*Cato*, 51) reporting that Cato had appealed to the Senate, "when it was believed that he [Caesar] had attacked the Germans even during a truce and slain three hundred thousand of them, there was a general demand in Rome that the people should offer sacrifices of good tidings but Cato urged them to surrender Caesar to those whom he had wronged, and not to turn upon themselves, or allow to fall upon their city, the pollution of his crime."

Cato was imploring the Romans not to celebrate but to "sacrifice to the gods, so that they do not turn the punishment for the general's folly and madness upon his soldiers, but spare the city." Plutarch put those words in quotation marks as if quoting the senator verbatim from some then-extant document. But—and this must be kept in mind—Cato's focus was on the sacrilegious nature of Caesar's defilement of a truce and its implications for the future of Rome, not on the slaughter, the genocidal act he had committed.

Not long after Cato presented his case, a courier from Rome arrived at Caesar's camp informing him how his opponent in the Senate had publicly defamed him. And though still involved in managing barbarian hordes during a war, the general felt compelled to write "a letter which he sent to the senate," Plutarch says, "when it was read, with its abundant insults and denunciations of Cato, Cato rose to his feet and showed, not in anger and contentiousness but as if from calculation and due preparation, that the accusations against him bore the marks of abuse and scoffing, and were childishness and vulgarity on Caesar's part." A war of ideologies was taking place in the Capitol over who Rome's true barbarian was.

Sounding somewhat like a wary Cicero, Cato continues, "it was not the sons of Germans and Celts whom they must fear, but Caesar himself, if they were in their right minds, and so moved and incited his hearers that the friends of Caesar were sorry that by having the letter read in the senate they had given Cato an opportunity for just arguments and true denunciations. However, nothing was done but it was merely said that it was well to give Caesar a successor." That is, that Caesar's proconsular command in the provinces ought to be rescinded.

All of Cato's seemingly pious political posturing, about what steps needed to be taken to deal with a renegade general, might have gained traction but, as Suetonius says (*Div* 24.3), "so great has been the success of his enterprises, that he had the honor of obtaining more days of supplication, and for longer periods, than had even before been decreed to any commander." The Roman hierarchy was celebrating the slaughter of peoples whose emissaries (*legatos*) were engaged in formal negotiations with Rome, a traveling band of foreigners searching for new lands to settle on.

To play on John Collins's acerbic take on the matter, "if there was a single Roman who felt morally outraged by the aggression of the proconsul of Gaul at any time, there is no trace of that person's sensitive conscience in the extant sources." Caesar was a rogue with carte blanche to kill.

Barbarian woman being stabbed in the chest by a Roman soldier while another is led away as a captive. Image is from the Column of Marcus Aurelius in the Piazza Colonna in Rome; photo from D-DAI Rome, institute negative 55.1120 (Photographer: J. Felbermeyer).

CHAPTER 3

IN PRINCIPIO:
The Shot Heard Round All Of Gaul

By the time Caesar engaged the Usipetes and Tencteri in 55, he had already been involved in campaigns of massacre for three years. His proconsular administration was designed to rid Gaul of the Gauls and Germany of the Germans or at least bring them into submission for the purpose of having them pay tribute in the form of manpower and natural resources such as tin and gold—and slaves. Plutarch (*Caes* 15.5) says he took a million or more prisoners and Velleius (2.47.1) that while, "more than four hundred thousand of the enemy were slain . . . a greater number were taken prisoners." At a certain point in his war-making, Suetonius (*Div* 54.2) says, "he had more gold than he knew what to do with, and offered it for sale throughout Italy and the provinces" at cut-rate prices. He went to Gaul a poor man in debt, returned enriched by precious ores and the bloody flesh of the slave trade.

Caesar's choice of particular targets followed a loosely-conceived design he had come to Gaul armed with. The classical historian Tenney Frank says (p. 339) that a plan "was apparently formed early in the first year's work, if not—as is more likely—even before Caesar approached Gaul." And the late French historian Gérard Walter claims (p. 142) that, "Since his arrival in Geneva his whole attitude pointed to the fact that he fully intended to make war." Some believe the attitude manifested itself when he had a dream of Alexander and deemed himself to be a mere miniature when measured against the great Macedonian. Cicero says it began when Caesar was aedile. It is our hypothesis that it began when Caesar, just turning 25, raised an army to punish pirates who had taken him for ransom—and even before that, when he first took up the mantle of his uncle Marius and later his father-in-law Lucius Cornelius Cinna.

In 58, the Helvetii were the first tribe to feel the brunt of Caesar's sting as they, assembled in a great caravan, were in the midst of migrating from Switzerland to southwestern Gaul. As ancient historians have chronicled, they had a long-standing relationship with Rome as formidable enemies. Indeed, some Romans never forgot their defeat of the troops of Lucius Cassius Longinus, and the cause of the general's death in 107, seven years before Caesar was born.[51] At the Battle of Burdigala, modern-day Bordeaux, Longinus and 10,000 of his troops had been handily defeated; the Romans said the brigade was ambushed. The remains of Longinus' army, then under the command of Gaius Popillius Laenas, were forced to surrender a large portion of their supplies to the enemy and then with great shame walk "under the yoke."[52]

Caesar never forgot the massacre for military as well as personal reasons. He says in the seventh chapter of Book I of his commentaries (*BG* 1.7.3), "*quod memoria tenebat L. Cassium consulem occisum exercitumque eius ab Helvetiis pulsum et subiugum missum, concedendum no putabat.*" A loose translation is, "he could not forget that Lucius Cassius, the consul, had been slain, that his army was badly beaten, and the residue [of the Roman army] subject to the humiliation of being put under the yoke like dumb oxen; and that those responsible deserved not the least consideration from Rome."

Although not given the same weight in the literature as his legendary "*alea iacta est*" dictum Caesar's "*memoria tenebat*" was an historical marker because it reflected Rome's and, in this case, Caesar's drive for vengeance no matter how far in the past the injury had been inflicted—and it was up to Caesar to determine how many Gauls and Germans and Britons needed to pay with their lives for the sake of atonement.[53]

If Caesar were among us today and we asked him to translate "*memoria tenebat*" I'm sure he would say, "I could not shake it." "I could not get it out of my mind." "It was driving me crazy." "They had to pay." All we can say is that he could not forget that Cassius and his army had been beaten by the Helvetii and that the barbarians had put the Roman army under the yoke and therefore were not worthy of human consideration, never mind *clementia*, under any circumstances. Caesar said they were a rootless people, hostile by disposition, and given the opportunity, would not be able to restrain themselves from engaging in further outrage and mischief "*temperaturos ab iniuria et maleficio.*"[54]

And on a personal level he was not able to shake off the fact that Lucius Calpurnius Piso Caesoninus, one of the legates of Cassius, was killed in that war, and was the grandfather of Caesar's father-in-law. Thus, a personal vendetta also drove him to rectify the harm-done.

When Caesar came upon the Helvetii in 58 as a newly-appointed proconsul, the tribe had already been wandering for three years. Their movement of course had not gone unnoticed by Rome. Two years earlier (March 15, 60) Cicero, in a sounding-the-alarm letter to Atticus (1.19) says, "for the moment the chief subject of interest is the disturbance in Gaul. For the Aedui—'our brethren'—have recently fought a losing battle, and the Helvetii are undoubtedly in arms and making raids on our province." With respect to what action Rome should take, he adds, "The senate has decreed that the two Consuls should draw lots for the Gauls, that a levy should be held, all exemptions from service be suspended and legates with full powers be sent to visit the states in Gaul, and see that they do not join the Helvetii." It was a martial-law-like call to arms.[55]

Nevertheless, a tribe engaged in such a mass pilgrimage, one lasting for years, was terribly vulnerable whether crossing the Rhine or Alps or from any one district to another. As the late Henri Hubert, a long-time scholar at the Musée d'Archéologie Nationale, (p. 150) notes, "a mass of men large enough to form a whole nation, with women and children, flocks and herds, a great number of chariots, and an indefinitely long train of very primitive wagons and pack animals, was an extremely difficult undertaking."

The Romans were always troubled by the potential threat to their sovereignty that any movement by any tribe at any time posed but they were also concerned about what might happen to lands left vacant by the evacuees. They saw the lands left vacant by the Helvetii as an invitation to troublesome German tribes or other aggressive nations to move in. Thus, the lands the Helvetii left came to be known as "the Desert of the Helvetii," new territory awaiting the much-feared Suebi.[56]

The great Helvetii migration began at least by 61 when the Helvetian nobleman, Orgetorix, made plans to resettle the tribe in southwest Gaul in the land of the Santones on the north side of the Lower Garonne, a tribe that, ages before, had migrated from Germany.[57] There still could have existed shared relatives within the two tribes however distant.

The date given for Caesar's first contact with the Helvetii is March 24, 58 and the number of travelers he estimated to be 368,000.[58] The exact size of the caravan could be determined Caesar says (*BG* 1.29.1-3) because later he had found a register written in Greek among the remains of the Helvetian camp.[59] The document indicated that the caravan was essentially a coalition of tribes: 263,000 Helvetii; 36,000 Tulingi; 14,000 Latobrigi; 23,000 Raurici; and 32,000 Boii. Of the 368,000, it was said that 92,000 were men bearing arms, 25 percent of the total, thus the rest were women, children, elders, and even the sick and infirmed.

It was a permanent move, an all or nothing situation for the migrating nation because, as Caesar tells us (*BG* 1.5, the Helvetii had, "set fire to their strongholds, in number about twelve; their villages, in number about four hundred, and the rest of their private buildings; they burned up all their corn save that which they were to carry with them, with the intent that by removing all hope of returning homeward they might prove the readier to undergo any perils; and they commanded every man to take for himself from home a three months' provision of victuals." And of course, as miners of gold, it is likely that some of their wagons were laden with the precious ore.[60] Such a fact would hardly have escaped Caesar's attention, a spendthrift who suffered from a case of *avaritia*.

In such a vulnerable position the confederation was not looking to start trouble. Géhard Walter (P. 142) seems to have grasped the situation at hand, "the Helvetii showed themselves to be so peacefully disposed there seemed to be nothing to prevent an amicable arrangement which would allow them to reach the end of their wandering without injury to Roman territory."

With winter mostly behind them, they had set out on a trek of about 450 miles, essentially the distance between Montreal and Philadelphia,

Pennsylvania. The starting point was the banks of the Rhone near Geneva. With all their belongings and people of different ages in tow, the tribes planned to be traveling on oftentimes mud-racked roads for at least two months, being able to move, under the best conditions, 10 miles a day.

When Caesar was informed of their departure, he tells us (*BG* 1.7.1-2), he saw the opportunity of a lifetime. He therefore hastened to Geneva with the utmost speed. Plutarch says (*Caes* 17.4) "he drove so rapidly that, on his first journey from Rome to Gaul, he reached the Rhone in seven days. Suetonius (*Div* 57.1) says his army covered "a hundred miles a day."

A Catonian cynic would say he smelled not just the gold of, but the blood of, opportunity, blood that would bring triumph, riches, and glory. Available documents say he requisitioned the greatest number of troops and ordered the bridge at Geneva to be destroyed (*rescindi*).

The Helvetii of course were not without reconnaissance. Hearing word of the governor's coming—what had they heard about the man?—they sent a group of the tribe's most distinguished citizens (*nobilissimi civitatis*)—surely a sign of respect—to meet with him. They told Caesar—which he already knew—that they were on their way to settle on new lands by the Santones and wanted permission to pass through a section of Roman-occupied Gaul. They promised that they would pass through without causing mischief of any kind (*sine ullo maleficio*). They offered no sign that they were in any way the threatening "enemy" Caesar defined them as.

It is here that Caesar enters into his report his famed *memoria tenebat* declaration, and to repeat, words as historically significant as *alea iacta est*. As if in a private Bill of Patriculars he was letting the Helvetii and posterity know that he had not forgotten the 107 BC debacle when the very same Helvetii killed the Roman general Lucius Cassius Longinus, forced his troops, the troops of the greatest nation on earth, to parade before a jeering enemy army like yoked oxen. Plus they had murdered a member of his wife's family. Needing to buy time until the full array of his troops arrived at Geneva, he told the *noblissimi* that he would take their request under consideration; they were to return on April 13. Of course a ruse.

When the envoys did return on the appointed day, they were told that a passage through the province was impossible (*BG* 1.8.4) causing disappointment and dismay to the Helvitii leaders. Not to be deterred they sought the assistance of an ally, the Aeduan chieftain, Dumnorix—a leader with strong anti-Rome sentiments—who managed to gain for them permission to pass through the territory of the neighboring Sequani. They began on the new route on April 26. And, to insure that they would pass through the territory without causing hardship or grief, they did in fact hand over hostages to the Sequani. For the conquering general the decision of the Sequani was a source of great displeasure not only because his plans for a confrontation were being dashed but also because a long time ago the Romans considered the Sequani as friends and allies of the Roman people.[61] They were now acting like traitors to Rome's wishes.

Thus, the seemingly endless caravan now found itself inching its way along the right side of the Rhône below the Jura, headed through the Pas de l'Écluse, about 20 miles downstream from Geneva. The road was so narrow in spots that Caesar says there was scarcely enough room for a single wagon to pass at a time. Estimates are that the caravan stretched for 15 miles.[62]

Despite the continuing disagreement modern scholars have over the length and composition of the wagon train, it is remarkable that several among them readily take the general's side in assessing the intent of the travelers and the effect their journey was having on the well-being of Rome and the nations near the path of the migrating train. Sounding like an advisor in Caesar's army, the Irish-born classicist, Thomas Rice Holmes says (*COG* p. 28), "The ultimate object of the emigrants was to settle in western Gaul, in the fertile basin of the Charente River. Thence they would be able to make raids upon the open corn-growing districts of the Province, and their mere presence would be a standing menace to Roman interests in Gaul." This threat was the pretext Caesar offered for taking up the instruments of war[63] and yet, as the late legal scholar Max Radin has noted (p. 17, 18) the tribe "had been much closer [to Roman territory] in their old lands ... [and] without imminent danger, the strongest statements of his reasons furnished at best a dubious justification." As early as 61, when the Helvetii had begun their journey, Cicero (*Att* 1.19.2) was in a way fanning the flames of war telling his friend Atticus, "fears of war in Gaul are the main topic ... the Helvetii are undoubtedly in arms and making raids on our province." What were his sources?

When the majority of the Helvetian caravan had crossed the Saône and headed toward the land of the Aedui, the latter, using their leverage as a friend and ally of Rome (*socius et amicus populi Romani*),[64] sent a delegation to Caesar asking him to stop the interlopers.[65] Thus, with a quarter of the caravan still on the east side of the river preparing to cross, in the middle of the night Caesar launched an attack, killing most of the travelers, causing the survivors to scatter. Those killed had been fingered as Tigurini, the very tribe history recorded as responsible for killing Lucius Cassius and forcing the Roman army under the yoke. Caesar had performed a retributive surgical strike and, for starters, Rome's thirst for vengeance was being slaked.[66]

The Helvetii must have thought Caesar lost his mind; they were in the midst of treaty negotiations, were *in colloquio*. To seek clarification they immediately sent a delegation to the general headed by one of their respected elders, Divico, which might have been a poor choice. As a young man, Divico was in fact the commander of the army that defeated Cassius and killed the general Lucius Piso as well as the grandfather of Caesar's father-in-law. It was tantamount to waving a red flag in front of a maddened bull. Nevertheless, not wishing to cause any conflict, the tribe was willing to take whatever route Caesar saw fit. (*BG* 1.13.3) Then, with face-saving bravado, they reminded him that they had already beaten a great Roman army and could do it again if they had to. All the maddened bull could bellow now was a resounding *memoria teneret* (*BG* 1.14.1).

Later in a report back to Rome covered in the first book of his *Commentaries*, Caesar informed the principal citizens of the city that he had taught the Tigurini and posterity—we are still talking about it—about the long arm and memory of Rome's retributive powers. In a kind of justificatory curtain-call he says (*BG* 1.12.5-7):

> This canton had in the memory of our fathers marched out from home alone and killed the consul L. Cassius, and sent his army under the yoke. Thus whether by chance or the judgement of the immortal gods, that part of the Helvetian state that had inflicted so striking a calamity on the Roman people first paid the penalty. By this event Caesar avenged not only public *iniuriae*, but private as well [*publicas sed etiam privatas iniurias ultus est*], because the grandfather of his father-in-law L. Piso, the legate L. Piso, the Tigurini had slain in the same battle as they had L. Cassius.

And, he added, the Helvetii were still causing havoc, first by trying to force their way through the Province and then by causing injury to Rome's allies, the Aedui, and their neighbors. He said he would consider a peaceful resolution to the current situation if the Helvetii gave hostages and compensated the Aedui and their neighbors for whatever damage they had done. Of course, a caravan of hundreds of thousands, no matter how well prepared from the start, would require (demand) sustenance from tribes it encountered along the way. They would have been an imposition of some import.

As indicated. Divico's response was—according to Caesar's account—that the Helvetii were accustomed to receive hostages, not to give them, and refused the general's demand for essentially a ransom. With that, Caesar told Divico that negotiations were over, and the tribal leader departed—Caesar not acknowledging that the Helvetii had already given hostages to the Sequani as surety for passing through their lands.

The next day, as the Helvetian caravan continued on its way, Caesar sent a cavalry of 4,000 strong—comprised primarily of Aedui and horsemen from neighboring tribes—to follow at a distance and observe the moving train, but the non-Roman auxiliaries got rambunctious and went at the Helvetii whose cavalry of 500 was able to inflict damage on the Roman contingent of Aeduan horsemen. With a mini-victory of sorts the Helvetii became emboldened and started provoking the Romans to engage them in skirmishes. For about two weeks, as the Helvetii caravan moved at a snail's pace, the Roman army, in a slo-mo-cat-and-mouse pursuit, followed several miles behind.

In the meantime, as the Roman army began to run out of supplies, Caesar boldly reminded the leaders of the Aedui that his army was dependent upon their nation for a regular supply of grain but nothing had been forthcoming, thus the Aedui had reneged on their reciprocal obligations as a friend and ally of the Roman people. They made excuses such as the crop was not ripe yet but Caesar soon learned that intra-tribal conflict among the Aeduan leadership was considerable. One faction openly expressed concerns about the motives and long-range goals of the Romans in Gaul, that the tribe should be wary of continuing to support the presence of an invasive army that had designs on their nation's future—never mind talk of friend and ally. What was doubly galling to Caesar was that, while he was in the midst of carrying on a war in the name of Rome, one of Her staunchest allies was hindering a general's operation. He Caesar berated the leaders of the tribe for reneging on their obligation reasserting that he had come to Gaul and "undertaken the war largely in response to their entreaties." (*BG* 1.16.6) By such reasoning he was shifting the pretext for the massacre-to-come to the supplications of the Aedui.

As the general was pondering how to handle the divisions within the tribe and move on with his plan, a chief magistrate named Liscus came forth to speak to him. Liscus explained (*BG* 1.16-18) there existed within the tribe a pervasive fear that, once the Romans defeated the Helvetii, Caesar and his army would continue their rampage and destroy and/or enslave the Aedui as well.[67] In other words, the Romans were not only a threat to the future of Gaul as a whole but also to the life of the very tribe the Romans called friend and ally. They said the potential threat of the Helvetii moving through their lands paled in comparison to what the potential enslaver-in-chief called Caesar had in mind for them. Thus, the general now had to deal with not only what he defined as an external threat, the Helvetii, but also an internal threat as well, destructive divisiveness within his own coalition.

The magistrate added that he was putting his own life at risk by telling Caesar these things. He said one of the two leaders of the tribe, Dumnorix, a smart businessman with considerable property and influence with the neighboring tribes, detested the Romans because they had helped his brother, Divitiacus, in his rise to power within the nation, thereby thwarting his own designs to be king.[68]

Such information was not idle intra-tribal gossip because, in terms of Caesar's planned military strategy, Dumnorix was in command of the Aeduan horse soldiers in Caesar's army, in fact it was he who started the retreat that caused a panic among the rest of the cavalry.[69] Equally important to know was that Dumnorix was married to a Helvetian woman of prominence, indeed the daughter of the late king Orgetorix who was the mastermind of the Helvetian migration. Caesar viewed himself as having a counter-offensive spy within his own ranks.

Liscus cautioned Caesar though, that if he punished Dumnorix for his seditious posture now, it would appear that his brother was the culprit and the existing divisions within the nation would only be aggravated. Caesar met with Dumnorix and confronted him on the matter, informing him that he would withhold punishment for now and then assigned a contingent of his intelligence unit to keep Dumnorix under constant surveillance.[70] He had in effect put the leader of a sovereign nation under lock and key and, with respect to his military operations, as indicated, was faced with a war on two fronts.

In the meantime the Aeduan cavalry continued to follow the Helvetian caravan at a safe distance looking for opportunities to stage hit-and-run encounters but were beaten off by the Helvetian soldiers. For a fortnight the caravan moved at most five or six miles a day. In a report back home—perhaps in a letter sent by messenger—Caesar made it clear that he was continuing to "oppose the robbery, pillage and devastation carried out by the enemy," a clear-cut propagandistic justificatory fabrication. The Helvetii had no designs for war, only to settle in new homelands by the Santones. When the Helvetii reached the foot of a mountain and halted, the Roman force was stationed just seven miles away.

By this time Caesar's army was out of supplies and, since food was still not forthcoming from his Aeduan allies, his options were to attack the caravan and take their supplies as spoils or to head to the Aeduan capitol of Bibracte and raid the stores there. As he approached the oppidum to confront the enemy, a miscue of intelligence forced Caesar to change his mind and direct his army toward the capitol. The Helvetians saw this as an opportunity to attack the rear guard of the Roman army and the war was on; it began mid-day and lasted until darkness halted Caesar's slaughter. As groups of Helvetii fled for their lives, the Romans took possession of their abandoned carts (*carri*) and provisions. Plutarch (*Caes* 18.4) says the "wives and children [of the Helvetii] defended themselves to the death" but were eventually "cut to pieces just like the men."[71]

As the fleeing Helvetii headed in the direction of the territory of the Lingones, Caesar sent messengers to the leaders of that nation, telling them that, if they dared help the Helvetii in any way, they too would feel the scourge of Rome's imperial power. Thus, no food was forthcoming from those quarters for the defeated travelers.

Without material support from any tribe, the Helvetian remnant sent a delegation to Caesar seeking mercy. Caesar says (*BG* 1.27.1) they, "threw themselves at his feet and speaking as suppliants sought peace with tears." He was letting history know that he had put the "yokers" under the yoke of Roman retribution. For the moment Caesar's thirst for vengeance had been satisfied. The Helvetii handed over hostages, threw down their arms, and returned the slaves who had deserted to their side. The disarmament lasted throughout the night.

The war was not over, however, because under the cover of night, 6000 Verbigenes, who had been part of the caravan, escaped in the direction of the Rhine; Caesar (*BG* 1.28.1), in another terror-charged message, "commanded the inhabitants through whose borders they had marched to seek them out and bring them back, if they wished to clear themselves from complicity in his sight." He had threatened civilians of neutral nations to serve as auxiliaries in his war effort. And "when the runaways were brought back," he adds (*BG* 1.28.1) "he treated them as enemies," his oratorical way of saying they were executed. Though they had thrown down their arms and surrendered upon their return, they were summarily slaughtered.

The Helvetian residue, which included Helvetii, Tulingi, and Latobrigi, numbered about 110,000 which meant, when compared to the numbers of travelers Caesar originally gave, he had slaughtered close to 250,000 tribesmen: women, children, infirmed, and elderly among them. Whatever the actual number of the travelers was originally and whatever the number killed, Caesar ordered the remnant to return to where they came from, to rebuild the settlement they had abandoned, and repopulate the desert they had created by their departure (*BG* 1.27-28) Plutarch (*Caes* 18.6) says, "He did this because he feared that if the territory became vacant the Germans would cross the Rhine and occupy it." He then ordered the Allobroges to supply enough food for the dispirited, unarmed, defeated travelers to make their way back home.[72]

In his *Commentaries* the general says that, when the neighboring tribes heard of the defeat of the Helvetii, their chieftains came from almost every part of Gaul (*totius fere Galliae*) to ask him about his further intentions—that is, how they might avoid a similar fate (*BG* 1.30.1). Caesar crowed that he had not only avenged the injustices done to the Romans in days gone by but also, for the present, produced great benefits for all of Gaul; he had saved Gallic nations from a marauding tyrannical nation. He reminded all who would hear his propagandistic shibboleth that, "the Helvetii had left their homes at a time of exceeding prosperity with the express design of making war upon the whole of Gaul and obtaining an empire." (*BG* 1.30.3) From the very beginning he had treated the Helvetian caravan as a warrior nation intending to make war on Rome, once again classic Caesarian pretextual fabrication.

Caesar then let all those back home know, especially those who were looking for an economic payoff to the new war, that, "out of a great number of possibilities in the Gallic territory, whatever area seemed most suitable and fertile . . . [he had turned] all the other nations into tribute-paying dependents." He then set his sights on another interloper, the German chieftain Ariovistus who was seeking to secure tribute-paying nations in his effort to extend the boundaries of his kingdom to the west side of the Rhine. He was cutting in on Rome's imperialistic cash-cow action. That story for another time.

The Roman drive to obliterate nations under the guise of a *memoria tenebat* ideology became culturally genetic. Thus, the Helvetian remnant, once back home, managed over time to create a vibrant community for themselves only to experience another Roman general under the empire who destroyed what they had created.[73] Massacred a second time, the Helvetian nation was wiped from the face of history.[74] We remember them now.

CHAPTER 4

Standards of Justice by Which to Address Caesar's Campaign of Terror

To our twenty-first century sensibilities, dear jurors, it would seem that a massacre of any proportions would be deemed sufficient grounds for dismissing a governmental employee even at the level of wartime general.[75] And that's the exact term French historians Camille Jullian and Michel Rambaud use in assessing Caesar's campaign against the German tribes of the Usipetes and Tencteri: they call it a "massacre."[76] And, as we just saw in evidence presented about Caesar's massacre of the Helvetii three years before that, he produced a massacre of equally horrific proportions.

When speaking of atrocities of such breadth, words like slaughter and massacre and even annihilation come to mind right away. But, because of the many human rights tribunals that have been impaneled over the years to establish the culpability of alleged perpetrators, we now have more specific definitions of "mass murder" to consult when seeking an indictment. It seems odd that so few historians and scholars in the canonical literature have spoken of Caesar's acts in terms of genocide or war crimes. We do find direct references to genocide tucked into paragraphs here and there but a noticeable shift occurred in 2020 when the U.S. historian Michael Kulikowski, in his review of James O'Donnell's new translation of Caesar's *De Bello Gallico*, refers to Caesar as "the first *génocidaire* in European history," moving Caesar's actions from the realm of routine campaign warfare to the horror of genocide.[77] Then the following year, even more directly, the Caesar historian Kurt Raaflaub led an assault, if you will, on Caesar's genocidal acts treating Caesar and genocide as inseparable peas in the same pod.[78] And of course in this grand jury, as you well know, weary Ladies and Gentlemen of the Jury, you have been considering evidence in this case since 2018.

Among the list of words used to describe mass atrocities, we find not only genocide but also mass killing, war crimes, massacres, ethnic cleansing, and crimes against humanity. And, we must add terrorism to the list because Caesar was a terrorist of grand proportions in his non-stop threats to tribal leaders and their citizens for not complying with his demands. When we look at the range of warring activities Caesar was engaged in during his extended proconsulship from 58 to 50 BC, every one of those words mentioned above applies to his actions in some way.

But in order to return an indictment based on the evidence presented, we must understand the meaning of each of the concepts that apply to atrocities. What about the claims of Michael Kulikowsk and Kurt Raaflaub and others who have accused Caesar of genocidal activity?

Article 11 of the United Nations Convention established in 1948 defined genocide as "acts committed with the intent to destroy, in whole or in part, a national, ethnic, racial or religious group" which might involve killing members of the group, causing serious bodily or mental harm to members of the group, and imposing living conditions on the group to bring about its physical destruction in whole or in part.

Looking at only the two Caesarian campaigns just discussed, we see that Caesar's acts fit every category mentioned.

And destruction associated with genocide also includes the dissolution of political and social institutions including cultural, language, and national feelings, acts that threaten personal security, liberty, health, and dignity. It does not necessarily entail the dissolution of political and social institutions but can reflect a coordinated plan to destroy the foundations of the life of a nation or tribe.[79] On just about every page of the *De Bello Gallico*, Caesar offers a confession of such destruction, oftentimes with self-congratulatory pride.

As we prepare to make judgments about Caesar's culpability in this regard then, let us look at what he says (*BG* 6.34) about the war he conducted in 53 against the Eburones, a Gallic-Germanic tribe living in the northeast of Gaul in what would now be the southern Netherlands, eastern Belgium, and the German Rhineland.

To save wear and tear on his own troops the general riled up a host of neighboring tribes, especially the Sugambri, and sicced them on the Eburones. That is, under the guise of the protector of the life of Rome, he became an engineer of international intertribal warfare, an inciter-in-chief, encouraging some tribes to prey on their neighbors and eradicate them from the annals of history. His destruction of the Eburones is another example of his *memoria tenebat* methodology whereby he sought revenge against a tribe who had killed two Roman generals and handily defeated their armies even though those generals were forcing the tribe, we assert, to face starvation during the winter to come.[80]

Describing how he decided to punish the Eburones, Caesar says of himself (*BG* 6.34.8), "He sent messengers round to the neighboring states and invited them all, in the hope of booty, to join him in pillaging the Eburones so that he might hazard the lives of the Gauls among the woods rather than the soldiers of the legions and at the same time, by surrounding it with a large host, destroy the stock and name of the tribe in requital for its horrid crime." He adds that, "A great number assembled speedily from every side." They responded speedily for fear that Caesar would turn on them if non-compliant. At times the Roman troops had trouble ferreting out tribal warriors who fled into marshes and woodland areas for safety, thus Caesar was especially pleased with the Sugambri for, as he says *(BG* 6.35.7), "No swamp, no woods can stymy these men who were born for war and depredations." A modern-day psychiatrist would characterize "born for war and depredations" as a classic example of Caesar's relentless projection.[81]

The Sugambri did have their way with the Eburones. Reveling in this vindictive triumph, Caesar (*BG* 6.43.2) describes how his marauding posse laid waste to everything, "Every hamlet, every homestead that anyone could see was set on fire; captured cattle were driven from every spot, the corn-crops were not only being consumed by the vast host of pack-animals and human beings, but were laid flat in addition because of the rainy season, so that, even if any person succeeded in hiding themselves for the moment, it seemed that they must perish for want of everything when the army was withdrawn."

Dutch archaeologist Nico Roymans (p. 45) says Caesar achieved an additional success when he carried off the tribe's gold which he melted down for easy transport. We can surmise that the general was elated since getting rich—working his way out of the grave of debt—was one of the goals of his governorship. But, with respect to the future of the Eburones, as the classical historian Edith Mary Wightman tells us, they, "disappear from the written record."[82] They are wiped off the face of history except for notations like these recalling their demise. As a terrorist Caesar always felt compelled to take more than what an "eye for an eye" called for.

The Aduatuci met oblivion in the same way after Caesar laid siege to their town in 57, the same tribe who mocked the Romans for their diminutive stature compared to the enormous engines of war they built to aid in their demolition of the tribe's walls. They might as well have been making fun of Caesar's baldness. The *Commentaries* say (*BG* 2.33) that after his troops had killed four thousand and the remainder "were flung back into the town" the next day, "the gates were broken open, for there was no more defense, and our troops were sent in."

There is no record of how many were massacred during the siege but Caesar reports that he "sold as one lot the booty of the town. The purchasers furnished a return to him of 53,000 persons."[83] As with the melted gold he carried away, and the profit netted from 53,000 captives sold as slaves, again, Caesar was using the human beings of Gaul not only to re-establish his financial footing back in Rome but also to lessen his dependence on the coffers of his fellow triumvir Marcus Licinius Crassus, the richest man in the city.[84] Killing a Gaul was a step toward financial freedom.

In the case of the Eburones the general incited inter-national war and with the Aduatuci he trafficked in human beings. The historian Dio (39.4; 1) reaffirms that the Aduatuci, "were all sold" adding that the destruction took place because they "belonged to the Cimbri by race and temperament" which Caesar confirms (*BG* 2.29): "the tribe was descended from the Cimbri and Teutoni." Wiping them from the written record was his exaction of revenge for what took place during the Cimbrian War more than 50 years earlier (from 113-102), and for the resulting "*terror cimbricus*" that the war produced in the Roman psyche like some unshakable Post-Traumatic Stress Disorder.

To emphasize what was said earlier, Caesar said at the beginning of *De Bello Gallico* (1.7) "*memoria tenebat*" which we can transcribe into the first person *memoria tenebam* where he is telling the world—the Romans of his day as well as posterity—I, Julius Caesar, have not forgotten, I cannot shake from my mind earlier harms done to Rome; Rome is an equal opportunity nation when it comes to revenge. How strange it is to hear modern historians take up Caesar's cause the way Plutarch did eons before and Thomas Rice Holmes does in his famed *Conquest of Gaul* when he says (p. 59): "Caesar was neither vindictive and cruel" but then adds, "to those who defied him, and especially those who broke faith, he was absolutely ruthless." Does not the record show that Caesar defined someone "breaking faith" as them having an opinion that differed from his imperialistic ideology?

At various junctures in his *Commentaries*, he does suggest that he was operating under a "just war" model of engagement, which means the Romans saw themselves justified in wiping out, by slaughter or enslavement, any tribe or nation that threatened the city's sovereignty—and this included non-combatants such as women, children, the aged, and infirmed. The heart of Caesar's MO, as was the case with Roman generals before him, was the pre-emptive strike and, once the gates of a stronghold were battered down, indiscriminate slaughter. Caesar had hundreds of years of precedents to justify his policies of slaughter and enslavement.

For example, in 212 when the gates of the City of Syracuse were torn apart, Roman troops began slaughtering anyone they came upon including the renowned mathematician Archimedes. Three years later, when Scipio Africanus stormed New Carthage, Polybius says (10.15.4-6), the general directed his troops, "according to Roman custom, against the people in the city, telling them to kill everyone they met and to spare no one ... The purpose of the custom ... to strike terror. Accordingly one can often see in cities captured by the Romans not only human beings who have been slaughtered, but even dogs sliced in two and the limbs of other animals cut off. On this occasion the amount of slaughter was very great." The generals saw themselves as justified terrorists.[85]

In 102, after slaughtering a small group of Ambrones in the deep of a river, Marius directed his troops toward the camp and wagons where women and children had taken refuge. Plutarch says (*Mar* 19.6-7), "Most of the Ambrones were cut down there in the stream where they were all crowded together, and the river was filled with their blood and their dead bodies; the rest, after the Romans had crossed, did not dare to face about, and the Romans kept slaying them until they came in their flight to their camp and wagons. Here the women met them, swords and axes in their hands, and with hideous shrieks of rage tried to drive back fugitives and pursuers alike, the fugitives as traitors, and the pursuers as foes; they mixed themselves up with the combatants, with bare hands tore away the shields of the Romans or grasped their swords, and endured wounds and mutilations, their fierce spirits unvanquished to the end." Tacitus (*Ann* 14.37) says 80,000 men and women were slaughtered along with their pack animals, and anything else that moved. Clearly Caesar's uncle provided justificatory precedent for his *memoria tenebam* rallying cry.

When we look closely at the acts he perpetrated during his campaign to destroy all of Gaul, we see them fitting into the categories of war crimes and crimes against humanity. Included among the latter are systematic and widespread harm directed against civilians during war or peace. And while a crime of murder, for example, can be responded to in a jurisdiction authorized to adjudicate such acts, murder defined as a crime against humanity can be tried in any "national" jurisdiction even though the criminal behavior is not codified in international law. But the might of Rome was the arbiter of all things "legal," the pre-emptive strike the procedural due process of the international tribunal.

"War crimes" are defined as serious breaches of international law that are committed against civilian or enemy combatants. This might involve the use of chemical or biological weapons, the mistreatment of prisoners, the destruction of civilian property, taking hostages, misusing a truce, among other brutalities. For such acts, to use a slang phrase, Caesar was their poster boy, the *carnifex Gallorum*.

Ethnic cleansing on the other hand, though it defies easy or simple definition, is criminal behavior that involves the systematic or systemic removal of ethnic, racial, or religious groups from one's homeland by a more powerful ethnic group. Those who engage in such behavior seek to remove physical and cultural evidence of the targeted group through the destruction of their homes, farms, and may involve the desecration of religious monuments such as places of worship. During his day Caesar was a cleanser in a league of his own but he was following the Roman ethic of the neutralization of enemy peoples when he engaged in slaughtering women and children of the Usipetes and Tencteri tribes. As indicated, he was miming a standard that his hero and uncle-by-marriage, Marius, had set in his slaughter of the Ambrones.

Of course, at this point we need to call attention to "presentist" dissenters who say that it is not appropriate to apply retroactively standards of justice that were developed over the course of 2,000 years. In one respect the archaeologist Simon James might agree in that the Romans had no or little sense that mass killing during warfare was unethical.[86]

Australian classical historian Jane Bellemore says that the massacres of the magnitude Caesar perpetrated were not only not vilified but accepted, we might say even celebrated with bigoted glee. In October 54 Cicero (*Fam* 1.9.12, in a letter to Publius Cornelius Lentulus Spinther speaks of "Caesar's brilliant successes" and in his *De Provinciis Consularibus*, a speech he delivered to the Senate two years earlier, he essentially gave Caesar *carte blanche* to wipe the barbarian off the face of the earth. Caesar had "with brilliant success, crushed in battle the fiercest and greatest tribes of Germania and Helvetia," Cicero crows, "the rest he has terrified, checked and subdued, and taught them to submit to the rule of the Roman people."[87]

When Cato challenged Caesar's defilement of a truce after the general massacred the 300,000, it, "came to nothing," Nico Roymans says, "the allegation against Caesar made no mention at all of his mass killings of the German population."[88] Killing or enslaving the different "other," defined as "the barbarian" was an ethic that ran through the ideological veins of all the Greco-Roman world. Indeed, Pliny the Elder (*HN* 29.14) says that Cato, in a treatise he wrote for his son Marcus, claimed that Greek doctors took oaths to kill Romans. "They take an oath among themselves to kill all the [Roman] barbarians with their medicine and this very thing they do for a fee, so they might win our confidence and kill us all the more easily. They also refer to us as barbarians, and they insult all more filthily than other groups by calling us Opici."[89]

Thus, in the ever-changing hierarchy of who was worthy to be called, and treated as, a victim—Greek, Roman, barbarian—"Caesar's willingness to tolerate brutality," as historian Kurt Raaflaub (2021 p. 64) notes, "is absolutely clear . . . his actions in Gaul also violated much that is barred in modern conventions limiting abuses in warfare (the so-called Geneva Convention adopted in 1929 and 1949), and represent 'war crimes' as they are defined in Article 8 of the Rome Statute of the International Criminal Court in the Hague in 2002."

In his review of James O'Donnell's translation of the *De Bello Gallico*, which we've called attention to several times, Michael Kulikowski says Caesar's treatise on Gaul, "is a bad man's book about his own bad deeds." But Raaflaub (p. 65) says "it is perhaps too simple to label him 'a very bad man.'" Is he implying that Caesar deserves some ethical wiggle room? And even though Adriaan Lanni (p. 470) emphasizes that the rules of war "were indifferent to considerations of mercy and the protection of noncombatants," Caesar saw himself not just as a *pater patriae* but also the *fons clementiae*. As already noted, they were going to build a temple to his kindness! In so many ways he said he knew better, that he was better than the rest but, as we know, his desire to be a king and to create a society over which he would rule as a superman, required him to annihilate all that stood in his way—Gauls, Germans, Pompey, recalcitrant Roman citizens. Hail, Caesar.

CHAPTER 5

MANGO MAGNUS DECAPITATORQUE:
The Great Slave-Trading Decapitator

WHEN JULIUS CAESAR PENNED his infamous *memoria tenebat* manifesto from his field headquarters in 58, he was letting his fellow Romans back home know, as well as posterity—here we are examining his case 2,000 years later—that he was a man who had a keen sense of history. Though a self-appointed retributivist, he was backed by a faction of the SPQR and especially by Cicero whose *De Provinciis Consularibus* speech delivered to the Senate in 56 gave him carte blanche to "carpet bomb" Gaul into oblivion. Cicero took his own advice when he adopted the same MO as governor of Cilicia in 51; without cause he erased a nation himself.[90]

With respect to the impetus of Caesar's underlying ideology, Cicero (*Off* 3.82) says the man liked to quote Euripides' "The Phoenician Women" (lines 524-525) on what political and military measures were available to an ambitious state functionary: "if one should perform a deed of injustice, then let it be performed for the sake of a kingdom." That is, for the sake of becoming a king, anything goes.

In the month of August of 57, the Belgae, the Suessiones, Bellovaci, and Ambiani fell to Caesar, some surrendered without engaging his army directly, others after seeing hordes of their family and neighbors slaughtered before their eyes. Caesar sums up his campaign with the Belgae as (*BG* 2.11.6), "without any danger our men slew as great a host of them as daylight allowed; when the sun went down they ceased, retiring to camp as they had been commanded."

When the general turned his attention to the Nervi who, under the command of Boduognatus, nearly defeated the Roman army, he finally at the Battle of Sabis, (*BG* 2.28.1), "brought the name and nation of the Nervii almost to utter destruction." At a certain point, seeing there was little sense in continuing the conflict, the tribal leaders of the Nervii, "sent deputies [*legatos*] to Caesar and surrendered to him." (*BG* 2.28.2) They had lost close to 60,000 warriors in the battle—there was scarcely 500 left—and "from six hundred senators they had been reduced to three" a loss of 99 percent of their leading citizens and political administration. Caesar had decapitated a nation.[91] As University of London historian, Hans van Wees, points out (p. 248), "Exiling or executing the ruling elite alone later became the Romans' standard procedure in dealing with rebellious cities."[92]

But, in telling of the destruction of the tribe's leadership, the *Commentaries* say the deputies informed him of this "disaster which had come upon the state." The language does not preclude Caesar having executed the senate outright or singled them out during battle—debilitating a nation by severing its political capital, as he was to do with the Veneti within a short time. At the very end of August, when the general was still engaged in warring with the Nervii, their neighbors the Aduatuci entered his line of sight, his war narrative, and the list of his continuing crimes against humanity. He was well aware that the

Aduatuci were (*BG* 5.29), "descended from the Cimbri and Teutoni." Dio (39.4) affirms that, with respect to their cultural geneaology, the Aduatuci "belonged to the Cimbri by race and temperament."

And, as a man of great historical memory, Caesar had not forgotten that it was the Cimbri who struck terror in the hearts of Romans until they were finally defeated in 101 at the Battle of Vercellae under the joint command of the consul Gaius Marius and proconsul Quintus Lutatius Catulus.[93]

In 57, when the Nervii were still engaged in battle with Caesar, the neighboring Aduatuci sought to aid them but, before they reached the place of battle, they learned that the Nervii had already been defeated at Sabis, near modern-day Saulzoir in Northern France, and decided it fruitless to continue with their plan; they headed home.[94]

Caesar was not about to let the Cimbrian offspring go without paying a price and ordered his troops to hunt them down. Aware that they were being hounded, the tribe abandoned (*BG* 2.29.2), "all their towns and forts, they gathered all their stuff in one stronghold." The general was not deterred; in September the siege of the town was begun.

Because of a great engineering feat, the Romans were able to overrun the battlements and the Aduatuci finally surrendered; and, because of the size of such machinery the Romans displayed, the tribe exclaimed that they "did not wage war without divine aid." (*BG* 2. 31.2) They knew they could not beat such odds, therefore they, as Caesar says (*BG* 2. 31.3-6), "resigned themselves and all their possessions to [Caesar's] disposal . . . [and] begged and earnestly entreated one thing, namely, that if perchance, agreeable to his clemency and humanity, which they had heard of from others, he should resolve that the Aduatuci were to be spared, he would not deprive them of their arms; that all their neighbors were enemies to them and envied their courage, from whom they could not defend themselves if their arms were delivered up: that it was better for them, if they should be reduced to that state, to suffer any fate from the Roman people, than to be tortured to death by those among whom they had been accustomed to rule." Where did they learn about such clemency and humanity? From the Nervii? Had they heard what happened to the Helvetii?

But the Aduatuci nation, fearful of facing the world without arms, did not fully surrender all their weapons, they kept a stockpile concealed inside the town. The night after their surrender, fully armed, they broke through the Roman line but their effort was quickly extinguished. In response to their assault, Caesar's troops killed at least 4,000 of the tribe and took 53,000 of the inhabitants captive whom the general sold into slavery or shared with his troops as spoils. His distribution of the slaves was quite possible because, as we know, in 52 he tells us outright that (*BG* 7.89.4), he had distributed "one of the remaining captives to each soldier throughout the entire army, as plunder." Regardless, once again Caesar was in the slave-trading business big time—a *mango* of great proportions.

Fully understanding the ignominy of marketing human beings this way, the Belgian-born painter **Rémy Cogghe** depicted the sale of the tribe in his dramatic painting of 1880 "Les Aduatiques Vendues à l'Encan." "The Atuatuci sold at the Auction."[95] As was the case with the Eburones, as Edith Wightman has noted, the Aduatuci disappear from the record of history. That is, Caesar had wiped another tribe off the face of the earth. Of course, a lingering question for the inquisitive student of Roman history, as well as those of human rights violations, is how the general-turned-businessman handled the exchange of 53,000 prisoners to the merchants traveling with the army. Again, it was Caesar the businessman, a *mango* of grand proportions, amassing a fortune via the backs of barbarian chattel.[96]

With the defeat of the Aduatuci coupled with the defeat of the Nervii, for a short period it looked as if Caesar had conquered all of Gaul.[97] He says (*BG* 3.7.1) "the Belgae were defeated, the Germans driven out, and the Seduni in the Alpine region conquered." As his troops were burying their comrades lost in the Nervian campaign, he sent Publius Crassus to Armorica to deal with the tribes along the Atlantic coast. He remained resolved to move against Britain because, "he had discovered that in almost all the wars with the Gauls succors had been furnished by our enemy from that country" (*BG* 4.20.1) but he first had to deal with the Veneti and their neighbors in Gaul who carried on trade across the channel with Britain.

But there are pieces to the puzzle that do not fit. First of all, with Crassus running interference, Caesar was sending a young, inexperienced, officer to Armorica and with only one legion, the Seventh, which had been badly bruised in the campaign with the Nervii, "harassed by the enemy." (*BG* 2.23.4; 2.26.1) Perhaps using a source other than the *Commentaries*, Plutarch (*Caes* 20.7), says the Nervii, had routed his cavalry, had "surrounded the seventh and twelfth legions and slew all their centurions." Appian (*Gall Wars* 4.23) says the Nervii not only, "made a very great slaughter' but also killed, "all of his [Caesar's] tribunes and centurions." However great the losses of officers and soldiers, Caesar was sending the young Crassus with a depleted contingent of 6,000 troops in dire need of time to heal their wounds.

Armorica was that part of Gaul between the Seine and Loire rivers and included the Brittany Peninsula. Today the region includes the French department of Morbihan and the southern part of Finistère with ports located across the English Channel from Britain. Caesar knew that, "These Veneti exercise by far the most extensive authority over the seacoast in those districts, for they have numerous ships, in which it is their custom to sail to Britain . . ." (BG 3.8.1) Their boats were built of oak timbers held together by thick iron pins strong enough to withstand the vicissitudes of the Channel. And, because of such powerful ships, the Veneti enjoyed a near monopoly in trade with Britain. The trade was highly lucrative and, when Caesar did set his sights on Britain, he had to deal with the Veneti for, as Strabo says (4.4.1) "they were already prepared to hinder his voyages to Britain since they were using the emporium there, a small centralized trading post, to carry on business."[98]

A major piece of the puzzle that does not fit is that there is no mention of a conflict of any kind between Crassus' army and the Veneti and their neighboring tribes. All we learn is that Crassus reported back to the general, "that all those states had been brought into subjection to the power of Rome." (*BG* 2.34) A win without a single *pilum* hurled?

And, in addition to the Veneti, Crassus had to contend with their neighbors in Armorica: the Venelli, Osismi, Curiosolites, Esubii, Aulerci, and Redones. In confederation these tribes far outnumbered a war-weary legion with an inexperienced leader. These tribes could put up defensive military numbers because in 52, five of them—the Curiosolites, the Redones, Osismi, Venelli, and Veneti (joined by the Ambibarii, Caletes, and Lemovices) sent a contingent of 35,000 troops to aid Vercingetorix at the Battle of Alesia (*BG* 7.75.4). They could have easily pitted more than 50,000 warriors against the worn-out army of a green political appointee.

That is, this Crassus, who was the son of the triumvir, was not even an officer, an official *legatus*. Indeed, Caesar refers to him as an *adulescens* and militarily as a *dux*, the word he used to denote tribal leaders.[99]

And because Caesar was successful in mowing down tribe after tribe in 57, especially after defeating the Nervii (who came close to defeating his army), he clarifies that (*BG* 2.35.1) "so mighty a report of this campaign was carried to the barbarians that deputies were sent to Caesar from the tribes across the Rhone, to promise that they would give hostages and do his commands." His campaign of terror was reaping fruit in expected ways. Perhaps all Crassus had to do was issue a threat to secure submission.

Whatever factors enabled Crassus to declare victory, he ordered his weary Seventh Legion to set up winter quarters among the Andes whose land was a short distance from that of the Veneti. As winter lingered on, food became scarce so Crassus sent a detail of commandants and tribunes (*praefectos tribunosque*) to the Veneti and neighboring tribes to beg, borrow, or cadge a supply of grain for his sequestered army. Titus Terrasidius went to the Esubii, Marcus Trebius Gallus to the Curiosolites, and Quintus Velanius and Titus Silius appeared before the Veneti chieftains. These were soldiers of some rank but in no way an official negotiating delegation (*legati*).

Of course the food supply was short among the Andes because many thousands of soldiers were demanding their daily bread from the Andean stores. And, if the shortage was due to a poor growing season, it meant that all the regional tribes would have been adversely affected. Either way, the *praefecti* and *tribuni* were asking the tribesmen to take food from the mouths of their children.[100]

There is no indication in Caesar's report about how the officers presented themselves to their respective tribes. It would appear the threat of force was sufficient for representatives of Roman might to have their demands taken seriously. It was a matter of assessing human worth, the worth of uncivilized savages—families—versus the worth of civilized Romans—armed troops. Crassus himself an *adulescens* could have sent *adulescentes* not only in age but experience as well to demand food, the cohort lacking in techniques of cordial negotiation—if cordiality were a factor.

Caesar tells us what occurred (*BG* 3.8.2), "It all began when the Veneti detained Silius and Velanius, thinking that by detaining them they might recover the hostages they had handed over to Caesar." Again, the propagandistic general playing the barbarian card, says nothing more could be expected from irrational actors, "for the Gauls are sudden and spasmodic in their design" meaning they did not sheepishly submit to the will of Rome, thereby offering Caesar a justification for any action he might take. Whether there was a coordinated effort on the part of the put-upon tribes to resist the demands of the *praefecti tribunique*, the Esubii and Curiosolites detained the party sent to them as well.

Something else happened which Caesar does not share, revealing only that the Armorican nations began acting as if they were in charge, acting with authority (*auctoritas*), challenging the only true authority in the civilized world. The Veneti, he says, "rapidly [dispatched] deputies among their chiefs, they bound themselves by mutual oath to do nothing save by common consent, and to abide together the single issue of their destiny." To defend themselves and their stores of winter rations against an invasive army, they had formed an ad hoc confederation. (*BG* 3.8.3) To pique further the *dignitas* of the future dictator, "they urged the remaining states to choose rather to abide in the liberty received from their ancestors than to endure Roman slavery." (*BG* 3.8.4) "As allies for the war [the Veneti] took to themselves the Osismi, the Lexovii, the Namnetes, the Ambiliati, the Morini, the Diablintes, and the Menapii; and they sent to fetch auxiliaries from Britain, which lies opposite those regions." (*BG* 3.9.10) In defence, the Veneti and their confederates had cast their die.

Caesar responded by ordering ships to be built, rowers to be drafted from the Province, and seamen and steersmen to be conscripted. Of course the Veneti confederation was well aware of these preparations. And the general says he was most justified in taking drastic measures because the Veneti had violated the *ius gentium*, international law, after they and the other tribes, "detained and cast into prison deputies, men whose title has been sacred and inviolable among all nations." Once again we see a sanctimonious Caesar pulling the law card. He was treating the prefects and tribunes he sent as if they were official envoys (*legati*) who were engaged in an official *colloquium*, that is, treating requisitioning officers, as Gelzer (p. 126) says, as if they were ambassadors. The man on the street in Rome reading, or hearing read to him, this encounter would never make any such distinction regarding the law; all he would see or hear was barbarian hordes treating Roman emissaries with lawless disrespect—even though they had come to snatch food out of the mouths of children and their mothers, and the aged and infirmed.

In an effort to prevent other tribes from joining in the fray, Caesar sent lieutenants to hot spots in Gaul to warn other tribes about the consequences of joining the confederation. He sent Titus Labienus, supported by a contingent of cavalry, to the Treveri who lived in the lower valley of the Moselle, a tributary of the Rhine. They were potential trouble-makers led by Indutiomarus, the spokesman for a strong anti-Roman faction in the tribe, which might better be called an enslavement-prevention unit. Labienus might have played on existing intra-tribal conflict because Indutiomarus' daughter was married to Cingetorix, leader of the pro-Roman faction in the tribe.

To further inhibit regional tribes from joining the Veneti confederation, Caesar sent the *adulescens*, Publius Crassus to Aquitania, Quintus Titurius Sabinus to the Venelli, Curiosolites, and the Lexovii, all of whom were under the command of Viridovix, chief of the Venelli. Viridovix was a source of great concern because he "held the supreme command of all the revolted states, from which he had raised an army and large levies [of men and ships] in addition." (*BG* 3.17.2) In great detail Caesar describes how his fleet was put together and how he managed to overcome the great sea-faring tribe of Veneti. "Accordingly, they surrendered themselves and all their belongings to Caesar." (*BG* 3.16.4)

And because the Veneti had defied the authority of Rome in Caesar's words—actually took steps to defend themselves against an army invading their homes—the general decided to make an example of them, thereby violating the *ius humanitatis* by commiting a war crime. He decided (*BG* 3.16.4) that "their punishment must be the more severe in order that the privilege of deputies might be more carefully preserved by the natives for the future. He therefore put the whole of the senate to the sword, and sold the rest of the men as slaves."[101] Mass murder followed by mass enslavement—Caesarian *clementia* and *humanitas* in action.

Here he was repeating the MO he had used with the Nervii by decapitating the political body of the tribe, and the same method he had used with the Aduatuci by selling off the tribe as slaves wholesale. Hail, Caesar, *pontifex maximus* of Rome, eraser of national identities. We are led to believe that the Veneti, like the Eburones had disappeared from history.

But further research shows that such was not the case. Indeed, the French historian, Patric Galliou (1984, p.15), offers a whole other picture. He says, "If we can indeed admit that Caesar had executed the ruling class of the Veneti (*BG* 3.16), the story that he tells us of the auction of all the people seems to stem from bragging or the lie of propaganda: the examination of later archaeological remains after the Conquest reveals to us, in truth, a heavily populated Venetia whose prosperity equals or surpasses that of their immediate neighbors (Merlat, 1959, André, 1960)."[102] Indeed, the history of the Roman Republic is filled with defeated tribes continuing to rise from their ashes seeking to avenge the wrongs done them, and then Rome repeating its carpet-bombing activities. Rome simply did not have the cultural wherewithal to deal with differences in cultures, that is, to employ methods to coexist with others through treaties and other forms of mutual agreement. As we have seen in the case of Caesar, Rome's main negotiation techniques were: slaughter; decapitation of an alien nation's leadership; and selling men, women, and children as slaves. For these methods as well Caesar was the poster boy.

CHAPTER 6

BEFORE GOING ON:
What Did Caesar Say He Was Up To?
THE COMMENTARII

OF COURSE, EVERY STUDENT IN EVERY CLASS OF "CAESAR," young and old alike, is interested in the personality of the dictator-to-be, how he grew up, his schooling, his relationships with his wives and children and mistresses, his sensitivity to his baldness, and all the other traits that comprised his personal life.[103] Outstanding among them was a rule he lived by: never show fear to the enemy. And of course as well, these very same students are interested in Caesar's public persona which includes the religious and official governmental positions he held as he continued along the *cursus honorum* to become dictator for life and Rome's first emperor.[104]

And the most important of all his official positions was his time in Gaul as proconsul which began in 58 BC and ended with a resounding victory against a pan-Gallic confederation at the Battle of Alesia in September 52. It was during those years—as alluded to at the outset—that he out-carnifexed the great carnifexer, Gnaeus Pompeius Magnus. The subtitle of this work pays "homage" to his *carnifexing*: Caesar the Killer.[105]

Every high school student who is taking, or has taken, Latin II—and since the 2012-2013 school year, every student in an Advanced Placement Latin class—is well aware that Caesar wrote a "book" outlining the strategies and tactics he used to lay waste to tribes and towns he saw as immanent threats to Roman sovereignty, as well as the reasons for taking such actions in the first place. That book, as we know by now, has for centuries been called *De Bello Gallico*.[106]

And so indelible are parts of that drama in the lives of some students—and the book might be considered just that—a dramatic presentation—that students I taught 60 years ago can still reel off its opening lines in Latin, "*Gallia est omnis divisa in partes tres, quarum unam incolunt Belgae, aliam Aquitani, tertiam qui ipsorum lingua Celtae, nostra Galli appellantur.*" And for those coming upon "Caesar" for the first time, the English is, "The entirety of Gaul is divided into three parts; the Belgae inhabit one, the Aquitani another, and the third part is inhabited by people who call themselves Celts but whom in our language we call Gauls."

The magnum opus, in which those opening lines are found, writers such as Cicero, while Caesar was still alive, offered great praise for. And while today we know the book as *De Bello Gallico* we have few clues as to what Caesar himself titled the work—though we do have a sense of when, and in what form, it appeared in Rome—and what he was trying to achieve by writing it—during a war he supposedly launched for his fellow Romans.

It is not insignificant, Ladies and Gentlemen of the Jury, that we trace down those clues to find out how Caesar described or titled the work which is very much related to whom he regarded as his intended audience. In this respect it cannot go without saying that a whole literature has developed calling the work he produced a grand dramatic piece of political propaganda.

If Caesar's intended audience was the SPQR, did he intend his reports more for the "S" or more for the "P," for the Roman Senate or the Roman people, keeping in mind that he was a rabid supporter of "the people," the *populares*—though I surmise only as a political strategy and not by heart? The short answer is: Caesar was "into" power and his view of the common people was as units of political support in his ideological battles with the optimates, the senatorial class.¹⁰⁷ Indeed, he would have out-Horaced Horace with his own take on his relationship with the populace: *odi et amo vulgus profanum et id arceo*.¹⁰⁸ "I love and hate the uncouth crowd simultaneously and keep it at arm's length."

Whatever the intended audience for the *Bellum Gallicum*—which we will discuss shortly—we know that Aulus Hirtius, a Roman writer and lieutenant of Caesar beginning in 58, was responsible for putting together Book 8 of the work before editing and overseeing the publication of the entire eight books of the corpus.¹⁰⁹ While telling us what the book was called, Hirtius tells us how the work was composed; in the Preface to Book 8 he says Caesar put the work together speedily and without great effort, "*Nos etiam, quam facile atque celeriter eos perfecerit, scimus*." The general's intelligence and dexterity with words has been well noted here so we are led to accept the editor's assessment at face value. As mentioned earlier, we are talking about a man who penned a dense tome on grammatical usage while crossing the Alps.¹¹⁰

Cicero did not hesitate to weigh in on the nature and quality of the work in his *Brutus* which appeared in 46, an essay that explored Roman oratory with a focus on the nature and expression of eloquence. It is also worth noting that he included Caesar among those who could express themselves with eloquence. In section 262 of *Brutus*, Cicero begins by remarking on Caesar's skill as an orator and then eases into an assessment of the general's "commentaries" which is what he calls the work: *commentarii*.

He says Caesar's, "orations please me highly, for I have had the satisfaction to read several of them. He has likewise written some commentaries [*commentarios*], or short memoirs, of his own transactions ... as merit the highest approbation: for they are plain, correct, and graceful, and divested of all the ornaments of language, so as to appear (if I might be allowed the expression) in a kind of undress."

The barrister goes on to say that, while Caesar, "pretended only to furnish the loose materials, for such as might be inclined to compose a regular history, he may, perhaps have gratified the vanity of a few literary embroiderers; but he certainly prevented all sensible men from attempting any improvement on his plan. For in history, nothing is more pleasing than correct and eloquent brevity of expression." That is, the *commentarii* were more than a compilation of notes intended for a future historian to shape into a coherent narrative; they might not be a history like Tacitus' work but they were and remain Caesar's take on the historical reality he engineered. And he never would have stood for anyone to rewrite his work. Repeat: he never would have stood for anyone to rewrite his work.

Clearly, Cicero was too abstract and euphemistic (politically) in his assessment, plus he does not say what Caesar was up to with the work. What was the general saying he was trying to accomplish overall? While a growing number of modern historians have weighed in on the purpose of the work, a considerable number continue to refer to it as, as just mentioned, an unabashed piece of propaganda.[iii] The more one explicates the text, the more one is led to see its stick-a-spear-in-your-face reality. We must never forget that Caesar knew what he was doing every step of the way, with every ablative absolute he began a sentence with.

Today, of course, the "*De Bello Gallico*" or "*Commentarii de Bello Gallico*" is translated as "About the war in Gaul" or "Commentaries on the Gallic War." Nearly every scholar of Caesar weighs in on the title in a similar vein. Arizona State University historian James O'Donnell, who came out with a highly-praised translation of the work in April 2019, calls his *De Bello Gallico* "The War for Gaul."

And the already-mentioned Irish-born historian, T. Rice Holmes (1855-1933) called his translation of the work "Caesar's Commentaries on the Gallic Wars" and it is worth noting that Holmes had put together a 846-page commentary and grand analysis of Caesar's activities as proconsul in Gaul called "The Conquest of Gaul." And while Holmes was in Caesar's corner all the way, he essentially depicts the general as a conquistador. As has been mentioned more than once, in his review of O'Donnell's translation in the *London Review of Books*, Michael Kulikowski does not kowtow to political euphemism, he agrees with the conquistador assessment saying, "Julius Caesar was the first *génocidaire* in European history."[112] He says Caesar was a "bad man."

Of course any student who lasts long enough to reach Chapter 7 of the first book of *De Bello Gallico* sees that Caesar speaks of himself in the third person when he says, "*Caesari cum id nuntiatum esset . . .*" Thus, we do not hear Caesar say "I did this" or "I did that" but rather projects a narrative in which he speaks about himself the way he might about his trusted cavalry commander Titus Labienus—though Florida State historian John Marincola contends that Caesar originally wrote in the first person but then, when the books were put into their final form for publication, switched to a third person voice.[113]

Regardless, the astute reader cannot help but wonder why Caesar would make either choice when we keep in mind that, besides being a genius military strategist and tactician, he was a political animal sans peer. What card was he hiding in the sleeve of his toga by distancing his first-person self from the text? *Cui bono?*

Long ago, the late University of Michigan classical archaeologist Francis Kelsey (1858-1927) suggested (p. 215) that Caesar wrote in the third person—seemingly anonymously—because it conferred greater glory on his efforts. The 45,000-word treatise was sent out blind, so to speak, because it was "more apt to be received without prejudice and so to carry greater weight than if it is known to have emanated from a conspicuous partisan." A hardly sustainable position today.[114]

But whether Caesar assumed a first- or third-person voice in his narrative, was it possible that he never titled the work from the very beginning and that the war reports or dispatches were meant only for private distribution for select senators and equites and their sons who were well aware who wrote it? In his (to some) controversial work, the French historian, Michel Rambaud, avers that, "César dicte les sept livres du Bellum Gallicum ... Il s'adresse au milieu politico-littéraire, compose de sénateurs, de chevaliers et de leur fils."[115] That is, the work was intended for the ears and eyes of "sénateurs, chevaliers et leur fils." That position is equally suspect today because our imagination—partially backed by documentation—suggests that, once Caesar's field notes, war reports, dispatches, *litterae*—call them what you will for now—made their way to Rome, every eye and ear was waiting eagerly to hear the news. Everybody knew who was in Gaul and everybody knew who wrote it, but again who was this every waiting-eye and waiting-ear? The S? The P? The SPQR without distinction?

We will take up this matter shortly but for now allow me to interject, with respect to the propaganda purposes of the reports, that, whoever finally heard or read Caesar's war notes, was exposed to a language that depicted the contests of war as if they were moves in a full-body-armor chess game. Caesar's bowdlerized account of the massacres muted the blood and guts of his campaigns even when he says war-making lasted until dark.

Historian Jacqueline J. Stimson, in her brilliantly-researched 2017 doctoral dissertation "Killing Romans: Legitimizing Violence in Cicero and Caesar," says Caesar carefully avoided blood and guts language so as not to further stir the ire of his enemies back home, especially those on Marcus Porcius Cato's end of the political spectrum. We will say more about Stimson's analysis later but for now suffice it to say that her data say that Caesar was describing not *cruor inimici recentissimus*, a term Cicero uses in his *Sextus Roscius* (7.19), but an over-heated session of the twentiety-century's Dungeons and Dragons game.[116]

And though the title of the work we have received through the ages is *De Bello Gallico*, Caesar does not use *bellum* in reference to the totality of his crusade, the *bello* part of *bello gallico*, but only to particular campaigns and, when he does, he refers to more than one campaign, as in "*bella.*"[117] He is not referring to the totality of the war. Again, Caesar wanted to get his point across about what he was engaged in but without reminding hostile parties in Rome, especially his political enemies, that he was engaging the republic in a protracted erasure of foreign threats by means of war—which some regarded as illegitimate.[118] His political rivals were waiting for—even trying to hasten—his return so they could, figuratively speaking, hang him. Thus, as historian Kurt Raaflaub (p. 206) notes, "From the moment he began his campaigns in Gaul, he thus needed to justify himself and to organize his defenses. In this political campaign, the commentaries played a major role."

But again, can we not find a hint as to what he called the reports he was sending back? As indicated, in his Preface to Book 8, Hirtius refers to the previous seven books as *commentarii*. *Caesaris nostri commentarios rerum gestarum Galliae* is what he says. And, to re-split the etymological hair, the commentaries describe Caesar's "*res gestae*" not "*Bellum*."

Hirtius was a most trusted ally of Caesar, having served as his administrative secretary and editor for years. He was said to be among those who dined with the general on the eve of January 10, 49, the day Caesar crossed the Rubicon. When he completed Book 8 to prepare the work for publication, Hirtius certainly had before him the entire texts Caesar wrote on his campaigns (*bella*). And, as a political ally, he well knew what Caesar said he was up to.[119] Not to be overly redundant but the first thing of note in Hirtius' Preface is his description of the genre of Caesar's work as *commentarii* and that the reportings were about "*res gestae*" in the province. If you will recall, Caesar also was responsible for holding courts of assizes in different parts of Gaul which were included in the *gestae*.[120] And to aver that Caesar, by speaking of his deeds as *res gestae* instead of *bellum* seems far-fetched, all we need to remember is that decades before he wrote, the dictator Lucius Cornelius Sulla titled his memoirs *commentarii rerum gestarum*.[121]

Kelsey's assessment, then, is that the original title of the seven books—with Hirtius' added in—was *C. Iuli Caesaris Commentarii Rerum Gestarum* which Caesar might have translated as "commentaries on the activities I was involved in while in Gaul." Or "Commentaries on my official duties while in Gaul." But he might never have used the word Gaul at all for his warring took place in so many other countries, for example, Germany, Switzerland, and Britain. And the citizens of Rome were treated to these "res gestae" every year of the general's campaigns. They came like clockwork bolstered with periodic reports during the year in the form of letters back home, *litterae*. How many we do not know but let us not forget that Caesar was a communicator nonpareil.

A man of Caesar's intelligence and literary bent was well aware of the limitations traditionally assigned to the genre of *commentarii*, that is, that it was often used to describe a collection or catalogue of mundane materials. Thus, in Cicero and other writers we find *commentarii* referred to as: (1) the records of priests; (2) family records; (3) a collection of memoranda (*Fam* 8.11.4) related to events in the city; (4) the papers of Caesar found after his death (*Phil* 1.2); (5) documents Antony was accused of forging (*Phil* 5.11); (6) a promise Caesar made in a memorandum (*Att* 14.13A.2); (7) collections of notes and memoranda (*Fam* 5.12); (8) an account of Caesar's consulship (*Att* 1.19.10); (9) technical books and outlines of lectures (*Fin* 5.12); (10) a family record (*Aulus Gellius* 13.20.17); (11) a collection of excerpts (*Caes vind* 6.2.1; 20.2.2) and a host of related ephemera.

But, as historians William Bastone and Cynthia Damon (p. 10), among others, have pointed out "by Caesar's day [the *commentarii* had become] an established form of apologetic history, history written and published by (or for) a public figure to affirm his achievements and defend his actions." Again, Caesar was not writing a history the way, say, Sallust or Tacitus might, so in a way, he invented his own genre or at least a variation on an already-existing theme.

History, as a literary genre, requires the dates of events, exact geographical locations where events took place, as well as their historical and cultural contexts and Caesar's work does not offer that kind of depth and expanse. As Stanford Professor of Classics Christopher Krebs (p. 212) says, the work does not meet such a standard because it is: (1) too narrow in its range of interest; (2) lacks any real detail; and (3) distorts, omits, and falsifies important events.[122] To continue with what Kurt Raaflaub (2004) said earlier, "their purpose, whatever the title, was to justify and glorify the author's achievements, present them from his perspective, and correct unfavorable propaganda or misinterpretations." And while Hirtius proudly speaks of the work's "*elegantia*," Cicero says (*Orat* 2.62) it transgressed the first law of writing history, which is that the "author must not dare to tell anything but the truth" and "dare not to omit anything that is true." Is the Canadian classicist Debra Nousek offering too much praise for Caesar's use of the genre when she says, "none has the same scope, literary panache, or fully developed historical narrative ... [his *commentarii*] demonstrate the wide range of Caesar's talents, from his knowledge of military affairs, his experience in Roman administration, his keen intellect and shrewd political awareness."[123] "For a man of Caesar's energy, literary training, and power of concentration," Kelsey (p. 217) adds, "the composition of the Gallic war could have been no great task." Again, keep in mind that he knew what he was doing right down to the very *sed etiam*.

Suetonius felt confident in using *commentarii* when referring to Caesar's writings but does so only when speaking of the texts on the Gallic and Civil wars together (*Div* 56). But there, as in other assessments of the *commentarii*, too little is offered about the non-stop massacre and slaughter involved. As we have said, Caesar never used "*bellum gallicum*" or "*gallicum bellum*" to refer to his *De Bello Gallico*, in fact when he was writing about his activities during the civil war, he does not refer to them as war, avoiding phrases like "*civile bellum*." In a letter to Cicero he says he was involved in civil strife or conflict, "*quam abesse a civilibus controversiis*" (*Att* 10.8.B.2) and, in his own writing on the war, he speaks of civil dissension "*civilis dissensio*" (1.67.3; 3.1.3). A general writing about war as a rhetorical exercise? And, though Caesar speaks of himself involved in *res gestae*, that idiom for all practical purposes was the linguistic equivalent of *bellum*. In *De Bello Civili* (2.32.5) he has Curio give a speech in which he uses "*res gestas*" as the equivalent of war. He says, "*An vero in Hispania res gestas Caesaris no auditis? Duos pulsos exercitus? duos superatos duces? Duas receptras privincias? Haec acta diebus XL, quibus in conspectum adversariorum venerit Caesar?*" That is: "Have you not heard of Caesar's exploits in Spain that he routed two armies? conquered two generals? recovered two provinces? and accomplished all this within 40 days after he came in sight of the enemy?" However one wishes to translate *res gestae*—exploits, feats, escapades, maneuvers—words like rout, conquer, recover, and enemy stretch beyond the bounds of "dissension" or "civil strife." They mean war and, from our perspective, Ladies and Gentlemen of the Jury, all those *bella* viewed as a whole, as we have heard, have all the markings of genocide, war crimes, and crimes against humanity.

Res gestae or *bellum*, *commentarii* or no *commentarii*, where does that leave us with respect to what Caesar says he was up to? Part of the answer lies in when the work appeared in Rome and when and how it was first promulgated. Of course, there has been a great and continuing debate over the years as to when the *De Bello Gallico* was written and published or at least disseminated; at what time and in what form did it make its way to Rome (and elsewhere)? Who were the first to see or hear about those heralded *res gestae*?

More than a few historians have argued that the work—whatever it was in fact called when Hirtius published the texts in his possession—was not written until Caesar finished his campaigns in 50. Among them are historians who wrote definitive works on Caesar such as Christian Meier and Matthias Gelzer.[124] But that cannot be the case because, as researchers have shown, there are glaring illogicalities or contradictions from book to book that make it impossible for Caesar to have written the work all at once. How could he have forgotten what he wrote a few chapters earlier? For example, he says that at the Battle of Sambre in 57 (*BG* 2.28.1), the Nervii were all but destroyed, only 500 were left standing. But in 53 we find the Nervii joining Ambiorix and the Eburones in a battle against Quintus Tullius Cicero (*BG* 5.38-52). Though we do not know how many Nervii joined in, the overall force was described as sixty thousand strong.[125]

Again, if Caesar were writing the entire work in 50, say, how could he have forgotten what he had said three books earlier? The answer of course is that, when writing Book Two, he had no idea what was going to happen in Book Five four years later in real time.

While historians continue to make and hear cases on both sides of the argument, several years ago Oxford historian, Peter Wiseman, said he had had enough of such talk and drew a line in the sand. He said, "The *prima facie* assumption ought to be that the books of the commentaries were written and published year by year, and the onus of proof ought to be on those who believe otherwise." QED, case closed.[126]

And, as just asked, who was the general eager to reach with those annual histories? Caesar blows more than a dog whistle by using the phrase "*populus Romanus*" more than 40 times in Book 1; his primary constituency knew from the start who he was fighting for. As Wiseman says, with a touch of sarcasm, (p. 4.), "It was also constitutionally proper that the People's general, carrying out the People's mandate, should regularly report what he had done in the People's name." After the first dispatch arrived in 58, Caesar's followers were taken in; they wanted more; they looked forward to each year's installment the way kids in a movie theatre years ago looked forward to the next installment of a cliff-hanging serial the following Saturday. And of course, the Senate and Caesar's nemesis, Cato, were partisanly interested to see if it was Labienus who penned the next installment informing the S and P that the general had been slain in battle.

And, is there any doubt that the annual reports made their way directly from the field to Caesar's two trusted lieutenants in Rome Lucius Balbus and Gaius Oppius and perhaps indirectly to the likes of Cicero? It is also likely that they received the *litterae* that Caesar sent from time to time with updates on the ebb and flow of the People's *res gestae*. Caesar himself mentions *litterae* on at least three occasions, in the most famous of which (*BG* 2.35.4) he informs the Senate that "*omni Gallia pacata,*" essentially that the war was over. And, as the Senate moved to grant him unprecedented honors for such an achievement, the governor went about attending to the back log of cases in his assizes courts.[127] Would that we had the minutes of those sessions to see how the chief administrator of the province handled the squabbles of the barbarian hordes. They would compare well to the results of a personality profile.

It is fair to say that the vast majority of Caesar's populist constituency were not readers, so they were not going to read their hero's *commentarii* once they made their way into print. Theirs were uneducated ears. Thus, we imagine these eager polloi gathering in the Forum by the Rostra or maybe assembling by the Temple of Castor or the Circus Flaminius, or perhaps in a make-shift theatre, where a lector enunciated in dramatic voice the facts of a campaign so that even those in the last row heard every noun loud and clear. To some, the reports were a fascinating travelogue of goings-on in exotic foreign lands. As indicated earlier, what taxi driver on the Appian Way ever heard of the Usipetes and Tencteri? How did they dress? Did they smell?

And Wiseman (p. 6) boldly asserts that, after the show made an appearance at Rome, it went on the road "reproduced on a smaller scale in the main piazza of every *municipium* and *colonia* in Italy—a skilled speaker, a rapt audience, and the cool, clear prose of a master of narrative." One wonders whether the interest of the suburbanites was more in hearing a good murder mystery or news about how their homes and wives and children were freer from the threat of barbarian anarchy.

And the general's followers did not come to hear the honey-dipped prose of a Cicero but the nuts and bolts prose of a savior-warrior, the level of language a second-year Latin student in 1950s America could handle (with a trot). Caesar knew how to handle his audience thereby offering a lesson to every future dictator—he said Sulla never got the dictator thing right—how they needed to speak to take control of a nation: "*tamquam scopulum sic fugias inauditum atque insolens verbum.*" That is, make sure "you avoid a strange and unfamiliar word as you would a dangerous reef."[128] When in Rome, speak not as the Romans do but in a way that the *populares* could digest the ideological underpinnings of the texts; be a salesman! "The political object in writing the Commentaries," as Holmes (*COG* p. 194) notes, "was not to apologize for his conquest, but to celebrate it ... The *Commentaries* were an *apologia*: they were not an apology." There are no *meae culpae*; dictators-to-be do not apologize.

The annual reports then, as Mommsen (*HR* 4, p. 605) concludes, were "to justify as well as possible before the public the formally unconstitutional enterprise of . . . conquering a great country and constantly increasing his army . . . without instructions." But that is only partially true because, as Long (3, p. 433) notes, the Senate had already commissioned the massacres, "the grant of *Gallia Comata* in general terms was equivalent to a commission to make war in the country."

What the future dictator failed to mention, but which was written in the subtext of every page, was his deep psychological need to surpass Alexander the Great who appeared to him in a dream and caused him great shame. He felt similarly when he measured himself against Gnaeus Pompey who seemed more destined to become Rome's Alexander having, at the age of 30, already been declared *Magnus*. Nor did Caesar mention that his proconsulship in Gaul was his means, his place, his once-in-a-lifetime opportunity to equal both those *Magni* while ridding Rome of barbarian filth and getting rich in the process. All Caesar had to do was slaughter a million or so, then he'd be a grand *imperator*, a *magnus* beyond compare and able to take the fight to Pompey in a civil war where Rome's slaughter would turn upon itself. Pompey might have been called, however unjustly deserved, an *adulescentulus carnifex* but Caesar became the *carnifex maximus* and arguably "the first *génocidaire* in European history."

Silver denarius from 44 BC depicting the tetrastyle temple the Senate decreed to honor Caesar's *clementia* but which was never built. On the obverse surrounding the temple is engraved *CLEMENTIAE CAESARIS;* on the reverse is depicted a galloping horseman, holding a whip in his right hand and the reins of the second horse in his left; a wreath and palm branch fill in the field; in relief is the name of the moneyer, P. SEPULLIUS above, and MACER below.

CHAPTER 7

HISTORY SAYS CAESAR WAS NOT *NATURA LENISSIMUS*

THERE ARE SEVERAL MODERN HISTORIANS—Thomas Holmes and even Theodor Mommsen come to mind—who have difficulty seeing the genocidist part of Julius Caesar's, if not nature, actions, a man who engaged in unbridled massacre during his near-decade tour in Gaul. Perhaps their assessment relied too heavily on the words of the ancient historian Suetonius who said Caesar was clement by nature. In the very first words of Chapter 74 of the life of the dictator, Suetonius asserts rather boldly, "*Sed et in ulciscendo natura lenissimus. . .*" That is, Caesar was "by nature most merciful" even when it came to "avenging wrongs"—the "*et*" here translated as even—when it came to dealing with those who had done him harm. So the statement implies he took into account the feelings of others generally but even when they were responsible for harming him. And, even if Caesar was moved to pardon his enemies during the civil war, we must put those actions in a whole other category from those that show how he treated the barbarians in Gaul and its surrounding nations—as "animals."[129] Of course it is difficult to pinpoint what the Senate had in its republican mind but in 44 BC it passed a resolution to erect a temple to celebrate Caesar's show of *clementia* during his life. The temple was to be called *Aedes Clementia Caesaris* ("The Temple of the Clemency of Caesar").¹³⁰ Clearly, the Eburones and Aduatuci had not been polled about the architectural design of the monument nor the ailing tribesmen who found their hands cut off after they surrendered to the general.

Thus, when *clementia* is mentioned as a characteristic of Caesar's personality and managerial strategies, a distinction must be made between his actions in his war against the barbarian hordes and those against his fellow citizens during the civil war. Indeed, we can say there were four phases in Caesar's life when it comes to patterns of his behavior: the first includes what he did up to becoming consul in 59; the second, what he did in Gaul from 58 to 50; the third, what he did during the civil war; and the last, his days as a dictator.

Caesar mentions *clementia* and/or *mansuetudo* only twice in the whole of the *De Bello Gallico* and not at all in the *Bellum Civile*. In the *De Bello* he depicts the Bellovaci (*BG* 2.14.5) asking him to "show your [his] customary mercy and kindness toward them" "customary" translated as "sua," implying that such an approach was already part of his managerial repertoire. A scholar so attuned to the nuances of language, as Caesar was, could easily have written the text without using a reflexive possessive adjective. But in both instances, Caesar is projecting an image of himself that has no basis in his history, in fact the opposite is true, so what was he thinking when he chose to project a public identity of himself as merciful before he entered Gaul? And from what source would the barbarians have heard of such merciful exploits once he was there?

With respect to the nature of Caesar's clemency after the Rubicon was crossed, Cicero tells his friend Atticus (*Att* 10.4.8) in April 49—three months after the die had been cast—that Caesar's inveterate supporter, Gaius Scribonius Curio, had stopped by his house and, when the subject of clemency was broached, there was talk about whether Caesar would engage in the massacre of fellow citizens. With respect to Caesar's disposition as a clement person, Curio told Cicero, "Caesar himself was not by inclination [*voluntate*] and nature [*natura*] averse to cruelty but thought mild measures [*clementiam*] would win him popularity. But, if the winds of the populace were to change, he would be cruel."[131] The previous month, though in a somewhat different context, in a letter to this same friend, Cicero (*Att* 8.16.2) refers to Caesar's tactics as "*insidiosa clementia.*" And in December 50, three weeks before the warring began, Cicero warns his friend (*Att* 7.7.7) about the course Caesar might follow, "For no one can be certain of the result once we come to fighting: but everyone is certain that, if the loyalists are beaten, this man will not be more merciful than Cinna in the massacre of the nobility, nor less rapacious than Sulla in confiscating the property of the rich."

The insurrectionist general provided an answer to the troublesome question in a letter to Oppius on March 5, 49, aware that Roman citizens feared he might adopt the same approach toward slaughtering at home that he used in Gaul (*Att* 9.7c1). He assured his friend that he would take "a new kind of conquering to strengthen one's position by kindness and generosity. As to how this can be done, some ideas have occurred to me and many more can be found." His hope was that through such, "moderation we can win all hearts and secure a lasting victory, since by cruelty others have been unable to escape from hatred and to sustain their victory for any length of time except L. Sulla, whose example I do not intend to follow." A wishful thinking smoke screen? Clearly, it is a stage of his personal and political development that differed radically from his evaluation of human life during his tour of duty in Gaul.

But, as the Notre Dame University classicist Luca Grillo so brilliantly clarifies, when Caesar advertises himself as a man of *misericordia* in his relations with the barbarians, what compels him to show clemency (pp. 99, 100) is "not care for their lives, but for his own good image, *ut videretur*, that he be seen a certain way." That is, "by Caesar's own admission, he feels no pity but extends leniency for practical ends." Seeking to out-Marius Marius, he sought to portray himself to folks back home as the ideal Roman general when, in fact, posterity now sees him as the ideal Roman showman. Even when he says he is showing mercy to the natives, the statistics show him upping the massacre ante. What must he have thought when he began writing Book 7 and had to portray his enemy, Vercingetorix, showing true mercy for his people in refusing to destroy a beloved town for the sake of military advantage? The issues behind the barbarian's decision can be found in the text but the long and short of it is that Vercingetorix accedes to the will of his fellow tribesmen—the text says he heard their prayers, *precibus ipsorum*—and showed compassion to the multitude—*misericordia vulgi*—the barbarian did not respond as an insurrectionist but as a respecter of the common good, as if he was part of a republic!

It also needs to be pointed out that, before Caesar entered the political arena, the concept of *clementia* was not a fully formed notion, assuredly not in political matters, and most assuredly not what it came to be in the Christian era. Historians Stefan Weinstock (p. 236) and Melissa Dowling emphasize that we hardly see *clementia* in use in the political realm before the first century. Going back to 160, Terence, in his *Adelphoe*, depicts a stern (*durus*) father who abandons his hard ways by choosing to show *clementia* toward those who have done wrong (Rozeboom, p. 85)—a paterfamilias taking a softer approach to his rule of the family. But, as Weinstock (p. 235) points out, the word *clementia* "never appears in Naevius, Ennius, Lucilius, nor in the fragments of early scenic poetry, history, or oratory." Plautus uses it only in the adjectival form of *clemens* and, while distinctions can be made about which words best reflect mercy, over time *clemens* and *clementia* came be associated, or even exchanged, with: *misericordia, lenitas, humanitas, mansuetudo, liberalitas, comitas, modestia, temperantia, magnitudo animi, modus,* and *moderatio* (Konstan, 341).[132]

Of course the first systematic treatise on the subject of mercy appeared in 55/56 AD when Lucius Anneaus Seneca (Seneca the Younger) penned *De Clementia* as a kind of apologia for the deadly actions of his intemperate pupil, the Emperor Nero. Previously the magister had delivered speeches on behalf of the boy-emperor that were supposed to reflect his mindset regarding clemency (Sullivan, 2017). Cicero had shown philosophical interest in *clementia* because he regarded it as a virtue, a trait that leaders should adopt who had an abiding interest in the commonwealth of a nation. In his *De Officiis* (1.88), which appeared in Oct-Nov 44, seven months after Caesar's death, the barrister—while still trying to reconcile the phases of the dictator's life—argues that *clementia* (as well as *mansuetudo*) are praiseworthy virtues in a leader. His explication is worth reading in full; he says, "Neither must we listen to those who think that one should indulge in violent anger against one's political enemies and imagine that such is the attitude of a great-spirited, brave man. For nothing is more commendable, nothing more becoming in a pre-eminently great man than courtesy [*placabilitas*] and forbearance [*clementia*]. Indeed, in a free people, where all enjoy equal rights before the law, we must school ourselves to affability and what is called 'mental poise;' for if we are irritated when people intrude upon us at unseasonable hours or make unreasonable requests, we shall develop a sour, churlish temper, prejudicial to ourselves and offensive to others. And yet gentleness of spirit and forbearance are to be commended only with the understanding that strictness [*severitas*] may be exercised for the good of the state; for without that, the government cannot be well administered. On the other hand, if punishment or correction must be administered, it need not be insulting; it ought to have regard to the welfare of the state, not to the personal satisfaction of the man who administers the punishment or reproof."

It is not surprising, therefore, that we find Cicero in three speeches made before Caesar, serving as judge in 46 and 45, making reference to *clementia* 13 times (Weinstock, (p. 236).[133] He was playing very hard on sensibilities that Caesar had manifested at several important junctures, for example, after his victory in 49 at Corfinium and at the Battle of Pharsalus in August of 48, the general telling his men on both occasions to treat with kindness those Romans they had defeated. We must give Caesar this.

That is, in June of 49, "When conditions of surrender were under discussion at Ilerda," Suetonius (*Div* 75.2) tells us, "friendly intercourse between the two parties was constant, Afranius and Petreius, with a sudden change of purpose, put to death all of Caesar's soldiers whom they found in their camp; but Caesar could not bring himself to retaliate in kind. At the battle of Pharsalus he cried out, 'Spare your fellow citizens,' and afterwards allowed each of his men to save any one man he pleased of the opposite party."

But, as intimated, Caesar had already clarified such a position in a letter to Cicero after Corfinium, (*Att* 9.16.1) "You judge me quite accurately—for my character is well known to you—when you say that nothing is more remote from my disposition than cruelty. For myself, as I take great delight in this policy for its own sake, so your approval of my action gives me a triumphant feeling of gladness. Nor am I shaken by the fact that those, who were allowed to go free by me, are said to have departed with the intention of renewing the war against me: for there is nothing I like better than that I should be what I am, they what they are."

Again, such an approach toward defeated fellow Romans raised the political eyebrows of people of all political persuasions in Rome, some still perplexed about whether Caesar would adopt the cruel measures of the Greek tyrant, Phalaris, or follow the ways of Pisistratus who, Herodotus said, had "administered the state constitutionally and organized the state's affairs properly and well." (*Att* 7.20.2). Of course, Caesar's partisans thought him a fool for taking such a stance, Cicero (*Att* 14.22.1) acknowledging that his *clementia* ultimately brought him down, saying, "his clemency did him harm; and that if he had not shown it, nothing of the sort would have befallen him."[134] Is that not why he spoke of Caesar's *clementia* as *insidiosa*? But today, with our understanding of the practice of "restorative justice" as a practice to heal divisions from harms and harms caused by divisions, we see Caesar's *clementia* during and after the civil war as a laissez-faire wishful-thinking poorly-orchestrated strategy of social control.

With respect to Caesar's policy and practices in Gaul, the Italian historian, Guglielmo Ferrero says that Caesar had no idea of "the risks and vicissitudes [they] might be likely to involve. He would make up his mind on the spot, when he was face to face with the situation ... Politics had become little more than the art of framing happy improvisations." That is, if the situation called for vengeance, he would be cruel. In this regard Willem der Boer (Balázs, p. 248 n30) says Caesar was essentially a jazz artist full of "ingenious improvisations" in contrast, say, to Pompey whose actions were far more measured. In trying to assess the sincerity of Caesar's motives in acting as a *homo clemens*, György Balázs (p. 248) hedges his bets, "there is no general consensus in present historical research as to whether the *clementia Caesaris* was a part of the great statesman or whether it can be regarded as a political and ideological phenomenon." But for Caesar, as Max Treu (p. 215) avers, neither *clementia* nor *misericordia* secure the well-being of the state or one's personal position in history, but only soldiers and money alone. He reminds us of Dio's assessment of the dictator (42.49.4), "he showed himself a money-getter, declaring that there were two things which created, protected, and increased sovereignties—soldiers and money—and that these two were dependent on each other. For it was by proper maintenance, he said, that armies were kept together, and this maintenance was secured by arms; and in case either one of them were lacking, the other also would be overthrown at the same time." From the time he was an *adulescens*, the dictator-to-be well understood the relationships among power and money and arms and the limited role *clementia* could play in such a triumvirate.

CHAPTER 8

THROAT-SLITTING AS A SHOW OF MERCY?

To gain the quintessential insight into Caesar's character (*voluntas*) and psycho-genetic disposition (*natura*) with respect to *clementia*, we need to return to the encounter the dictator-to-be had with pirates off the island of Pharmacusa in the winter of 74-73. There he proved Suetonius wrong; he was not *natura lenissimus*, clement by nature, especially when it came to *et in ulciscendo*. That was the year he slit the throats of pirates as their payment for capturing him on the open seas and holding him for ransom. In assessing the chronology of Caesar's adventure with Cilician pirates in 74, as well as the cast of characters involved, Georgetown historian Josiah Osgood offers valuable insights. But a short way into his analysis (p. 322) he sets up a troublesome roadblock when he says that, "Modern writers, too, have had a tendency to use the tale as a glimpse of what is to come." That is, the actions the young Caesar took to deal with the pirates, once he was free from their clutches, cannot be considered an indicator of how he would behave in the future. That is not so, indeed it is the first significant piece of data we have about the development of Caesar's *memoria tenebat* view of righting wrongs with violence. It cannot be stressed enough that the young Caesar was not a man of *clementia* by nature or otherwise.

The story is: in 74 or the winter of 74-73, the 26-year old nobleman, while sailing to Rhodes to continue study with the famed rhetorician Apollonius Molon,[135] was captured by a band of Cilician pirates. "Cilician" was the generic term used to describe all the pirates who sailed the Mediterranean to seize cargo ships and important Romans for whom they might demand lucrative ransoms. Plutarch (*Pomp* 24.4-5) says the pirates had more than 1,000 ships and over time were able to put 400 cities under their control. Dio (36.20-21) explains how such a thing came about; he says pirating of that scale emerged as one of the insidious side-effects of Rome's endless wars. Thus, it can be said that the 26-year old found himself a victim of his country's own imperialist policies that he later would champion and raise to the level of insurrection. And, while nearly all the ancient historians have accounts of the incident, some stretch the bounds of credibility with overly dramatic details of the seizure and emancipation so that they find themselves out on the limb of truth. Osgood suggests the dramatic, somewhat fantastic, details of the event could have come from a gloating young Caesar himself when he shared the story with his secretary Gaius Oppius after returning safely to Rome. At any rate, the young Julius Caesar found himself a victim of the insidious side-effects of war[136] as did other prominent citizens who found themselves in the clutches of anarchic bands of pirates.[137]

While ancient historians Suetonius (*Div* 8.23.1); Plutarch (*Caes* 1.4.2); Polyaenus (*Strat* 8.23.1); and Velleius Paterculus (*Hist* 2.41.1; 2.42.1) all take up the matter with differing narratives, the core facts are: (1) once captured, Caesar was held captive for 38 days; (2) the Cilician horde sent a contingent of Caesar's skeletal crew to Miletus to secure a ransom of 50 talents of silver for his release; (3) upon their return with the ransom money, Caesar was freed; (4) boiling with vengeance, the young nobleman headed to Miletus and, as a private citizen (*privatus*), begged and borrowed ships and a crew; (5) backed by a small armada he returned to the scene of the crime and took a large number of pirates captive whom he imprisoned in Pergamum; (6) he went to the governor of the region (Asia and Bythinia), Marcus Junius Juncus, and impudently demanded that the state take action again the brigands; (7) an over-worked Juncus said he would take the matter up in due time, intimating he himself might take the captives and sell them off as slaves; (8) dissatisfied with the decision, a disgruntled Caesar hastened to Pergamum, extracted the robbers from prison, and crucified them, which is what he warned them he would do when they held him; Velleius (2.42.3) says he, "returned to the coast with incredible speed and crucified all his prisoners before anyone had time to receive a dispatch from the consul in regard to the matter;" (9) and, as a show of mercy toward the brigands, Suetonius says (*Div* 74.1), Caesar slit their throats—the very chronicler who boldly stated that Caesar's personality was merciful by nature, even when it came to dealing with those who had harmed him.

First of all, with respect to Caesar's capture and the pirates' demand for ransom: after the reward had been paid, Caesar could have treated the whole thing as a bad experience and been on his way to Rhodes to see his teacher, "lumping it" as legal anthropologists say (Felstiner p. 81), that is, "ignoring the dispute, by declining to take any or much action in response to the controversy." But that was not to be for a man whose fundamental ethic at that age was already one of *memoria tenebat*. Thus, the late Austrian-born classical scholar Ernst Badian (p. 19) seems to be more in tune with the nature, and meaning, of Caesar's response to his capture generally and specifically to the punishment measures he embraces. That is, he says it is, "the first example of his callous ruthlessness that was to reach its climax in the Gallic War."

Secondly, and more importantly, Caesar wanted the brigands to be punished *quam celerrime*—his calling card—so he could receive satisfaction or justice and be on his way. In terms of the punishment measures available, Juncus indicated that selling the pirates into slavery would have been just-desserts enough. And, even though they'd be enslaved for life—though many slaves were freed—they would remain among the living. They would not be subject to the finality of capital punishment. Thus, being sold as a slave was comparable to being sentenced to prison for life with or without a cell. But that was not sufficient for Caesar who opted for the death penalty via crucifixion. And he was not about to wait days to watch the brigands slowly languish on the cross, he sought immediate satisfaction which explains the throat-slitting to be an act of expediency not mercy. If he had left with the pirates hanging on the cross, it was possible that Juncus—disagreeing with the young man's vigilantism—could have taken the hanging souls down and sold them as he indicated he wanted to do. Again, Caesar, as a private citizen, appropriated the state's function and assumed the role of punisher-in-chief. Meier (p.109) is being too generous when he says, "there is no doubt that such self-sufficiency and arrogance were exceedingly unusual: such decisive action in the name of Roman rule, or at least in its interest, in the interest of bold efficiency and as a demonstration of Roman power—and executed with such energy!" It can be said that, as a young man, Caesar was already declaring: L'état, c'est moi. Moi!

And not long after Caesar arrived in Rhodes, he heard that Mitradates had refused to recognize Nicomedes IV's bequest of his kingdom to Rome and launched an invasion into Bithynia. And while the Senate in Rome took action by assigning the consuls Lucius Licinius Lucullus and Marcus Aurelius Cotta to head east and put out the administrative fire, Caesar, still a private citizen, took it upon himself to sail from Rhodes to the mainland and once again raise a private army which he led into battle. He wanted to avoid, as Suetonius (*Div* 4.2) says, "the appearance of inaction when the allies of the Roman people were in danger." He enjoyed some success in that his auxiliaries drove, Suetonius continues, "the king's governor out of the province, retained in their allegiance the cities which were wavering and ready to revolt." But as a private citizen! And, oddly enough, Caesar was not done with the pirate problem for, when Marcus Antonius Creticus—elected praetor in 74—was commissioned to stem the threat of piracy on the open seas in 73, Caesar joined his staff and became part of a mission that turned out to be an abject failure.[138]

It is worth noting that, by raising an army as a private citizen on two back-to-back occasions to punish evil-doers, Caesar could have claimed there was precedence for such action in the Republic. Indeed in 509 BC, at the very birth of the Republic, Rome's first consul Lucius Brutus engaged in a similar act for a seemingly similar reason. Cicero (*Rep* 2.46) says he, "freed his fellow citizens from the unjust yoke of cruel servitude. And though Brutus was only a private citizen, he sustained the whole burden of the government, and was the first in our state to demonstrate that no one is a mere private citizen when the liberty of his fellows needs protection." And, a decade before Caesar's exploits (in 83), a 23-year old Pompey had raised an army as a private citizen and joined Sulla's efforts during his civil war. As Appian (*BC* 1.80.1) says, Pompey had come forth with "a legion he had collected from the territory of Picenum owing to the reputation of his father . . . A little later he recruited two more legions and became Sulla's righthand man in these affairs." A private citizen raising three legions?

Precedent or not; Caesar was acting the part of a vigilante on two occasions. Again we turn to Cicero's incisive assessment of the man's character, which we find in Plutarch, (*Cicero* 4.8), "At all events, the man who is thought to have been the first to see beneath the surface of

Caesar's public policy and to fear it, as one might fear the smiling surface of the sea, and who comprehended the powerful character hidden beneath his kindly and cheerful exterior . . . that in most of Caesar's political plans and projects he saw a tyrannical purpose."

And, while we have no words of Caesar to indicate what was going through his mind when he raised an army in Asia to execute lawless pirates in opposition to the wishes of the State in the person of Juncus, we do have his view of accountability and punishment in 63 when the Senate was deliberating about what punishments were to be meted out to five insurrectionists who had joined Catiline in his effort to overthrow the government. To harness these five individuals, the senate had enacted a *senatus consultum ultimum*, its most powerful tool to respond to a situation it believed had threatened the life of the Republic; it was tantamount to imposing martial law in response to a declared act of treason.

Caesar, then a praetor-designate, knew exactly how Catiline's accomplices should be handled. He stood up among the senators and directly contradicted the reasoning behind the measures he took when he responded to the pirates who had captured him for ransom. With respect to the insurrectionists, who had threated the life-blood of the State by seizing it for ransom, he argued against the death penalty, saying that death was no penalty at all, that it was mild in comparison to life imprisonment and thus the men should be imprisoned. He said the death penalty was against the principles of the Roman people and, if the Senate went down this path, their vengeance would come to haunt them and their children in the future, that people would remember the punishment and forget the crime involved. He was retroactively admitting that he acted against the principles of the Roman people when he executed the pirates.

His solution was to have the Senate take away everything the culprits owned and, as Appian (2.6) says, "distribute the culprits among the towns in Italy," which was essentially sentencing the accused to house arrest in different parts of the region. This he regarded as the severest penalty? In his fourth Catilinarian speech (7-10) Cicero reports that Caesar, to give teeth to his position, added that any public official in one of the towns where a prisoner was kept, who allowed a detainee to escape, would be dealt with harshly. And, as Sallust (*Cat* 43) clarifies, no one was even to "refer this case to the senate or bring it before the people under pain of being considered by the Senate to have designs against the welfare of the state and the common safety." That is, the records of the case, indeed any reminder of it, were to be sealed forever. It was a kind of *damnatio memoriae* whereby those convicted of a crime would be deleted from Rome's collective memory—and the whereabouts of the prisoners forgotten. Of course, voluntary exile remained an option which was tantamount to imprisoning the insurrectionists elsewhere for perpetuity. Thus, the man whom Suetonius described as most lenient when it came to responding to harms-done, was arguing for the most severe sanction possible for Catiline's accomplices—life in prison—the very measure he argued against nine years earlier when responding to brigands who had threatened his life.[139] And while people's views on punishment and correction change over time, we suggest that when Caesar said imprisonment was no punishment at all, it was his transactional nature in operation. Because of the modest punishment Caesar recommended for the insurrectionists, and for other reasons as well, it is understandable why more than a few Romans believed that Caesar, however indirectly, was somehow behind Catiline's insurrectionist effort.

CHAPTER 9

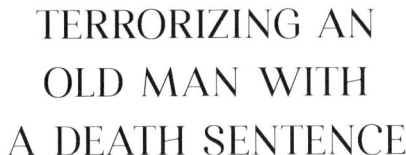

TERRORIZING AN OLD MAN WITH A DEATH SENTENCE

THE DEVELOPMENT OF CAESAR'S non-*clementia*-producing *memoria tenebat* managerial style, if you will, can also be traced to a prosecution he instigated in 63 against an aged and seemingly undistinguished senator nearly 40 years after the man had been accused of murdering a tribune of the people. It was no small matter; Dio (37.26.1) says it "caused the greatest disorder." As far as prosecuting cases in the courts of Rome, Caesar was no newcomer. In 77, as a 23-year old, he took on the former consul Gnaeus Cornelius Dolabella, accusing him of extortion during his governorship in Macedonia. The following year he brought suit against a former lieutenant of Sulla, Gaius Antonius Hybrida, for extortion while stationed in the Greek province of Achaea.[140] Taking up cases like this, Lily Ross Taylor says (1941, p.119), was "a well-established custom of the young Roman who wished to secure political advancement." Nevertheless, we must keep in mind that 63 was an especially significant year because that was the year when Caesar was elected Pontifex Maximus and when various Senators accused him of being in cahoots with Catiline, however indirectly, and his insurrectionists.

But what could have been the political payoff for a young politico for taking so dramatic a step as to accuse an aged senator of high treason through an antiquated legal procedure called *perduellio*? If convicted, a person so charged was subject to death by hanging from the fated *arbor infelix* or by being cast off the dreaded Tarpeian Rock to stones several stories below. In addition, the families of the dead man were forbidden to mourn his passing, and his house was to be razed to the ground. The late classicist Ernest George Hardy (p. 13) says the politically green Caesar took up the case because he, "still needed a rallying cry to unite the populares against the senatorial government which the new consul [Cicero] was known to favor, and with which it was not impossible that Pompey on his return might ally himself." Ultimately Caesar was arguing that the state could not use its power to issue a *senatus consultum ultimum*—a state of emergency tantamount to martial law—against its *populares* opponents which it had done 37 years earlier; a procedure rarely used in the Republic's history and then only to deal with major crises. If he was successful, by using an old man's life as expendable political bait, the state's *ultimatum* power to defend itself against those who threatened its continuity would be sorely diminished.

Although there are divergencies in the telling of the story, some significant, the basic facts of the case are as follows: Gaius Rabirius, the senator in question, was being accused all those years later for killing, or participating in killing, a tribune of the people Lucius Appuleius Saturninus in 100, a man with a highly-checkered past to say the least.[14] In 63 the charge was brought against Rabirius by a current tribune of the people, Titus Labienus—the same Labienus who effected changes in the law to make it easier for Caesar to become *pontifex maximus* and who, in five years time, would become Caesar's arch-lieutenant in his Gallic campaigns. Though Caesar was behind the proceeding, Labienus seemed a good choice to serve as his prosecutorial surrogate because Labienus' uncle had been killed with Saturninus and others of his populist faction.

The story continues: In 100 Saturninus was serving as tribune of the people for the third time, the same year Marius entered upon his sixth term as consul, and that Gaius Servilius Glaucia, a collaborator of both men in legislative matters and otherwise, was serving as praetor.[142] The three acted as a kind of conspiratorial triumvirate. Glaucia, whom Cicero (*Brutus* 224) called "the most abandoned wretch that ever existed" hoped to run for consul the following year but the law stipulated that active praetors had to wait at least two years before throwing their toga into the ring. Glaucia ran nevertheless, and against Gaius Memmius, who kept saying Glaucia's candidacy was illegal because he failed to meet the requirements of the law. To silence him Saturninus and Glaucia hired a hitman who murdered Memmius openly in the comitia. Appian (*BC* 32.1) says, "they sent a gang of ruffians to attack him with clubs while the election was going on, who fell upon him in the midst of the comitia and beat him to death in the sight of all." It was nothing new for Saturninus who, when running for his tribuneship the year before, had his opponent Aulus Nonius murdered which opened up a seat for him.[143] Ancient documents say so. Valerius Maximus (9.7.3) says, Saturninus' supporters forced Nonius "to flee to his own house; and then dragging him out from there, they slew him; so that by the slaughter of an honorable citizen, they might make way for that pernicious man to gain power."

The day after Memmius was murdered, the senate issued a *senatus consultum ultimum* against Saturninus and Glaucia. As noted, the *consultum* was an emergency measure for the preservation of the state that was tantamount to declaring martial law. The long form of the decree was written as "*consules darent operam ne quid detrimenti res publica caperet*" or "*videant consules ne quid res publica detrimenti capiat*" "let the consuls take a measure to ensure that the state suffers no harm." Orosius offers a dramatic take on the confrontation between the then-consul, Marius, and the killers (his friends) whom he was sent to take into custody. He says (5.17.6-10) Saturninus, "after daring to commit these infamous deeds, held a meeting at his own house and there was acclaimed 'king' by some and 'general' by others" which emboldened him. The brigands were not going to surrender peacefully. Orosius says a "battle took place in the forum but Marius forced Saturninus to take refuge in the Capitol." Marius then, he says, "cut the pipes which furnished that place with water. Thereupon a savage battle took place at the entrance of the Capitol. Many around [Gaius] Saufeius [the quaestor] and Saturninus were slain. Saturninus cried out loudly and called the people to witness that Marius was the cause of all their difficulties. Marius next forced Saturninus, Saufeius, and [Quintus] Labienus to flee for refuge in the senate house, where some Roman knights broke down the doors and killed them." Glaucia fled and "was dragged from the home of Claudius and killed . . . Cn. Dolabella, the brother of Saturninus, while fleeing with L. Giganius through the Forum Holitorium, was put to death." The threat to public order was over. And, as the law required, Furius, the tribune of the people "decreed that the property of all these men should be confiscated."[144]

Appian's version of the end of the melee (*BC* 1.32) is, "As everybody demanded that they should be put to death at once, Marius shut them up in the senate-house as though he intended to deal with them in a more legal manner. The crowd considered this a mere pretext, tore the tiles off the roof, and stoned them to death, including a quaestor, a tribune, and a praetor, who were still wearing their insignia of office." Glaucia, who managed to escape to his home, the committee—among whom was Rabirius—pursued, dragged him out of the house, and killed him.¹⁴⁵ Rabirius was part of the posse responsible for executing the state's "warrant" and was charged with the murder.

As indicated, Labienus did not prosecute Rabirius in a court that dealt with violence (*questio de vi*) or even in a court designed to hear murder and assassination cases (*questio de sicariis*) but in a special court of high treason for the crime of *perduellio*. And Caesar was well aware of the purposes and jurisdiction of the different tribunals because the year before, 64, he had served as *iudex quaestionis* and was involved in all sorts of cases including those of *de sicariis*. A lesser crime would be heard before a jury but under the charge of treason, Rabirius was brought before two ad hoc judges called *duumviri perduellonis*, one of whom turned out to be Caesar, the other his cousin (and consul the previous year), Lucius Caesar.¹⁴⁶ We need to interject at this point that Sceva, a slave of Quintus Crito, was credited with the killing for which he was awarded his freedom. In effect, the culprit had been caught and Caesar knew about it.

Although Rabirius had the great Quintus Hortensius as his attorney, he was found guilty—Caesar being one of the two judges rendering the verdict. It was a set-up. On appeal, with Cicero now his lawyer, Rabirius appeared before the people's assembly, the *comitia centuriata*, where the decision of the duumviri would assuredly be upheld. And once convicted in such a court, as mentioned, the convicted person would be tied or nailed to a wooden post or cross called the *arbor infelix* or thrown off a 80-foot cliff on the south side of the Capitoline Hill known as the Tarpean Rock. And, as we find in *Digest* (3 tit. 2,s 1), the house of the *perduelle*, was to be razed, and his relatives were forbidden to mourn him having been defined as an enemy (*hostis*) of the people.¹⁴⁷ So these were no small potatoes.

But, as Cicero was arguing his essentially lost-cause case before the people's assembly, a *deus ex machina* appeared in the person of the current praetor, Quintus Metellus Celer, who hastened to the Janiculum and took down the military flag that flew atop it. In accord with an ancient tradition, when the flag was taken down, all public deliberations were disbanded.[148] Thus, the trial was over; Rabirius had cheated death. Of course, Labienus had the right to continue the case on appeal but did not; Caesar had made his case which he prosecuted "with such eagerness" Suetonius (*Div* 12.1) says, "that when Rabirius appealed to the people, nothing was so much in his favor as the bitter hostility of the judge." Walter (p. 67) calls it "a belated thirst for vengeance." It was another example of Caesar honing his *memoria tenebat* strategy: *natura lenissimus*?

Whether taking up the case met Caesar's need for political recognition and the furtherment of his political cause or not—it did—the late classicist Max Cary (p. 489) says, "Caesar, whose instincts of showmanship got the better of his discretion, gave the proceedings a dramatic turn which in effect reduced them to a farce." But was it a farce? Caesar had issued a warning to the Senate and the *optimates* faction that they were not to interfere with the populist movement and execute a tribune without consequence—even in a case like that of Saturninus and Glaucia who had murdered a political enemy.[149] To repeat, if Rabirius had been convicted, it might have constrained the Senate's power to override procedural due process in time of crisis for the benefit of the state's well-being. Of course, the Senate did continue to issue ultimatum decrees; indeed that very year, one was decreed in response to Catiline's insurrection against the Republic. By taking action against Rabirius, Caesar was more than intimating that the nuclear option of the state (the *consultum*) had been challenged with a nuclear option of his own (trial by *perduellio*). Through his own sustained insurrection beginning 14 years later, he became the state and began to fashion a society consistent with his own dystopian or fascist ideals—what is the bon mot here? But first he had to go to Gaul to raise the money and an army to make that happen, massacring hundreds of thousands of barbarian hordes as foreign *perduelles*. For the young ambitious Caesar, extinguishing the life of an old worn-out undistinguished senator for the sake of a cause was no more than squishing a noisome gnat that got in through the screen door on a summer day. This from a man whom the Senate would decree a temple of mercy to celebrate his thoughtfulness. Would he have gone through with the execution of Rabirius if Metellus had not orchestrated his *deus ex machina*? Sorry to query this way, Ladies and Gentlemen of the Jury, but is not the answer yes?

CHAPTER 10

THREATENING TO DELETE A PERSON FROM HISTORY

A CRITIC OF CAESAR MIGHT SAY THAT, when it came to exacting revenge and retribution, Julius Caesar was as predictable as the annual coming of the Ides of March. Gérard Walter saw into Caesar many centuries after Cicero did, recognizing his (p. 79), "good memory, especially when it came to settling certain personal accounts." Indeed, as we see from the evidence offered thus far, Ladies and Gentlemen of the Jury, vindictiveness was a key element in Caesar's personality. Not only did he eradicate persons, cities, nations ex post facto but did so through pre-emptive strikes. How many times does he say in his *De Bello Gallico* that, if he hadn't taken steps to destroy someone or something, he would have had a bigger headache on his hands in days to come? The same cynic might lay upon him as an appropriate moniker, therefore, *Imperator Memoria Tenebat*, General Punishment. But in a court of law, cynicism is not evidence. The evidence says that Caesar's vindictive memory reared its head in 62, when, in his new position as praetor, he made an attempt to remove the name (*abolitio nominis*) of Quintus Lutatius Catulus from the annals of history. It was a kind of *damnatio memoriae*, the culmination of years of enmity between the two men, with Caesar finally organizing his psyche in a *triplex acies* formation to make it seem Catulus never existed.[150]

First of all, the year before, in 63, as already said, Caesar had been elected to the coveted position of Pontifex Maximus an honor, all things being equal, that should have gone to one of two prominent well-known elder statesmen and senior colleagues of Caesar in the College of Pontiffs. Both had served as consul: Publius Servilius Vatia Isauricus, in 79, and the aforementioned Quintus Lutatius Catulus Capitolanus the year before (and Caesar, if you will recall, had served under Servilius in Cilicia). Plutarch's view was that (*Caes* 7.1), "though they were most illustrious men and of the greatest influence in the senate, Caesar would not give way to them, but presented himself to the people as a rival candidate." Thus, at 26, Caesar was elected to the highest position in Rome's priestly class.[151]

And because Caesar's candidacy (Plutarch *Caes* 7.4) "made the senate and nobles afraid that he would lead the people on to every extreme of recklessness," Catulus offered him money (a bribe?) to drop out of the race, this from a man who was the leader of the Senate (*princeps senatus*), and who also served as *censor* in 65.[152] Dio says (37.46.3) he was a "man who always, more conspicuously than anyone who ever lived, preferred the common weal to everything else."[153] This is indeed high praise in an era when factional politics often resulted in crippling violence and even murder. Cicero (*Sest* 57.122) called Catulus a man of balance, "accustomed at times to reprove and attack the precipitate counsels of the people, and the blunders of the senate as well, with great freedom." And Plutarch in his Life of Crassus (13.1) referred to him as "the gentlest of the Romans."[154] And because Catulus was held in such esteem, he was given the monumental task of restoring the Capitol that had been severely damaged by fire.

And even though he was Sulla's pick for consul in 79, Catulus told the dictator to cool it on the killing part of his program of proscription, that there wouldn't be an able-bodied man left to serve in the army. Orosius says (5.21.2), "When all the citizens were loudly and openly bewailing the fate that each one individually feared, Q. Catulus then said publicly to Sulla: 'If we kill armed men in time of war and unarmed men in time of peace, who will survive with us?'" And yet when Sulla died in 78, it was Catulus who orchestrated a lavish funeral for the dictator.[155]

There are several instances when these men—Caesar and Catulus—crossed ideological swords, but an event in 69 stands among the most memorable and one for which Caesar was going to make the former consul pay. That year, when Caesar's aunt Julia died—the wife of the great populist hero and general, Marius—he used the opportunity to sing her praises in a speech, though some historians have seen the event as a time when Caesar sought to bring Marius back to life and, by doing so, stir up rebellious sentiments among the *populares*.[156] In dramatic fashion Caesar, Plutarch (*Caes* 6.1-7) says, "had images of Marius secretly made, together with trophy-bearing Victories, and these he ordered to be carried by night and set up on the Capitol. At day-break [passersby] beheld all these objects glittering with gold and fashioned with the most exquisite art (and they bore inscriptions setting forth the Cimbrian successes of Marius)." Marius, like the Lazarus of scripture, was given new life.

But in one respect the event was all about Caesar's future. All who passed by the exquisite display, as Plutarch continues, "were amazed at the daring of the man who had set them up (for it was evident who had done it), and the report of it quickly spreading brought everybody together for the sight. But some cried out that Caesar was scheming to usurp sole power in the state when he thus revived honors which had been buried by laws and decrees, and that this proceeding was a test of the people, whose feelings towards him he had previously softened, to see whether they had been made docile by his ambitious displays and would permit him to amuse himself with such innovations." It made no difference to the "partisans of Marius [who] encouraged one another and showed themselves suddenly in amazing numbers and filled the Capitol with their applause. Many, too, were moved to tears of joy when they beheld the features of Marius, and Caesar was highly extolled by them, and regarded as above all others worthy of his kinship with Marius."

But not all were moved by the partisan display for, "when the senate met to discuss these matters," Plutarch adds, "Catulus Lutatius, a man of the highest repute at that time in Rome, rose up and denounced Caesar, uttering the memorable words: 'No longer, indeed, by sapping and mining, Caesar, but with engines of war do you now capture the government."

Caesar, the supreme politician and ideological warrior, and never one to shirk from a challenge in the Senate or elsewhere, Plutarch says, "defended himself against this charge and convinced the senate, whereupon his admirers were still more elated and exhorted him not to lower his pretensions for any man, since the people would be glad to have him triumph over all opposition and be the first man in the state." By first man in the state, did the frenetic ideologues in Caesar's camp already have dictator in mind?

Thus, Catulus had lost twice, first in an election to Caesar in 63 for the position of supreme pontiff, and six years earlier in an ideological battle Caesar never forgot. In both instances, as Dio (37.37.3) says, Caesar, "showed himself perfectly ready to serve and flatter everybody, even ordinary persons, and shrank from no speech or action in order to get possession of the objects for which he strove. He did not mind temporary groveling when weighed against subsequent power, and he cringed as before superiors to the very men whom he was endeavoring to dominate." With Caesar willing to sell himself this way, it is understandable why in 63 Catulus tried to situate the groveler among Catiline and his band of insurrectionists as they sought to overthrow the state.[157]

Thus, on the morning of January 1, 62, "the first day of his praetorship," Suetonius (*Div* 15.1) reports, "he [Caesar] called upon Quintus Catulus to render an account to the people regarding the restoration of the Capitol, proposing a bill for turning over the commission to some other person." Dio (37.44.1-3) clarifies who that other person might be, "Caesar, who was now praetor . . . had been endeavoring to secure the removal of the name of Catulus from the temple of Jupiter Capitolinus . . . and to have Pompey entrusted with the construction of the remainder of the edifice." Thus, it appears that, "When the consuls went to the Capitol to offer sacrifice at the commencement of their term of office (on January 1), their friends escorted them to the temple and back to their homes. Caesar took advantage of the absence of the aristocrats for his attack on Catulus." That is, he grabbed hold of the mic.

By Capitol, of course, is meant the Temple of Jupiter, also known as the Temple of Jupiter Capitolanus, which dated back to the first year of the Republic in 509.[158] On July 6, 83 the building was severely damaged by fire during the Social War between Marius and Sulla,[159] and Quintus Lutatius Catulus, during the reign of Sulla, was assigned the task of restoring it.[160] And because of his work on the restoration, he received as a *cognomen ex virtute*, the moniker "Capitolanus."[161]

And, when a dedication ceremony was held in 69, Catulus' name had been chiseled into the stone as the restorer of the building; passersby would see something like *"Catulus curator restituendi Capitolii,"* but for all the talk (with respect to the inscription) the job was still not completed when Caesar became praetor in 62.[162] Caesar's attack was politically-based of course, though Catulus has been subject to criticisms for some of the aesthetic choices he made in the restoration.[163]

Dio says (37.44.1-2) that Caesar, "had been endeavoring to secure the removal of the name of Catulus from the temple of Jupiter Capitolanus, charging him with embezzlement and demanding an account of the expenditures he had made, and to have Pompey entrusted with the construction of the remainder of the edifice; for many parts, considering the size and character of the work, were but half finished, or at any rate Caesar pretended this was the case, in order that Pompey might gain the glory for its completion and inscribe his own name instead." In no way did the dictator-to-be want the name of an arch enemy go down in history as accomplishing such a great feat in the eternal city, hence, the public accusation of embezzlement, of [Catulus] using public funds for his own benefit.[164]

It is worth going back to look at the picture the late historian Gérard Walter painted of the first act of the first day of Caesar's praetorship when he took the opportunity to humiliate his opponent. He says (p. 79), "It was the first of January in the year 62. A solemn ceremony was in progress in the Capitol. The Senate was receiving the new consuls in the presence of all the magistrates of the *curia*—praetors, aediles and quaestors who likewise had been appointed that day. Instead of taking his place among his colleagues in conformity with the traditionally established rules of etiquette, Caesar went straight to the Forum and, mounting the platform reserved for him, without much ado launched a formal accusation against Catulus. The reason for the indictment appeared sufficiently compromising for the reputation of the 'most venerated of Romans.'"

As indicated, the indictment had nothing to do with the progress of the temple; it was a vast undertaking. There were still other far deeper issues involved. As indicated as well, Catulus had accused Caesar of being involved in Catiline's insurrection during Cicero's administration in 63. The historian Sallust, an inveterate devotee of Caesar, says in his *The Conspiracy of Catiline* (49.1-2), probably written in 42, that Catulus put pressure on Cicero to indict Caesar for his part in the insurrection: "at the very time Quintus Catulus and Gaius Piso tried in vain by entreaties, influence, and bribes to induce Cicero to have a false accusation brought against Gaius Caesar, either through the Allobroges or some other witness. For both these men were bitter personal enemies of Caesar."[165]

Catulus, when he was informed that he was being accused of wrongdoing on the morning of January 1, hastened to the Forum to speak in his own behalf. Caesar, always ready to grind a political opponent's face in the mud, would not allow the head of the Senate (*princeps senatus*) to speak from the Rostra but from the floor like a plebian. But here is another, and perhaps more important, matter that drove Caesar into his *memoria tenebat* mode. As has been said, Caesar was Marius's nephew by marriage through his aunt Julia, but Marius had another nephew, Marcus Marius Gratidianus, who served as tribune of the plebes in 87 and 82, and it is through Gratidianus' death that we see Catulus in a new light, a light that doubly fueled Caesar's ire.

In 87 Gratidianus, who had developed a small cult following of his own, began prosecution of Catulus' father—of the same name—for a charge of treason (*perduellio*), the same charge Caesar brought against

Rabirius. Although the elder Catulus was counsul with Marius in 102, he opposed him during the Social War and was proscribed. Those convicted were subject to being punished by scourging till death.[166]

Rather than face the ordeal of a legal fait accompli, the senior Catulus took his own life. Velleius Paterculus (2.22.4) says that when the old man, "was being hunted down for death, he shut himself in a room that had lately been plastered with lime and sand; then he brought fire that it might cause a powerful vapor to issue from the plaster, and by breathing the poisonous air and then holding his breath he died a death according rather with his enemies' wishes than with their judgement."[167]

And, while ancient sources vary on the details of what steps Catulus' son, the consul of 78, took to avenge the death of his father—though they got more gory as time went on—there is agreement that Catiline had been hired by Catulus to avenge the death of his father. Plutarch (*Sull* 32.2) says, "Then Catiline, returning this favor of Sulla's, killed a certain Marcus Marius [Gratidianus], one of the opposite faction, and brought his head to Sulla as he was sitting in the forum, and then going to the lustral water of Apollo which was near, washed the blood off his hands." Some sources say the mutilation took place at the burial ground of the older Catulus. Thus, Caesar—in going after Catulus who had avenged the death of his father—on the first day of his praetorship, was avenging the death of a cousin.[168]

Two points are worth mentioning: the first is that Orosius (6.3.1) says Catiline was able to escape an earlier charge made against him of violating the Vestal Virgin, Fabia—half-sister of Terentia, Cicero's wife—with Catulus' help, that Catulus "exerted influence in his behalf and through that he escaped punishment." That is, Catiline's involvement with Gratidianus was the fulfillment of a quid pro quo; the second is a letter from Catiline to Catulus which was read in the Senate, the text of which Sallust (*BC* 35.1-6) offers and is worth reading in full for the insight it offers into the insurrectionist: "Lucius Catilina to Quintus Catulus. Your eminent loyalty, known by experience and grateful to me in my extreme peril, lends confidence to my plea. I have therefore resolved to make no defense of my unusual conduct; that I offer an explanation is due to no feeling of guilt, and I am confident that you will be able to admit its justice. Maddened by wrongs and slights, since I had been robbed of the fruits of my toil and energy and was unable to attain to a position of honor, I followed my usual custom and took up the general cause of the unfortunate; not that I could not pay my personal debts from my own estate (and the liberality of Orestilla sufficed with her own and her daughter's resources to pay off even the obligations incurred through others), but because I saw the unworthy elevated to honors, and realized that I was an outcast because of baseless suspicion. It is for this reason that, in order to preserve what prestige I have left, I have adopted measures which are honorable enough considering my situation. When I would write more, word comes that I am threatened with violence. Now I commend Orestilla to you and entrust her to your loyalty. Protect her from insult, I beseech you in the name of your own children. Farewell."

The web-like complexity of the relationships involved is daunting but for Caesar, who was able to see the nuances in relationships when he wished, saw Catulus in black and white. Thus, he sought to erase his name from history in the same way he would erase the Eburones from the face of history in a few years thence. Here we have an earlier example of Caesar's vindictive punitive streak which excludes him from being associated with *clementia*. He was never really *natura lenissimus*, as Suetonius claimed, especially *et in ulciscendo*, when he found himself wronged in some way.

CHAPTER 11

TRYING OUT MASSACRE AT AN OUT-OF-TOWN VENUE

In 61, Caesar began his year-long appointment as propraetor in Further Spain (*Hispania Ulterior*), a territory he knew well because eight years earlier, as quaestor, he went from town to town to oversee the province's finances and its administration of justice in the assizes courts. This time, endowed with *imperium*, he was supplied with his own army, his first as a public official—and how he handled himself here proved to be a harbinger for his years of massacre in Gaul.[169] Now, heavily in debt, the man who in two years was to pass a law prohibiting the bilking of the provincials—*lex Julia de repetundis*—set his sights on cadging a little something for his own money and glory coffers. The late German historian Wilhelm Drumann says the promoter of the law, "was the same man who was going to corrupt with Gallic gold all the electoral elections in Rome during the years that were to follow."[170] The praetorship was an out-of-town warm-up for the big show in Gaul three years thence.

And the budding politician needed to make a name for himself as a military leader. He needed military credibility as well as money. And though with the new appointment he was moving an additonal step up on the ladder of the *cursus honorum*, he was well aware of how far behind he was to the real-life person he envied most in the glory and *dignitas* departments, Gnaeus Pompey, who years before had been saluted by the dictator Sulla as Magnus, the great one.[171] At this point Caesar was hardly anyone.

Indeed, in September of Caesar's administration in the hinterlands, Pompey was slated to celebrate his third triumph in Rome, a man who, as Pliny the Elder was later to tell (*HN* 7.97) had already in his 30-year career, "slain or received the surrender of 12,183,000 people, sunk or taken 846 ships, received the capitulation of 1,538 towns and forts, subdued the lands from the Maeotians to the Red Sea." He seemed the true heir to Alexander.[172]

Dio (37.52.1-2) provides some insight into Caesar's mind as he crossed the Alps on the way to his new assignment, that is, "He was eager for glory, emulating Pompey and his other predecessors who at one time or another had had great power, and his aspirations were anything but small; in fact, he hoped, if he should at this time accomplish something, to be chosen consul immediately and to display mighty achievements." He needed a war; he needed barbarian victims; he needed money—and he wanted a triumph.

And the only way to accomplish these feats was with an army. As indicated, it would be the first time he would have troops at his disposal as a public official in a foreign land; he had raised troops twice before as a *privatus*, the first time to punish pirates who had captured him for ransom, the second to push back incursions of Mithridates in parts of Asia, but here he was acting as an official magistrate of Rome.

As he entered Corduba, a capital town situated on the Quadalquivir River, Caesar had 20 cohorts waiting for him from the previous administration, about 10,000 soldiers, the equal of two legions.[173] He immediately set about recruiting from the locals 10 additional cohorts, essentially another legion; thus he had three legions under his command for making a name for himself through war. History tells us he wasted no time in marshalling his forces for, as Plutarch (*Caes* 12.1) says, "as soon as he reached Spain he set himself to work, and in a few days raised ten cohorts in addition to the twenty which were there before." Appian (*BC* 2.81) is critical of these priorities because, he says, Caesar "neglected the transactions of public business, the administration of justice; and all matters of that kind because he considered them of no use for his purposes, but he raised an army and attacked the independent Spanish tribes one by one until he made the whole country tributary to the Romans." A euphemism for massacre.

There are no records of how fast Caesar dove into the barbarian coffers but Suetonius (*Div* 18.1) says that, when he was writing his history, he was privy to writers who said Caesar "took money from the proconsul, who was his predecessor in Spain, and from the Roman allies in that quarter, for the discharge of his debts." He says the Pontifex Maximus of Rome (*Div* 54.1), "rifled the chapels and temples of the gods, which were filled with rich offerings, and demolished cities oftener for the sake of their spoil, than for any ill they had done. By this means gold became so plentiful with him, that he exchanged it through Italy and the provinces of the empire for three thousand sesterces the pound."

With respect to money-grubbing, shall we say, Caesar acted without scruple. Suetonius (54.1) says, "he not only begged money from the allies, to help pay his debts, but also attacked and sacked some towns of the Lusitanians although they did not refuse his terms and opened their gates to him on his arrival." He had come to the province to earn military credentials, thus, any pretext for war was suitable enough. He turned to troublesome tribes living in the mountain areas which he used as a straw man for military action. Dio says (37.52. 3-4), he "ordered the inhabitants [of the Herminian Mountains] to move into the plain, in order, as he claimed, that they might not use their fastnesses as a base for marauding expeditions, but really because well he knew that they would never do what he asked, and that as a result he should have some ground for war. This was exactly what happened. After these men, then, had taken up arms, he overcame them."[174] Dio (35.521-20 offers a motive for his pursuit, "he might without any great labor have cleared the land of brigandage, which probably always existed there, and then have kept quiet . . . [but] was unwilling to do so. He was eager for glory, emulating Pompey and his other predecessors who at one time or another had had great power, and his aspirations were anything but small; in fact, he hoped, if he should at this time accomplish something, to be chosen consul immediately and to display mighty achievements." Again, he was triumph-hunting.

Plutarch (*Caes* 12.1) says, "he led his army against the Callaici and Lusitani; overpowered them, and marched on as far as the outer sea, subduing their tribes which before were not obedient to Rome." Suetonius sees Caesar's action as a kind of massacre for he (*Div* 18.1), "plundered at the point of the sword some towns of the Lusitani [and Callaici], notwithstanding they attempted no resistance and opened their gates to him upon his arrival before them." Repeat: "attempted no resistance and opened their gates to him upon his arrival." Just as the Romans remembered their hurts from eons before, so the Lusitani and Callaici remembered theirs, especially when the Roman general Decimus Junius Brutus devastated their towns from 138 to 136 earning him the honorific *Callaicus* for his carpet-bombing efforts.[175] And while a strong cause-and-effect argument cannot be made, it is no coincidence that the two tribes Caesar first pursued, the Callaici and the Lusitani, were among those who took the side of Carthage during the Second Punic War. Caesar had not forgotten; supplied with his first official army, he was able to successfully complete a *memoria tenebat* mission without interference from the powers that be, the *Senatusque populi Romani*.[176]

Indeed, his status upon his return to Rome was the direct opposite of what it was during his departure. As Plutarch says, (*Caes* 12.4) "In high repute for this administration he retired from the province; he had become wealthy himself, had enriched his soldiers from their campaigns, and had been saluted by them as *Imperator*." That is, he had not simply solved his debt problem—and no longer had to rely on Crassus for financial backing—but had been hailed as a general worthy of praise. The warrior who received the *corona civica* as a teenager was now hailed a "*Magnus*" of sorts; his men had recognized his abilities as a military leader somewhat on the same plane as Pompey.[177]

With respect to returning to Rome as a rich person, it can be said that, as a student of history, ethnography, and geography, Caesar was well aware of the rich mineral deposits in the towns the Lusitani and Callaici inhabited. It was a known fact since the Second Punic War. Pliny (*HN* 4.112) says, "The whole of the district mentioned, from the Pyrenees onward, is full of mines of gold, silver, iron, lead and tin."[178] He adds that (*HN* 33.78), "According to some accounts Asturia and Gallaecia and Lusitania produce in this way 20,000 pounds weight of gold a year, Asturia supplying the largest amount. Nor has there been in any other part of the world such a continuous production of gold for so many centuries." And gold generally he says (*HN* 33.80) "contains silver in various proportions, a tenth part in some cases, an eighth in others. In one mine only, that of Gallaecia called the Albucrara mine, the proportion of silver found is one thirty-sixth, and consequently this one is more valuable than all the others."

Added to the gold, silver, and tin deposits as bounty was a refitting of his cavalry with the finest Lusitanian horses for, as Justinus (44.3.1) says, "In Lusitania near the river Tagus, many authors have said that the mares conceive from the effect of the wind; but such stories have had their origin in the fecundity of the mares, and the vast number of herds of horses, which are so numerous, and of such swiftness, in Gallaecia and Lusitania, that they may be thought, not without reason, to have been the offspring of the wind." And no general in history sought to equal the wind more than Gaius Julius Caesar. Indeed, he gave new definition to *quam celerrime*.

The praetorship in Spain, however much truncated, had been a grand success. Matthew Gelzer (p.63) sums it up thusly, "In Spain we already have the complete Caesar of the Gallic War." He adds that Caesar "conducted affairs like a born general and ruler, but never lost himself in this activity on the periphery of the Empire: what mattered was always its effects on Rome." That is, how he was playing to the *popularis* audiences back home. The complete Caesar of the Gallic War? Not exactly but practically. He had opened his show out of town and its success in the hinterlands proved that he was ready for the bright lights of the great white way of Gaul.

Plutarch (*Caes* 11.3-4) offers a story which, although regarded by some writers as legend, does shed light on the early drive of Caesar to surpass every contender for personal glory, and it is worth repeating here. While he "was crossing the Alps," [on the way there], Plutarch says," and passing by a barbarian village which had very few inhabitants and was a sorry sight, his companions asked with mirth and laughter, 'Can it be that here too there are ambitious strifes for office, struggles for primacy, and mutual jealousies of powerful men?'" Whoever the companions were, it is a most interesting musing. Was political conflict inherent in social life? Caesar's response to the query was "in all seriousness, 'I would rather be first here than second at Rome.'" That is, he would never settle for second place in any venture, even it meant having to massacre more than one million barbarians during his governorship of Gaul and conduct a civil war against fellow Romans. In Spain, with his first army, he realized he could get legally away with murder in grand style. The tribes had heeled like obedient dogs and he slaughtered them anyway.

The triumph he was awarded for his unnecessary massacre was never celebrated; his ambition to run for consul took precedence. Appian (*BC* 2.8) says, "He was making preparations outside the walls for a most splendid procession, during the days when candidates for the consulship were required to present themselves. It was not lawful for one who was going to have a triumph to enter the city to register, then leave, and go back again for the triumph. As Caesar was very anxious to secure the office, and his procession was not yet ready, he sent to the Senate and asked permission to go through the forms of standing for the consulship while absent, through the instrumentalities of friends, for although he knew it was against the law it had been done by others. Cato opposed his proposition and used up the last day for the presentation of candidates, in speech-making. Thereupon Caesar abandoned his triumph, entered the city, offered himself as a candidate, and waited for the comitia."

What Roman poet or writer ever sang of the spirits of the dead Caesar left in Spain *ad maiorem gloriam Caesaris*? We do not have a single record of where the graves of the slain inhabitants might be, even if buried en masse, or who they were or how they felt when Caesar turned their lights out, all for the greater glory of an Imperator who could not forget past harms. And the tribes had opened their gates for him when he arrived!

CHAPTER 12

POMPEY OFFERS A MODEL OF EFFECTIVE STRUCTURAL CHANGE

Supporters of Caesar's work in Gaul, and certainly those who winked at the extent of his massacres elsewhere, are ready to assert upon questioning that the general was adhering to the *mos mairoum* of his ancestors and the times. That is, dating back to Marcus Claudius Marcellus, aka "The Sword of Rome," the wholesale massacre of foreign nations was not only the most practical but the most cost-effective way to protect the luxury of a satirical poet strolling down the Via Sacra musing about an annoying fellow come his way.

History book after history book, both ancient and modern, show a city, a nation, mired in a deep and ineluctable neurosis. On one level, the history of Rome is a sad sad story. The classicist, Erich Gruen, offers evidence of Rome' efforts to make treaties and mutual defense contracts with foreign nations but, as Iain Francis points out, "The Romans created a discourse of primitivism and barbarism to define and guide their military, political and social relationships with other Italian people with whom they came into conflict in the years of Rome's struggle for dominance among the Italian cities and regions." The Italian historian,

Gaetano De Sanctis, says (p. 237) the loss of dignity began or at least accelerated with the death of Scipio Aemilianus (in 129 BC); he says, "there was no longer anything that could stop the fierce strife between revolutionaries and reactionaries. Therefore, the people who were the masters of the world hastened to pay for their own imperialism, by bowing their head under the yoke of military monarchy." And Caesar, who made a foreign nation pay for yoking a Roman army eons before, was now most instrumental in forging a military yoke that helped hobble the social ethic of the Roman nation.

If structural solutions to the "barbarian problem" did exist, Caesar did not embrace them. Perhaps in some quarters, and even with posterity, he might have received kudos for ingenuity in "crime prevention" but he knew there was no immediate payoff for such in the *gloria* department.

But in Caesar's arch rival, Gnaeus Pompey, we do find at least one radically viable alternative that shouts for recognition because it demonstrates that it was possible, even toward the end of the Republic, to deal with testy situations without all-out violence. In at least one instance we can refer to Pompey as *lenissimus*, acting—if not with *humanitas, temperantia, mansuetudo*—certainly with crime-prevention intelligence, even though his actions, as Plutarch (*Pomp* 29.1) tells us, "could not escape the envy and censure of his enemies." Hermann Strasburger (1965 p. 51) says, "The measure of Pompey's broke with a long tradition of Roman behavior towards enemies considered as criminals." Too radical an alternative for the ancients to digest then and, in the case of some modern historians, too much of a perceived propaganda stunt to swallow whole now. While it is not possible to minimize Pompey's part in Rome's annihilation business, he does show us that there were alternatives to prevent crime in the future.[179]

In 68 the Port of Ostia was sacked by bands of pirates; the port was set afire, the consular fleet was destroyed, and two senators were kidnapped, Rome was duly shaken.[180] Almost immediately the 39-year old Pompey was called upon to put an end to Rome's "pirate problem" once and for all. A tribune of the plebs, Aulus Gabinius, (whom Dio (23.4) describes as "a most base fellow") passed a law—the *lex de uno imperatore contra praedones instituendo*—that gave Pompey unprecedented imperium over all provincial matters within 50 miles of the Mare Nostrum.[181] Though the pirates were a perennial problem—as the young Caesar could attest to—the governmental administration took such drastic measures in 67 because the fire had greatly affected the supply of grain to Rome and subsequently the price of bread. In a paper summing up Pompey's mopping up measure, the classical historian, Manuel Tröster, hits the nail on the head with a subheading that reads, "*Humanitas* and resettlement: a political solution to a socio-economic problem." That is, Pompey took action to deal with a problem structurally. Through a brilliant chess-board-like strategy—as historians ancient and modern have confirmed—the *Magnus* had made short order of the piracy problem in three months. But what is most striking about his solution was not only the speed with which he "dispatched" thousands of the brigands but also his response to those who sought mercy. Plutarch (*Pomp* 28.2) says, "he did not once think of putting [them] to death" but developed a relocation strategy that would please a modern-day penologist.

When, Plutarch (*Pom*, 27.4) continues, "Some of the pirate bands . . . begged for mercy . . . he [Pompey] treated them humanely, and after seizing their ships and persons did them no further harm, the rest became hopeful of mercy too, and made their escape from the other commanders, betook themselves to Pompey with their wives and children, and surrendered to him. All these he spared, and it was chiefly by their aid that he tracked down, seized, and punished those who were still lurking in concealment because conscious of unpardonable crimes." One wonders what Caesar would have done with the women and children whom on more than one occasion during his campaign in Gaul, he slaughtered as if they were armed ferocious warriors. His tactics were more in line with the treachery the likes of which Titus Didius exhibited in Spain.[182] Didius was not adverse to slaughtering multitudes of entire families to whom, in supposed good faith, he promised a future of safety.

Pompey, on the other hand, had an awareness of the structural conditions that drove people to piracy—he said poverty—as well as of what steps needed to be taken for a permanent solution to the problem, that is, he chose to integrate the sea-warriors into land-based communities. It was like taking fire away from an arsonist. Plutarch (*Pomp* 28.3-4) says Pompey knew, "that by nature man neither is nor becomes a wild or an unsocial creature, but is transformed by the unnatural practice of vice, whereas he may be softened by new customs and a change of place and life; also that even wild beasts put off their fierce and savage ways when they partake of a gentler mode of life, he determined to transfer the men from the sea to land, and let them have a taste of gentle life by being accustomed to dwell in cities and to till the ground." What an epitaph for one's grave.

Thus, the general, Plutarch continues, transported, "Some of them . . . into the small and half-deserted cities of Cilicia, which acquired additional territory; and after restoring the city of Soli, which had lately been devastated by Tigranes, the king of Armenia, Pompey settled many there. To most of them, however, he gave as residence Dyme in Achaea, which was then bereft of men and had much good land." In addition to Dyme he sent one group to Calabria, Italy and others, Appian adds (*Mith* 14.96), were transferred to Mallus, Adana, Epiphaneia, and other thinly populated towns in Cilicia Tracheia. As history student Joshua Robinson (pp. 44-45) points out, "Epigraphic evidence also points to colonies of ex-pirates in Cyrenaica . . . Those pirates there show a variety of ethnic backgrounds among the 'Cilician' pirates settled there. The stone inscriptions name men and the lands they were given by Pompey through the authority of his legate Cn. Cornelius Lentulus Marcellinus in 67 BC."[183]

Dio (36.37.5) also picks up on Pompey's understanding of the poverty complex, "those who were defeated by his troops and experienced his clemency went over to his side very readily. Besides other ways in which he took care of them he would give them any lands he saw vacant and cities that needed more inhabitants, in order that they might never again through poverty fall under the necessity of criminal deeds." It was a manifestation of *clementia* unlike that Caesar showed toward his enemies because it had a recidivism prevention component affecting where people lived.

When Caesar responded to the pirates who had captured him—granted he was on his way to Rhodes to study and did not have an official command—he did not want to dally watching hardened criminals wither away on a cross they had been fastened to; he slit their throats and was off. And, while it is possible, as mentioned, had he left them alive on the gibbet, someone could have come and taken them down to save them or sell them as slaves—as the then-governor of Asia Junius Juncus threatened—the reality is he was interested in staging a pageantry (*spectaculum*) to demonstrate to his foreign base, his potential *clientele* in Asia, "that he was concerned for its well-being." (Osgood, 332)

To repeat once again, Cicero had it right in his assessment of Caesar's character in that he was (Plutarch *Cic* 4.8), "the first to see beneath the surface of Caesar's public policy and to fear it, as one might fear the smiling surface of the sea, and who comprehended the powerful character hidden beneath his kindly and cheerful exterior . . . that in most of Caesar's political plans and projects he saw a tyrannical purpose."

Part of Pompey's story is that he had visited his teacher, the great Stoic philosopher Posidonius of Rhodes, during his campaign against the pirates in 66. It might seem a stretch of the imagination but we are left to wonder if the latter's Stoical values of community, did not rub off on the commander. If so, Posidonius was able to engender a greater sense of *clementia* than Apollonius of Rhodes was able to achieve in his ever-aggrieved student, Julius Caesar. As indicated, Caesar did not take to philosophy.

Pompey visited Posidonius again in 62. As a Stoic philosopher Posidonius did not place the "civilized" Romans higher on a scale of humanity than "less civilized" peoples. Strabo (11.1.6) says that, at the end of one of the lectures Posidonius had presented, Pompey asked the philosopher if "he had any orders to give, and Posidonius replied, 'Always be the best you can and distinguish yourself by being above others.'" "Above others" did not mean being supercilious but in doing the right thing. Morrell (p. 85) suggests that "Posidonius drew a pointed contrast between Pompey's settlement of the pirates and the harsh (and ultimately unsuccessful) methods of Roman commanders in Spain."[184] Didius and Caesar immediately come to mind.

Hermann Strasburger (1965, p. 52) says, "the endeavor of Pompey in the period of his glory seems more modern and promising than Caesar's . . . Scholars who like to lay stress on Caesar's fine education should not fail to observe that no connection between him and any philosopher or his doctrine is attested." In this respect, despite their political differences, Caesar and Cicero stood in the same camp in that the latter showed, as Strasburger (1965 p. 53) continues, "total indifference to the fate of the wretched mountain tribe which brought a gay auction of human prey to his soldiers and to himself the hope of a triumph." We spoke about that earlier. And, while in the situation with the resettlement of the pirates, Pompey's personal goals, as Strasburger adds, "were undoubtedly an important factor, this should not obscure the fact that the campaign successfully combined military and non-military instruments and thus not only removed a pressing threat to Rome in the short run but also prepared the ground for a more lasting settlement that might allow the vanquished pirates to be reintegrated into civilian life ... In other words, the hard power of military resources was applied along with the soft power of inducing the pirates to surrender and accept the order to be established by the hegemon."

And while scholars like the University College Dublin historian, Philip DeSouza, (p. 176) minimize Pompey's efforts because, "It is abundantly clear that Soli and Dyme, the main cities turned over to the pirates, were ideally situated not for farming, but for piracy" we must ultimately accept such a position as, *"Parturient montes, nascetur ridiculus mus."* DeSouza must provide data that say the sequestered pirates returned to their former lives of crime, that is, that they had recidivated and Pompey's strategy failed.

- Caesar, unlike Pompey, was either unable or unwilling to grasp the teachings of a Posidonius who liked to point out everywhere, as Strasburger offers (1965 p. 48), "that even barbarians and slaves might be endowed by nature with the highest qualities of human dignity, that normally they became brutal only as a result of brutal treatment." Caesar's treatment of the nations in Gaul, Germany, Britain, and elsewhere is a clinic in how to dismiss hundreds of thousands of the heart of humanity for the sake of a kingly coronation. It might sound harsh to some but that was, and remains, the reality a *memoria tenebat* ideology generates.

CHAPTER 13

L'ÉTAT C'EST MOI

IN OUR EFFORT TO BRING AN INDICTMENT AGAINST JULIUS CAESAR, Ladies and Gentlemen of the Jury, I have suggested that we must keep in mind the four phases of the dictator's life. Let us not be led astray by listening to what ancient historians, and Caesar himself, had to say about the *mansuetudo* he showed toward some of his enemies during the civil war and think that that is the Julius Caesar of Gaul. Gaul was a stepping stone to an insurrection, a civil war, a dictatorship, and the creation of an ideal society which we allege Caesar had in mind after he was abused by pirates as a young man of twenty-five, perhaps even before that encounter. For some, the assertation about an ideal society will require further study but the seeds for such a statement already exist.

And, with respect to Caesar's *clementia* phase, if you will, on March 1, 49, less than a month after he crossed the Rubicon, he sent a letter to his assistants and political allies, Gaius Oppius and Lucius Cornelius Balbus, which came into Cicero's possession; he tells them he was going to take their advice on how to handle his enemies because it meshed with his own thinking. He says, (*Att* 9.7c) "I had spontaneously resolved to display the greatest clemency and to do my best to reconcile with Pompey. Let us try in this way if we can recover the affections of all parties, and enjoy a lasting victory; for others, owing to their cruelty, have been unable to avoid rousing hatred, or to maintain their victory for any length of time, with the one exception of Lucius Sulla, whom I have no intention of imitating. Let this be our new method of conquering-to fortify ourselves by mercy and generosity." He did not want to see a Sulla-like proscription list posted among the *acta diurna* on the public bulletin board, and subsequently see the bloody heads of the proscribed arranged on pikes across the Forum.

In a letter to Atticus toward the end of the same month (March 26), Cicero enclosed a letter Caesar had sent him expounding on leniency as a way to deal with enemies. The letter was addressed "imperator to imperator." The dictator *imperator* says (*Att* 9.16), "You judge me quite accurately—for my character is well known to you—when you say that nothing is more remote from my disposition than cruelty. For myself, as I take great delight in this policy for its own sake, so your approval of my action gives me a triumphant feeling of gladness. Nor am I shaken by the fact that those, who were allowed to go free by me, are said to have departed with the intention of renewing the war against me: for there is nothing I like better than that I should be what I am, they what they are." It seems like an odd logic in retrospect but he viewed pardoning as a method of social control, believing that those pardoned would view the act of clemency as an impetus to mend their ideological ways, perhaps even join his side in the contest. As Cicero says (Att 10.4.8), "he thought clemency would win him favor," that is, would pay off for him politically and militarily though his soldiers complained that the policy prolonged the war.

In his narrative of the civil war he initiated (*BC* 1.22), Caesar tells us he told the former consul Publius Cornelius Lentulus Spinther who fought on the side of Pompey—that it was never his aim to hurt people—he meant Romans—because he had, "not come out of the bounds of his province, with an intent to injure anybody; but to repel the injuries done him by his enemies; to revenge the wrongs of the tribunes; and to restore to the Roman people, who were oppressed by a small faction of the nobles, their liberties and privileges." The phrase "to revenge the wrongs of the tribunes" is operational. That is, he had ordained himself a political minister, a savior (*soter*), to make straight the crooked ideological path of the *optimates*. Incessantly whining at his alleged mistreatment, the insurrectionist says he, "conjured them to defend against the malice of his enemies, the honor and reputation of a general, under whom they had served nine years with so much advantage to the commonwealth, gained so many battles, and subdued all Gaul and Germany." That is, his *dignitas* ought to be shown more respect and, in his own form of Caesar-speak, he kept saying it was he—the man who was tearing down the Republic—who was standing up for the constitution.

And although Titus Ampius Balbus was a political foe of Caesar, his commentary on what the *res publica* actually meant to Caesar contains more than a kernel of truth. Suetonius (*Div* 77.1) tells us, "No less arrogant were his [Caesar's] public utterances, which Titus Ampius records: that the state was nothing, a mere name without body or form; that Sulla did not know his A. B. C. when he laid down his dictatorship; that men ought now to be more circumspect in addressing him, and to regard his word as law. So far did he go in his presumption, that when a soothsayer once reported direful innards without a heart, he said: 'They will be more favorable when I wish it; it should not be regarded as a portent, if a beast has no heart.'" To mix metaphors, the *pontifex maximus* would determine what the tea leaves of the future had in store. And by saying, "men ought now to be more circumspect in addressing him, and to regard his word as law," he was indicating he was having a hard time controlling the restless wagging tongues of the Roman populace that soon would morph into wagging daggers.

With respect to the mere-name-without-body-or-form Senate, Cicero (*Att* 10.4.9) notes that, "Caesar hates the Senate like poison, and declared that all such authority will proceed from him." Indeed, he had informed the Senate in January 49 that he would run the government the way he warred against the tribes associated with Gaul, as a military commander. In the first book of his civil war diary (1.32.7) he tells us what he said in his address to the Senate at the time, that is, he "exhorts and charges them to take up the burden of state and administer it with his help." He taunts his supposed colleagues with, "*Sin timore defugiant . . .*" that is, "if fear deters you from getting involved in administering the affairs of state," then "*illis se oneri non futurum . . .*" "I will not lay such a burden on you . . ." thus, "*et per se rem publicam administraturum.*" "I will run things on my own." But the "*sin,*" the "*if,*" is a false offering; there was never going to be an "if," a sharing of power; that was not why he massacred a million or so in Gaul. Cicero tells Atticus (9.18.3) in a March 28, 49 letter that, at the end of one conversation he had with Caesar, the dictator said to him with respect to administering the state "though I might not use your [Cicero's] advice, I will use what advice I can, and do what needs to be done by any means necessary." That is, he would do in, finish off, the *res publica* one way or another.

Indeed, when he took charge of the affairs of State, Caesar flooded the Senate with laws and decrees as if he were dictating four or five letters to his secretaries simultaneously. Matthias Gelzer says (p. 290), "the number of decrees which he issued himself was so great that there was not enough time to keep to the usual complicated procedure. In particular, he often shortened the transactions of the Senate by merely informing the senior members of his plans and, if he called a meeting of the whole body, he simply announced his decisions to it and without any discussion these were entered in the archives as senatorial decrees." He might now utter not only *L'état c'est moi* but also *le ciel c'est moi, la terre c'est moi,* even *tout le monde c'est moi.* Above the cross of the crucified Christ was inscribed INRI, Jesus of Nazareth King of the Jews, above Caesar's throne of gold and ivory we can project ISRR, *Julius Suburra Rex Romanorum,* Julius of Suburra King of Rome.[185]

And he made sure the numbers were there to grease the skids, if you will, for, as Dio says (43.47.3), "he enrolled a vast number in the senate, making no distinction whether a man was a soldier or the son of a freedman, so that the sum of them grew to nine hundred."[186]

And with respect to the quality of these appointees Suetonius (*Div* 72) says, "he advanced some of his friends to the highest positions, even though they were of the humblest origin, and when taken to task for it, flatly declared that if he had been helped in defending his honor by brigands and cut-throats, he would have requited even such men in the same way." When Augustus took over the administration of the empire, one of his first tasks was to rid the empire of the hordes of Senators of "low-birth," to weed out the brigands and cut-throats.[187]

And with respect to the traditional and long-fought-for authority of the tribunate—*tribunicia potestas*—which Caesar said he would defend to his dying day, for which he said he went to war to protect, in 48 the Senate granted him all tribunal power for life. This, as the late University of Chicago classicist, Frank Abbot, (p. 135) says, "enabled him to interpose a veto and to convoke the plebeian assembly, and made his person inviolable" and that "the control which he exercised over the nomination of other members of the college, would protect him against serious interference with his plans." And woe to those who showed independence of judgment. Indeed, when a situation arose that exposed his latent desires before the gathered crowd—as in his desire to be king—in dramatic fashion he eviscerated the power of the tribunes of the plebs by stripping two tribunes of their office before the Senate, before a stunned populist faction. It was another sign that he had betrayed the cause he once heralded as the essence of the spirit of Rome.[188]

That is, in the same way that Caesar erased the Eburones from the face of history and the earth and, in the same way he sought to erase the name of Lutatius Catulus from Rome's cultural history, he erased the names of the tribunes Gaius Epidius Marullus and Lucius Caesetius Flavus from public life—public servants who in fact sought to protect him—thereby making a mockery of the *popularis* tradition he championed for decades. Dio's account is worth noting because it is another example of Caesar beginning to lose his emotional balance. Indeed, we might suggest at this point that Caesar did not suffer from epilepsy, as modern medical professionals have offered, or even from a series of strokes as others aver, but from PTBS, Post Traumatic Battle Syndrome, which manifested itself periodically in debilitating anxiety attacks.[189]

Anxiety attacks or not, he was beginning to lose his mind, or to be more accurate, a consciousness of a self that was part of a collective, a *res public*, as Ampius declared— and the Senate added fuel to the fire of madness by pouring one sedition-based honor after honor upon him. As Matthias Gelzer (p. 278) points out, "On his arrival in Rome, the Senate decreed him new and unprecedented honors: a festival of thanksgiving for forty days' duration for his victory; the dictatorship for ten years; seventy-two lictors for his triumphs; control over morals for three years (an enhancement of one of the powers belonging to the censors); the right of designating even extraordinary magistrates for popular election, and in the Senate the right of sitting on the curule chair between the consuls at all meetings and of speaking first on all questions. Further, he was to give the signal at all games, and his name was to replace that of Catulus on the Capitoline Temple. Inside the temple, a triumphal chariot was set up, on which stood a statue of Caesar with the globe at its feet and an inscription, later removed on the dictator's orders, recalling his descent from Venus and Anchises and describing him as a demigod."[190]

Caesar had been exposed to the value of being treated as a god during the nine months he spent with the Queen of Egypt; he developed an understanding of the mentality of a populace who willingly submitted themselves to a king (queen) who was a god or a god who was an earthly monarch. He came away from Egypt with, as Lily Ross Taylor (p. 62) says, "a new conception of the ruler as a being legitimized by the gods whose son he was, a sharer with them in the house of their temples, and at the same time the ideal representative of the people in every secular and religious act." Taylor suggests that every divine honor bestowed on him came with parallel prerogatives in his daily life. When transacting the business of the empire, he was given a throne of gold and ivory to sit upon; he wore a laurel crown, and donned the ceremonial garb usually reserved for triumphs, the costume of a Roman king. Toward the end of 45, when senators came to present him with decrees that made him a *dictator perpetuus*, he did not rise to acknowledge their public worth, their *dignitas*.[191] Plutarch's account (*Caes* 60.4) is: "after sundry extravagant honors had been voted him in the senate, it chanced that he was sitting above the rostra, and as the praetors and consuls drew near, with the whole senate following them, he did not rise to receive them, but as if he were dealing with more private persons … This vexed not only the senate, but also the people who felt that in the persons of the senators, the state was insulted, and in a terrible dejection they went away at once." Livy (*Epit* 116.2) adds that because of this slight, "several grudges rose against him . . . [he] had caused hostility toward him, arguing that he was aiming at one man rule, that is, as a king." And even though Plutarch says Caesar told the senators that "his honors needed curtailment rather than enlargement," fuel had already been poured on the fire of counter-insurrection.[192] Brutus and Cassius were watching like Cerebus, the multi-headed hound of Hades to see when Caesar should be sent, brought, into the netherworld for his just reward.

But Cicero, conflicted more than any other intelligent observer of the changes in the *res publica*, had spoken in godly terms years earlier in the famous speech he gave in behalf of Marcus Claudius Marcellus in 46 when he tells Caesar that his (*Marc* 8), "actions [were] of such a nature, that the man who does them, I do not compare to the most illustrious man, but I consider equal to God." On earth that equates to a king and his enemies, picking up on that, sought to turn public sentiment, and even his best friends, against him by exposing in public his repressed but adamant desire to be king.

Thus, on January 26, 44 when the dictator was riding from the Alban Mount at the end of the annual celebration of the *Feriae Latinae*, some men in the crowd began shouting "Rex! Rex!" When Caesar heard it, he countered right away with "My name is not 'Rex' but 'Caesar.'" While sloughing off the shout-out as inane, he did nothing to securely put the matter to rest. To raise the ante and expose his ulterior motives, the dissidents secretly placed the diadem of a king on his statue on the rostra. When the tribunes, Gaius Epidius Marullus and Lucius Caesetius Flavius, just mentioned, took it down Dio (44.9.3) says, "he [Caesar] became violently angry, although they uttered no word of abuse and moreover actually praised him before the populace as not wanting anything of the sort. For the time being, though vexed, he held his peace."

Nevertheless, Caesar said (Dio 44.10.1-4), "these very officials were really stirring up sedition against him." He took action when these men, as Dio (44.10.1-4) continues, "issued a proclamation declaring that they were unable to speak their mind freely and safely on behalf of the public good, he became exceedingly angry and brought them into the senate-house where he accused them and put their conduct to the vote. He did not put them to death, though some declared them worthy even of that penalty, but he first removed them from the tribuneship, on the motion of Helvius Cinna, their colleague, and then erased their names from the senate." They were then exiled. Erasure then exile; out of sight, out of archives. Understandably, many began to question Caesar's sanity for whereas, "he should have hated those who applied to him the name of king, he let them go and found fault with the tribunes instead."[193] Caesar, the duplicitous public official who claimed he started a civil war to protect the sanctity of the *tribunicia potestas*, stamped out this power on behalf of his conflicting ego-drives. Indeed, he even excluded the *tribuni aerarii* from serving on juries, a right they enjoyed since the Lex Aquileia was passed in 70.[194] Under the cover of night, Casca continued sharpening the blade of his tyrannicidal sword.

When Caesar saw the adverse reaction his unwarranted punishment produced among the populace, as well as the Senate, as Appian (*BC* 2.109) points out, "he repented, and, reflecting that this was the first severe and arbitrary act that he had done without military authority and in time of peace, it is said that he ordered his friends to protect him, since he had given his enemies the handle they were seeking against him. But when they asked him if he would bring together again his Spanish cohorts as a bodyguard, he said, 'There is nothing more unlucky than perpetual watching; that is the part of one who is always afraid.'" Being hailed as an "unconquerable god" not only reduced his once-savvy political sense but increased his isolation from others.

What the thin-skinned unconquerable god was not able to conquer was his drive for vindictiveness. With respect to one of the two tribunes he judged acting against him, Valerius Maximus (5.7.2), says he went to Caesetius' father and told him to disinherit and disown his son to show support for Caesar. All the father could say was, "You shall rather take from me, O Caesar, all my sons, than compel me by my own actions to disinherit any one of them." How ironic that, in the same way that Caesar sowed tribal dissention, the seeds of genocide, by inciting nations to attack neighboring nations for the general's benefit in Gaul, he sought to incite hatred of a father against his son. So perhaps the governing principle in Caesar's life was consistent through all phases of his life, that is, that there really were not stages but simply different editions of the same controlling retributive *memoria tenebat* ideology.[195]

By degrading the dignity of the tribunes, Caesar was further signing his own death warrant which began to manifest itself in small but significant ways. When his chariot was passing the tribunes' bench during his triumph over Spain in October 45, Pontus Aquila, a tribune for that year, refused to rise to honor the *triumphator*. Suetonius (*Div* 78.2) says, "when he himself in one of his triumphal processions rode past the benches of the tribunes, he was so incensed because a member of the college, Pontius Aquila, did not rise, that he cried: 'Come then, Aquila, take back the republic from me, you tribune;' and for several days he would not make a promise to anyone without adding, 'That is, if Pontius Aquila will allow me.'" Five months later Aquila was among those who murdered Caesar on the Ides of March; so much for political *clementia* as a form of social control.[196]

When a statue of Caesar was set up on the Capitol among those of the kings of Rome, his ego might have been boosted but not his longevity. And although Weinstock (p. 145) says that it was not another step toward full kingship for Caesar, his adversaries could not see straight because of the fury generated by seeing his statue among the kings of yesteryear. He had already been called "*Liberator*" and "Savior" (*Soter*), but to insert himself among the kings was another example of his out-of-bounds hubris. Cicero (*Deiot* 33) says, "that men were exceedingly offended at your [Caesar's] having been placed among those of the kings." Not only had the destroyer of the Republic hubristically set himself among the kings of the past but his statue was near that of Lucius Junius Brutus, the founder, and one of the first consuls, of the Republic. Plutarch (*Brut* 1.1) says the, "bronze statue, with a drawn sword in its hand, was erected by the ancient Romans on the Capitol among those of the kings, as a sign that he was most resolute in dethroning the Tarquins." How ironic that a Brutus of a different stripe helped bring down the purple-robed Tarquin of 44.

Whether Caesar felt his new-found position among the kings of Rome was favorable to him or not, reality spoke otherwise. In 44 Cicero, in his famed essay *De Officiis*, composed as a blueprint for his son on how to become a moral and just person, says Caesar overthrew all laws, sacred and profane (1.26) and later enslaved Rome (*Off* 3.84) "how many more foes, do you think, had that king—who with the Roman People's army brought the Roman People themselves into subjection and compelled a state that not only had been free but had been mistress of the world—to be his slave?" Cicero, bitterly disappointed over seeing his Republic disappear as well as the talent of someone he had the highest esteem for, lamented on January 1, 43 (*Phil* 5.49), that Caesar "wasted all the power of genius which he had in a most brilliant degree, in a capricious pursuit of popular favor. Therefore, as he had not sufficient respect for the senate and the virtuous part of the citizens, he opened for himself that path for the extension of his power, which the virtue of a free people was unable to bear."

Ever the self-appointed self-apologist extraordinaire, Caesar says in his treatise on the civil war (1.32.3) that, "He [Caesar] set before them his moderation, in voluntarily proposing that both parties should lay down their arms, by which he must have been himself divested of his government and command. He displayed the malice of his enemies, who sought to impose terms on him, to which they would not submit themselves; and chose rather to involve the state in a civil war than part with their armies and provinces. He enlarged upon the injury they had done him, in taking away two of his legions, and their cruelty and insolence, in violating the authority of the tribunes. He spoke of his many offers of peace, his frequent desire of an interview, and the continual refusals he had received." No, it was he who had violated the authority of the tribunes and their constitutionally-ordained power.

As we've continued to assemble the existing pieces of the Caesarian puzzle, it has become increasingly clear that Caesar had within himself a vision of an ideal society which he hoped to create and manage in every detail. Why otherwise massacre a million barbarians? We can project that a placard on the front of Caesar's statue aligned with those of the ancient kings of Rome would read "MAKE ROME GREAT AGAIN!" In this sense, he was like the Alexander he sought to emulate, for both of them, as Lily Ross Taylor (p.76) says, "godhead was not adulation. It was a necessary part of a type of monarchy that had functioned in the past and might be expected to function again. Under the ideal of government which they had in mind they were themselves the authors of their own divinity." When in 58 he hastened from Rome to challenge the Helvetii, we aver that he already had an ideal society embedded in his soul; he knew he was beginning on a path that one day would lead to him being king of the world.

In Plato's "Republic" Socrates posited an ideal, utopian city-state, Callipolis, ruled by a philosopher king. In his "Laws," written not long after, Plato shared his dream of a utopian society called Magnesia. Caesar had a view of a Roman society with himself as the Übermensch or Superman, a role he practiced hard for when he slaughtered hundreds of thousands of Usipetes and Tencteri in 55. Dio (43.25.3) says, "since it was by ruling the Gauls for many years in succession that he himself had conceived a greater desire for dominion."

He took to reforming the civil service, once again we surmise to ensure that an infrastructure existed to ensure the implementation of his proclamations so that it appeared he was still working for the benefit of the people. Matthias Gelzer (p. 310) says, "he was chiefly concerned to create a large and devoted imperial civil service. With so many plans awaiting realization there was not enough time for all the formalities prescribed by law. In fact, the constitutional forms only continued to be used very superficially." He had already disbanded the practice of allocating provincial governorships by way of lottery. Cicero (*Fam* 6.12.2) says that by November 46 he already had in place a kitchen cabinet comprised of his closest associates Gaius Vibius Pansa, Aulus Hirtius, Lucius Cornelius Balbus, Gaius Oppius, Gaius Matius, and Marcus Curtius Postumus. And with respect to his non-constitutionally-assured procedurals—elections were mere formalities. Paradoxically, amid the growing imposition of imperial power from above, an anarchic free-for-all was in full swing below.

Thus, during the time of his third and fourth consulships, Suetonius (*Div* 76. 2-3) says, "he substituted two consuls for himself for the last three months, in the meantime holding no elections except for tribunes and plebeian aediles, and appointing prefects instead of the praetors, to manage the affairs of the city during his absence. When one of the consuls suddenly died the day before the Kalends of January, he gave the vacant office for a few hours to a man who asked for it. With the same disregard of law and precedent he named magistrates for several years to come, bestowed the emblems of consular rank on ten ex-praetors, and admitted to the House men who had been given citizenship, and in some cases half-civilized Gauls. He assigned the charge of the mint and of the public revenues to his own slaves, and gave the oversight and command of the three legions which he had left at Alexandria to a favorite of his called Rufio, son of one of his freedmen." He called Rufio an "*exoletus*," a boy favorite. He did say, did he not, that he would install "brigands and cut-throats" if that's what it took to get the job done? Cicero (*Att* 10.8.6) opines, "what kinds of associates and servants can he employ? Are men to rule provinces and direct affairs not one of whom could steer his own fortunes for two months?"[197] Again, Matthias Gelzer is spot on when he says (p. 311) that Caesar had a "grand design for government." The problem with such a statement is that Gelzer did not go far enough in his assessment. Caesar had a grand design not just for government but for a Roman society that within his purview would no longer be Roman but Caesarian.

Thus, more study is needed on Caesar as an economist, as a master of cost-effectiveness, of the quid pro quo politics of benevolent fascism. Suetonius says (*Div* 23.2.), "to secure himself for the future, he took great pains always to put the magistrates for the year under personal obligation, and not to aid any candidates or suffer any to be elected, save such as guaranteed to defend him in his absence. And he did not hesitate in some cases to exact an oath to keep this pledge or even a written contract."

Is it overstatement then to claim that Caesar's no-Rome Rome was headed toward a benevolent fascism? He began to dictate who could travel outside of Rome and for how long, and stipulated the kinds of clothes people could wear. Suetonius (*Div* 43.1-2) says, "He denied the use of litters and the wearing of scarlet robes or pearls to all except those of a designated position and age, and on set days." And although he spent lavishly on his triumphs and other public activities, "he enforced the laws against extravagance, setting watchmen in various parts of the market, to seize and bring to him dainties which were exposed for sale in violation of the law; and sometimes he sent his lictors and soldiers to take from a dining-room any articles which had escaped the vigilance of his watchmen, even after they had been served." Indeed, as Cicero reported in a letter to his friend Atticus on June 9, 45, (13.7.1), Caesar feared leaving Rome for "fear that if he went away his laws would be disregarded, as his sumptuary law was." Big Brother had to be there to ensure that his, not utopia, but dystopia was functionally efficient. And when it came to handling matters with speed and efficiency, Caesar had no equal.

And for those who went astray of the law, "he administered," as Suetonius (*Div*. 43.1) says, "justice with the utmost conscientiousness and strictness." In the case of "Those convicted of extortion he ... dismissed from the senatorial order. He annulled the marriage of an ex-praetor, who had married a woman the very day after her divorce, although there was no suspicion of adultery." And to insure that grass-roots organizing and querulous rebellion-instigating dissension were minimized, as Suetonius (*Div* 42.3) reveals, "he dissolved all the associations, except the ancient ones" which meant political clubs were verboten.[198] He also forbade extended terms of political office, as Gelzer (p. 289) says, "as a precaution against future revolutionary governors."[199] Caesar was well aware of the threat a power-hungry governor could be upon his return to Rome because, during his own provincial governorship, he had sown the seeds of insurrection by constituting himself as a revolutionary unconquerable general.

To bring in the thinking of a modern author who has studied the nature of a totalitarian society, Michel Foucault, he might say Caesar sought to create social institutions that produced "docile bodies" who paid undying homage to an insatiable king. Having to stay in town to insure that people observed his laws on how and what to eat, he became the leader of a Caesarian Panopticon society where the eyes of the god-king see all. Brutus and Cassius, and all those who refused to accept this level of disciplinization they experienced personally, knew the only way to cut such a scenario short was to blind the sight of the overseer.

In Gaul he had an army to insure that his wishes and ideals were carried out without question in almost every instance;[200] but in Rome without an army—he had just disbanded his Spanish bodyguard—he had to rely on controlling the populace through disciplinizing institutions. In a way, this is what he was laying the ground for in the rules of speech he set out in his *De Analogia* where all Romans would mouth Caesar-speak, sending the Roman tongue to its grave; and, because of increasing fluctuations in Roman society, Cicero said Rome had lost its sense of ironic wit, a topic worthy of doctoral research.[201]

Thus, Ladies and Gentlemen of the Jury, we have to make a decision not only about Caesar's genocidal actions in Gaul but also about his crimes against humanity when he moved Rome toward a friendly-fascist state, when he dissolved the SPQR in favor of JCRA, *Julius Caesar Rex Aeternus*. For all that his brilliance saw, little did he see that the raised sword of Brutus, the first citizen of the Republic, displayed on a statue next to his on the Capitol, was waiting to strike on the Ides of March with a lesson on the cost of despotic hubris. What say ye, Ladies and Gentlemen of the Jury: thumbs up or thumbs down?

CHAPTER 14

AFTERWORD

As we sift through and analyze one last time the evidence presented in this case, let us disregard the cynicism of those radical realists who assert that Caesar was not assassinated but took, or at least helped take, his own life after becoming psychologically blind and deaf. The very first sentence of Matthias Gelzer's legendary text on the life of Caesar says the most important quality of a statesman is to have "a quick grasp of and prompt reaction to circumstances with which he is faced: this can serve the needs of the moment by allowing him to take account of existing trends with a clear head." It can be said that Caesar had such a grasp in 58 when he hastened to Gaul as a lean and hungry general but, once the Roman Senate flooded him with non-stop waves of adulatory identities, he lost himself; the radical-realist, preventer-in-chief *imperator*, who destroyed nations in the interest of becoming a king, died long before his fated Ides of March.[202]

In Chapter 80 of his life of Caesar, Suetonius provides a list of ominous signs that prefigured something bad was in store for the man. After the deed was done the wagging tongues kept asking how a person once noted for his quick grasp of circumstances could have been so dense. And, while it is possible two millennia later to mock the superstitious and metaphysical-like omens the Romans guided their lives by, there were as well real-life, *caligae*-on-the-ground happenings that portended ill for Caesar that were not discerned or, if they were, were not attended to with an urgency that would have prevented, or at least forestalled, the emperor's death. Caesar's story became that of the blind soothsayer Tiresias of Rhodes in Sophocles' "Antigone." In a psychological way he became blind like Teresias but he also became deaf like those who refused to heed the seer's warnings about the ill that was about to occur. Those familiar with the story of the rebellious young woman know the unheeded warnings resulted in the deaths of cherished loved ones—by suicide and otherwise.

First of all, toward the end of his biography of Caesar, Suetonius says that when builders of new homes for colonists in Capua began demolishing the ancient tombs they found there, they came upon a tablet inscribed in Greek that said, "Whenever the bones of Capys shall be moved, it will come to pass that a son of Ilium shall be slain at the hands of his kindred, and presently avenged at heavy cost to Italy." Everyone knew Caesar traced his lineage to Troy—and finding the message was not a hoax as the historian assures us, because Caesar's trusted lieutenant, Cornelius Balbus, verified the occurrence.

Then, there was the matter of the horses Caesar dedicated and let loose to roam free as part of a spontaneous *caerimonium* when he crossed the Rubicon in 49. Suetonius (*Div* 81.2) says that not long before Caesar's death, "he was told the herds of horses which he had dedicated to the river Rubicon when he crossed it, and had let loose without a keeper, stubbornly refused to graze and wept copiously." The smile of *Fortuna* was beginning to frown on her favored son. And then something strange occurred when the Etruscan soothsayer Spurinna was offering sacrifice and was, as Valerius Maximus (8.11.2) reports, "interpreting the warnings of the gods . . . [which] he foretold to C. Caesar, that he should beware of the deadly aspect of the next thirty days, the last of which was the Ides of March." Such an omen might be viewed as quackery by a religious sceptic of today but the story continues, "Upon that day in the morning, when they were both in the house of Calvinus Domitius, Caesar exclaimed to Spurinna, 'Do you realize that the Ides of March have now come?' And he replied, 'Do you realize, that they have not yet passed? The one had cast off all fear, believing the time of danger was over; though the other did not think even the last minute to be void of danger. Would to heaven the diviner had rather failed in his augury, than that the Parent of our country had been mistaken in his security!'" Suetonius says the *pontifex maximus* started, "laughing at Spurinna and calling him a false prophet."

And the day before Caesar's death, legend has it that a kingbird flew into the Curia of Pompey—the spot where Caesar would die—carrying a piece of laurel in its beak; all of a sudden a band of birds flew in behind it and, pouncing upon the kingbird, tore it to pieces. That night Caesar had a dream in which he—who had his own statue in the *cella* of Juppiter Capitolinus—was taken high above the clouds and grasped the hand of Juppiter in person. Then Caesar's wife, Calpurnia, had a dream in which, as Julius Obsequens (*Prod* 67), says, "the pediment of the[ir] house ... fell down. At night when the doors of the bedroom were closed, they opened of their own accord, so that the light of the moon came inside and awoke [her]." Nicholas of Damascus (*Augus* 130.83) says she was so terrified that, "She clung to him and said that she would not let him go out on that day." But tragically, Valerius Maximus (1.7.2) says, he would not be "moved by a woman's dream ..."

Again, modern-thinking people write off such omens as psychological projections but they are not able to do so with signs that were actual physical happenings which were not heeded or minimized to the point of being disregarded. Disaffected citizens had been whispering for some time, talking in the streets about the dictator's campaign for a kingdom, despite Caesar forbidding citizens to gather in groups. But disaffected *hoi polloi* kept at it. When the former general Quintus Fabius Maximus, whom Caesar appointed consul in October 45 to finish out the year, appeared in a theatre, his lictors asked the audience to stand and show respect for the magistrate; but the anti-Caesareans refused and started shouting, "He's no consul! He's no consul!" To add fuel to that fire, "When Fabius died on the last day of his consulship," as Dio (46.43.3) reports, "he [Caesar] straightway named another man, Gaius Caninius Rebilus, in his place for the remaining hours."[203] The *gravitas* of a consul's job had been reduced to that of a streetsweeper.

Doubly-impaired with the loss of sight and hearing, Caesar violated the most important quality Gelzer ascribed to a statesman: having a quick grasp of, and prompt reaction to, circumstances at hand. That is, other signs were missed as well. For example, after Caesar had dismissed from office, and then exiled, Caesetius and Marullus—tribunes who sought to cover for him in an awkward social situation—the pair received write-in votes for the next year's consul making a mockery of the dictator's rashness. And then there appeared on the Capitol at the foot of the statue of Lucius Brutus—the first consul and an endless source of pride for the Republic—a placard with the plaintive plea: "*Utinam viveres!*" "Oh, Brutus, how badly we need you now!"

Among the designees Caesar appointed to the Senate when he raised its number to 900, were unorthodox citizens.[204] Whether or not they were the cut-throats Caesar said he would appoint if necessary, people began to chant the ditty:

> *Gallos Caesar in triumphum ducit: iidem in curiam*
> *Galli braccas deposuerunt, latum clavum sumpserunt.*[205]

> **Caesar paraded his Gauls in the street**
> **for a triumph; these same**
>
> **barbarians replaced their trousers**
> **for the purple strip of the Senate.**[206]

And then at some point there actually did appear below Caesar's statue on the Capitol a placard with the words:

> *Brutus, quia reges eiecit, consul primus factus est;*
> *Hic, quia consules eiecit, rex postremo factus est.*

> **Brutus, after he threw out the kings,**
> **became the first consul;**
>
> **This guy, after he threw out the consuls,**
> **became a king himself.**

Saying that Caesar took his own life rather than had it taken, might seem like wild conjecture but Suetonius implies that Caesar's mental and physical health kept waving on the conspirators to whet the edges of their blades. But then, when we listen to the historian's words more closely, we think perhaps Caesar was not so deaf and blind after all. In Chapter 86 he confirms that, "Caesar left in the minds of some of his friends the suspicion that he did not wish to live longer and had taken no precautions, because of his failing health; and that therefore he neglected the warnings which came to him from portents and from the reports of his friends . . . because he had full trust in the last decree of the senators and their oath . . . he dismissed even the armed bodyguard of Spanish soldiers that formerly attended him." Appian (*BC* 2.107) says, "He dismissed the praetorian cohorts that had served as his bodyguard during the wars, and showed himself with the ordinary civil escort only." His closest friends Pansa and Hirtius told him, Velleius (2.57.1) says, he needed to reactivate the regiment as soon as possible.

Others said the dictator had grown weary of all the talk of plots against his life, thus, Suetonius continues, "he elected to expose himself once for all to the plots that threatened him on every hand, rather than to be always anxious and on his guard. Some, too, say that he was wont to declare that it was not so much to his own interest as to that of his country that he remain alive; he had long since had his fill of power and glory; but if anything befell him, the commonwealth would have no peace, but would be plunged in strife under much worse conditions." It's like Caesar saying: the Republic I am killing cannot live without me.

And after he had read Xenophon's account of how things went for Cyrus the Great "in his last illness [giving] directions for his funeral, he expressed his horror of such a lingering kind of end and his wish for one which was swift and sudden. And the day before his murder, in a conversation which arose at a dinner at the house of Marcus Lepidus, as to what manner of death was most to be desired, he had given his preference to one which was sudden and unexpected."

In Shakespeare's "Richard III," the king facing death on the battlefield, shouts "A horse, a horse! My kingdom for a horse!" Despite all the honors showered upon him, Caesar's plea became "Peace of mind, peace of mind! My kingdom for some peace of mind!" In micro-managing every detail of his new kingdom he had worn himself thin and into isolation.[207] The great historian Theodor Mommsen says (4. 570-571), "The Imperator naturally decided in person every question of any moment ... Caesar had no helper at all in his work who exerted a personal influence over it or was even so much as initiated into the whole plan . . . he was . . . the sole master-workman." Even Cicero, one of the two or three most prominent citizens of Rome at the time, had to sit hours in a waiting room to see Caesar on a friend's behalf. The Imperator, one of the sharpest minds Rome ever saw, was relegated to uttering a remedial *mea culpa*. In the disrespect shown to Cicero, the barrister himself reports that (*Att* 14. 1.2) when Caesar found out what happened, he said, "Can I doubt that I am heartily detested, when Cicero sits waiting and cannot visit me at his convenience? Yet, if ever there was a good-natured man, he is one. However, I have no doubt that he detests me." For all the power he displayed, a streak of awkward touchiness ran through him.

What else is there to say in closing about the new-born king, especially when it comes to the accuracy of his account of his operation in Gaul, the *De Bello Gallico*, the work, the war, that made him king, and the subject of this essay? In 1954, the highly-respected classicist John H. Collins reviewed the first earth-shattering critique of Caesar's veracity as a recorder of facts *L'art de la déformation historique dans les Commentaires de César"* by the French historian Michel Rambaud. Monsieur Rambaud did not exactly call Caesar a liar but said it might be better if the librarians of the world shelved the *De Bello Gallico* somewhere in the fiction section.

Collins acknowledged the power of Rambaud's cutting-edge critique but felt compelled to defend Caesar, thereby throwing his lot in with the unabashed Caesar-defending historian Thomas Rice Holmes. On Page 244 of his *Conquest of Gaul*, Holmes approvingly recalls Montaigne's assessment of Caesar's war account: "*le plus net, le plus disert, et le plus sincère historien qui fut jamais;*" that is, that Caesar was "the clearest, the most eloquent, and the most sincere historian who ever lived."[208]

And yet only a few lines before in his review, Collins says that Holmes had been bewitched by Caesar—perhaps paving the way to justify his own submission to the dictator's wizardry—when he muses, "*Wen hat er nicht bezaubert?*" Who has not been bewitched by him?" Collins was; he sums up the review with, "Caesar was . . . as everyone knows, spectacularly, steadily, overwhelmingly successful" and the balance sheet is there to prove it: "two great wars fought and won, a province established, a government reorganized, and a Roman empire founded . . ."[209]

And what are we to make of the words of the equally-cherished and spectacularly-disciplined Caesar scholar Lily Ross Taylor when she says of the dictator's life (1957 p. 17) "in his statesmanlike measures, Caesar, with understanding of the problems of empire, manifested a deep concern for the welfare of the people of Rome, of Italy, and also of the provinces that he tried to amalgamate with Italy--in short, of all the people over whom, in everything but name, he had established a *regnum*." Deep concern for the welfare of the people of Rome? Caesar was an imperialist insurrectionist waging war against his own country and then began managing the details of every citizen's life down to the piece of pork they put in their mouth for dinner.

In 63, in his fourth oration against Catiline, another insurrectionist of consequence—delivered no less in the *Aedes Concordiae*, the temple of the goddess of social harmony—Cicero (*Cat* 4.9) reminds Caesar of the great ethical choice facing every person in life but especially someone of his stature: to act like a dictator or a citizen working for the common good. "It's understood," he reminds Caesar, "that there is a difference between the capricious ways of a dictator and the spirit of someone committed to the well-being of every citizen."

As we have seen in the evidence presented in this case, Caesar was not a liberator but an imprisoner; he was not a savior but a taker; he was not the father of a country *(pater patriae)* but the maker of a fascist dystopia; he was not a man of *lenitas* or *clementia* but a sower of discord, ill-will and death. His life and what happened to Rome during his regime is a sad story like the sad stories the lives of Sulla, Cinna, and Marius were as they hacked away at the foundation of the Roman Republic. We have tried our best to do justice to Caesar in this inquiry; let us make a decision now on what crimes we shall charge him with for his massacre of so many human beings and his destroying the Republic which he saw as standing in the way of his projected society with him as king.

CHAPTER 15

EPILOGUE

IN THE DEEPEST LEVEL OF DANTE'S "INFERNO," the ninth circle of his imagined hell, the great Italian epic poet depicts Satan—the once-upon-a-time magnificent angel Lucifer—encased in ice, turned upside down, sporting three gaping mouths. Stuffed in each mouth is a sinner constantly being chewed with an insatiable vehemence and, as they are consumed, they grow back so they experience the undying pain of eternal damnation.

Dante was seeking to portray the worst possible punishment for those he judged to be the most wicked souls ever born—the betrayers—the Italian is *Tradimento*. Two had violated the trust humans have with each other, and the third betrayed the trust of his God. Lucifer of course is the insurrectionist who claimed to be equal to God and sought to take control of the government of heaven.

Satan's left mouth is chewing on the infamous Marcus Junius Brutus and the right is gnawing at the body of the equally infamous Gaius Cassius Longinus, the two responsible for engineering the murder of Julius Caesar. In the center mouth is Judas Iscariot the man who betrayed Jesus Christ for 30 pieces of silver. While being consumed, Judas' back continues to be flayed the way Jesus' was when scourged before his death. For Dante the sin of these men was worse than what Cain did to Abel, worse than what Ptolemy, son of Abubus, did to his father-in-law, Simon, when he took his life and the life of his two sons during a banquet. How ironic that Caesar's arch-enemy in life, Cato the Younger, finds himself situated in Purgatory with a chance of someday gaining a place in heaven.

In retrospect it seems strange that two of Dante's most despicable criminals are Brutus and Cassius, killers of Caesar, and not Caesar himself. Not to justify violence in any way—tyrannicide or otherwise—but Caesar's contemporary and political opponent, Marcus Tullius Cicero, said Caesar got what he deserved; there was no murder involved. In his essay on "Duties" (*De Officiis* 3.32) he says those who "jeopardize the health of the other parts of a body . . . [are] fierce and savage monsters in human form . . . [and] should be cut off from what may be called the common body of humanity." Neutralize, terminate are the words he'd use today for what Brutus, Cassius, Casca and all the rest did to end the reign of the King of Rome.

If he were among us today, we'd have to ask Dante why he let Caesar—a genocidal killer of barbarians and later his fellow Romans; a destroyer of his nation's electoral political system (regardless how close to the brink of demise it was); and a creator of a society where people were managed like dystopian drones—escape the grip of Satan. Are not such crimes worse than that of a soul confused about the values of peace and justice within the kingdom of God? Does not Caesar deserve to take center stage away from Judas *in perpetuum*?

We know so little of Caesar's youth and his mindset when he finally decided to become a political warrior, even though that was the usual route for a young man desirous of becoming a player in Roman society in the late Republic. And, because the young Gaius had as an uncle the great Roman general Gaius Marius, who showed him up close what was possible to achieve in the glory department, we can assume the boy had little choice in careers. But now, because of that choice, he is faced with being convicted of crimes associated with genocide. Indeed, the late historian Ernst Badian (p. 89) called Caesar "the greatest brigand of them all, applying and perfecting the lessons of Pompey both at home and abroad, with a single-mindedness not weakened (as in Pompey's case) by scruples about traditional forms or by desire for the approval of his peers." Caesar said the *res publica* was an empty shell; for him everything—including Rome's constitution—was up for grabs. He was, as Christian Meier noted (p. 23) an "outsider" who "was isolated in Roman society." Nevertheless, his involvement in everyday affairs allowed him to see things not only up close but also from up above—he saw things up close and from up above simultaneously—as poets see. The problem with Caesar is that he was armed not with metaphor but with deadly weapons and an army and a vindictive disposition. To repeat, for the umpteenth time, he was not, as Suetonius declared, merciful by nature.

We are left to wonder what Caesar might have done for the betterment of humankind had he chosen to become a poet or a philosopher or grammarian, a Roman Plato, for instance, or another Cicero or Vergil envisioning a Rome where the needs of all were taken into account. It is not as far-fetched as one might think, for as Theodor Mommsen points out (*HR* 4 p. 591), when Caesar started reforming the laws on the distribution of grain in Rome, that is, determining who was and who was not a worthy recipient of free grain, he converted a "political privilege into a provision for the poor, a principle remarkable in a moral as well as in a historical point of view ... [for it] came for the first time into living operation." It's more complex but that's all that needs saying for now.

We know that, as an orator, Caesar was the near-equal of Cicero and, with practice, might have bettered the famed barrister.[210] As a philosopher he might have written his version of a "Republic" laying out a society where diversity and having a say in one's daily life were part of the social agenda. A man of his intelligence who wrote a two-volume text on grammar while on his way back from war could have envisioned a society where the needs of all were taken into account. Caesar's intelligence can never be underestimated.

We do know that, like many a school boy, he tried his hand at literature; Suetonius (*Div* 56.7) tells us of works like the poem the "Praises of Hercules," and a tragedy called "Oedipus," and a "Collection of Aphorisms," quotable sayings he copied in notebooks, some most likely from the mouth of Alexander.[211] And, although Pliny the Younger minimizes (*Ep* 5.3.5) Caesar's ability to handle Latin meter, the general was capable of free-association-writing because, on a 24-day trip from Rome to Spain, like a twentieth-century Kerouac or Ginsberg, he penned a poem about the journey he was on called "Iter." Caesar had a bohemian hiding within.[212]

Nevertheless, as a wily trickster, he was not about to show his heart for all to see. We do know he was an inveterate letter writer; Suetonius says there were "letters of his to Cicero, as well as to his intimates on private affairs," which would have told us so much about his state of mind at different junctures in his life, but Suetonius cautions that "if he had anything confidential to say, he wrote it in cipher, that is, by so changing the order of the letters of the alphabet, that not a word could be made out." But people did figure out the scheme for, as the historian continues, "If anyone wishes to decipher these, and get at their meaning, he must substitute the fourth letter of the alphabet, namely D, for A, and so with the others."

What a paradox he was therefore, that is, though far from embracing the philosophy of stoicism, he was more stoical in responding to the complexity of the political, military, and religious situations confronting him than Rome's celebrated Stoic, Cato the Younger, ever was. Thus, what are we to make of his response to hearing that Pompey was killed and beheaded? We know that, as an up-and-coming political warrior, Caesar wept when he came upon a statue of Alexander because he felt he had accomplished little in comparison to the Macedonian great. Then, when the head of a present-day Alexander was brought to him, we find him besotted with tears again. Plutarch says (*Pomp* 80.5), "he turned away with loathing, as from an assassin; and on receiving Pompey's seal-ring, he burst into tears." But the historian does not say what kind of tears they were. Were they tears of joy and relief that the last obstacle to him becoming king was finally removed and the prize he had sought all his life was finally in reach? Were they the tears an actor sheds on stage when presented with an award for dramatizing some great literary work?

Tears or not, he had a vindictive streak to contend with that never abated—and a case can be made that this held true when he engaged in his so-called acts of *clementia* during the civil war. It has already been mentioned that, when in his mid-twenties he had been harmed by pirates, he responded with a vindictiveness he later said reflected his *memoria tenebat* ideology. He could not forget a harm-done no matter how far in the past it had been perpetrated. He took it upon himself not just to incorporate Rome's collective memory, her master narrative, but also to act as the city's executioner when that narrative called for retributive justice. *Memoria tenebat* was a constant justification for his violence whether reactive or preventive. With respect to Rome's collective social memory then, he demonstrated what the memory expert

Paul Connerton says (p. 18) is characteristic of rulers and statesmen alike, that "above all things, they must prevent any further power from ever achieving an ascendency . . . [they must] remind themselves that nothing like the old wars . . . must be allowed to recur." Thus, Caesar would not allow, as Ernst Badian (p. 5) says, "the independent existence of other powers and their right to run their affairs without intervention from the outside . . . right from the start there was the determination to dominate whatever was within reach and to build up strength to extend that reach." And as a constant lifelong learner he made "every attempt . . . to build up power where it had shown itself deficient." Those who failed to grasp the power of the intelligence that came with his double vision suffered greatly from its sting.

In their never-ending flow of extraordinarily brilliant work on Caesar and the Roman Republic generally, classical historians over the years—for whom I am forever grateful—have more than hinted at who Caesar was but a profile that has fully captured his personality remains in absentia. I am suggesting that, in the way that biblical scholars created a "Jesus Seminar" years ago to find out with the greatest certainty possible what Jesus said and did, classical scholars need to form a "Caesar Seminar." This might include, at the very least, selecting a psychological inventory, such as the MMPI, and then situating Caesar on a spectrum of, say, good and evil or some other dimension the personality profile affords. Does he deserve to replace Judas in the pit of Dante's hell?[213]

And, because Caesar was such a propagandist, when writing about his own feats as a warrior-general, perhaps his works should be read only in military citadels like the United States Military Academy at West Point or the Royal Military Academy Sandhurst in the UK where fledgling military officers can study and argue about the wisdom of his strategies and tactics against barbarians and later, his fellow citizens at Rome. Was the civil war he brought against Rome in any way preventable for a man whose ideology increasingly became *ad maiorem gloriam Caesaris*?

And for students of any age—even the citizen on the street—who begin reading "Caesar" without a contextual trot—such as the one offered here in the form of grand jury evidence—the task of grasping the propaganda and ruthlessness quotient of the works is near impossible. There would be no way to decipher the subtexts Caesar presents with a carefully-orchestrated dog whistle. Reading "Caesar" should not be a game of deciphering one letter for another to gain comprehension about the slaughter he engaged in. Whose side was the literary scholar J. W. Mackail on when he said Caesar, "used the Latin language with a purity and distinction that no one else could equal."? He certainly had Cicero to thank, for the inveterate republican in his *Brutus* (261) says Caesar in his writing "was guided by the principles of art," that "he has added all the various ornaments of eloquence," that "he has such extraordinary merit even in the common run of his language," and in "his manner of speaking, both as to his voice and gesture, is splendid and noble, without the least appearance of artifice or affectation: and there is a dignity in his very presence, which bespeaks a great and elevated mind." That from one of the smartest minds in Rome.

During his triumph in the streets of Rome in 46, following his victory over Pontus, Caesar had his people display a placard (*titulum*) that filled the eye of every bystander with amazement. Suetonius says (*Div* 37.2), "among the show-pieces of the procession an inscription of these words, VENI VIDI VICI was seen by all, not indicating the events of the war, as the others did, but the speed with which it was finished."[214] No matter how the *titulum* is read ideologically, it is a confession of ease at slaughtering. Twentieth-century corporate advertisers claimed to have invented the fast in "fast food" forgetting that Caesar with his *VENI VIDI VICI* had invented the fast in fast-slaughter. Thus, the placard, as we have contended from the very title of this work, should have read *VENI VICI TRUCIDAVI*. I came, I saw, I slaughtered.

But in the war of such sound bites, so much is left out as Jacqueline Stimson says in her brilliant analysis of the language Caesar used in his *De Bello Gallico*. She says on pages 111-112 of her work, "Instead of celebrating the violence that would naturally occur in a war narrative as Rome inexorably conquered Gaul, Caesar suppresses the majority of it, and carefully employs the little violent language that is present." Thus, she adds, "The dearth of violent language in the *BG* is a clear demonstration of this phenomenon. Indeed, over the course of the seven books, well over 40,000 words, less than 200 of these can be considered to be violent or graphic. This striking statistic, in a narrative dedicated to recounting battles, deaths, and conquests, indicates a concerted effort on Caesar's part to suppress the normal occurrence of violence." In a way, with respect to Caesar's language, she has produced a "*De Analogia*" of her own, arguing that Caesar was involved in a self-promoting cover-up.

As we prepare to reset Caesar's bones back into his grave, let us not cheat him of his success in equaling the feats of the great Macedonian. What Ian Worthington says of Alexander holds true for Caesar in spades. Worthington queries (p. 303), "does a man deserve to be called 'The Great' who was responsible for the deaths of tens of thousands of his own men and for the unnecessary wholesale slaughter of native peoples? How 'great' is a king who prefers constant warfare over consolidating conquered territories and long-term administration? Or who, through his own recklessness, often endangered his own life and the lives of his men? Or whose violent temper on occasion led him to murder his friends and who toward the end of his life was an alcoholic, [though Caesar did not drink] paranoid, megalomaniac, who believed in his own divinity? These are questions posed by our standards of today of course, but nevertheless they are legitimate questions given the influence which Alexander [and Caesar] exerted throughout history—an influence which will no doubt continue." Exit Presentists stage right.

Perhaps the evidence that has been offered to you, Ladies and Gentlemen of the Jury, will lessen that influence in Caesar's case. But, no matter how it evolves, this is a sad sad story: an insane nation, the City of Rome, producing insane presidents [consuls], who waged insane wars decade after decade. In the midst of all this insanity we ask Caesar, as he sticks a knife into the heart of the Roman Republic: *Et tu, Gai?*

ENDNOTES

PREFACE

1... Dio (37.8.1-2) says Caesar, "exhibited both the *Ludi Romani* and the *Megalenses* on the most expensive scale and furthermore arranged gladiatorial contests in his father's honor in the most magnificent manner. For, although the cost of these entertainments was in part shared jointly with his colleague Marcus Bibulus, and only in part borne by him individually, yet he so far excelled in the funeral contests as to gain for himself the credit for the others too, and was thought to have borne the whole cost himself. Even Bibulus accordingly joked about it, saying that he had suffered the same fate as Pollux; for, although that hero possessed a temple in common with his brother Castor, it was named after the latter only." However, Suetonius (*Calig* 22.2) correctly notes that it was called "the temple of Castor and Pollux." Deniaux (p. 185) says, "At times, aediles would spend their own money, that of their friends, and that of their clients for grain distribution during times of scarcity." There is at least one example when the aedile was so poor that he sought to resign the position. Appian (*BC* 4.41.1) says that in the case of Marcus Oppius, "In admiration of his piety the people in later days elected the young man to the aedileship, and since his property had been confiscated and he could not defray the expenses of the office, the artisans performed the work appertaining thereto without pay, and each of the spectators tossed such money as he could afford to give into the orchestra, so that he became a rich man." Dio's version is (48.53.4-6), "When a certain Marcus Oppius planned to resign the aedileship because of poverty (for both he and his father had been among the proscribed), the populace did not permit it, but contributed money to meet the various necessities of his living and the expenses of his office. And the story goes that some criminals, too, actually came into the theatre in masks as if they were acting a play, and contributed their money also. Thus was this man loved by the multitude while in life, and at his death not much later he was carried to the Campus Martius and there burned and buried." However, "The senate ... feeling vexed at the utter devotion of the masses to him, took up his bones, on the plea that it was impious for them to lie in that sacred ground; they were persuaded by the pontifices to make this declaration, although they buried many other men there both before and after this."

2... *Cursus honorum* is literally translated as course of honors. It was in fact ascending rungs on a ladder to the Roman presidency, a consulship. And there was a minimum age for each step, and a required time lapse between one rung and the next. In the last years of the Republic, however, there were notable exceptions to the rule. Romans who sought to achieve each political office up the ladder prided themselves on achieving each step as soon as their age allowed. It was referred to as *suo anno*. Cicero, a *novus homo*, was exceedingly proud in having accomplished this feat. In *De Officiis* (2.59) he says he is happy to "make this boast my own . . . [that] I was unanimously elected at the earliest legal age." First of all, all Romans of senatorial rank were expected to serve in the military—in most cases as many as 10 years—to qualify for political office. The first political position they tackled was quaestor which they could assume at age 30. The office of aedile was next which might be assumed at 36. Three years later, at 39, the candidate could become praetor which came with the power of *imperium*. After serving in the office, the praetor went to one of the provinces to serve as a propraetor which gave him an army and administrative power in the province. At 42 a candidate could run for the country's highest office which was consul—two selected each year. After the consulship, the commander was assigned one of the Roman provinces for a period of time, in some cases lasting for years. Then, after completing all these steps, the politician could serve as a censor for a period of 18 months. And, while serving in the senate, a politician might be chosen to serve as its head, *princeps senatus*, for a period of five years which might be renewed for another five-year term. The senate numbered between 300 and 500 politicians—which Caesar raised to 900—a position a person held for life. Senators were not elected but appointed by consuls and later censors. After a Roman magistrate (an elected official) served his term, an appointment to the senate was almost automatic.

3... Of course, the assertion here is that an ordinary person has a hard time reading under well-controlled circumstances, how could Caesar write a most exacting book when bullets [*inter tela volantia*] were flying around his head? Here are lines 1-11 from Fronto's text to provide context:

> Quod te vix quicquam nisi raptim et furtim legere posse
> prae curis praesentibus scripsisti, fac memineris et cum animo
> tuo cogites G. Caesarem atrocissimo bello Gallico cum alia multa
> militaria tum etiam duos 'De Analogia' libros scrupulosissimos
> scripsisse, inter tela volantia de nominibus declinandis, de ver-
> borum aspirationibus et rationibus inter classica et tubas. Cur
> igitur tu, Marce, non minore ingenio praeditus quam G. Caesar
> nec minus ordine insignis nec paucioribus exemplis aut documentis
> familiaribus instructus, non vincas negotia et invenias tibimet
> tempora non modo ad orationes et poemata et historias et praecepta
> sapientium legenda, sed etiam syllogismos, si perpeti potes, re-
> solvendos?

4... Plutarch (*Caes* 17.4) says that when Caesar was being "conveyed to garrisons, cities, or camps, one slave ... was accustomed to write from dictation as he traveled sitting by his side." He adds (*Caes* 17.7) that "in the Gallic campaigns he practiced dictating letters on horseback and keeping two scribes busy, or as Oppius says, even more." It's not surprising that Caesar was (Plutarch, *Caes* 17.8) "the first to devise intercourse with his friends by letter, since he could not wait for personal interviews or urgent matters owing to the multitude of his occupation and the great size of the city." Cicero later remarked (*Fam* 7.5.2; *Fra* 2.14.3) that Caesar even took the time to concern himself with a person Cicero had recommended to him for a position.

5... Working while at play was a practice Augustus sought to avoid, as Suetonius (*Aug* 45.1) records, thus, "whenever he was present [at a public function], he gave his entire attention to the performance, either to avoid the censure to which he realized that his father Caesar had been generally exposed, because he spent his time in reading or answering letters and petitions."

6... Pliny (NH 16.5) notes, "Nor is the same honor any greater if the rescued person is a general, because the founders of this institution wished the honor to be supreme in the case of any citizen. The receiver of the wreath may wear it for the rest of his life; when he appears at the games it is the custom for even the senate always to rise at his entrance, and he has the right to sit next to the senators; and he himself and his father and his paternal grandfather are exempt from all public duties. Siccius Dentatus, as we have mentioned at the proper place, won fourteen Civic Wreaths, and Capitolinus six, one in his case being actually for saving the life of his commanding officer Servilius. Scipio Africanus refused to accept a wreath for rescuing his father at the Trebbia. How worthy of eternity is a national character that rewarded exploits so distinguished with honor only, and whereas it enhanced the value of its other wreaths with gold, refused to allow the rescue of a citizen to be a thing of price, thus loudly proclaiming that it is wrong even to save the life of a human being for the sake of gain!" Gellius (*AN* 5.6. 11-12) says, "The crown is called 'civic' which one citizen gives to another who has saved his life in battle, in recognition of the preservation of his life and safety. It is made of the leaves of the esculent oak, because the earliest food and means of supporting life were furnished by that oak; it was formerly made also from the holm oak, because that is the species which is most nearly related to the esculent; this we learn from a comedy of Caecilius [Statius], who says: 'They pass with cloaks and crowns of holm; ye Gods!'"

Dio (44.5) says there were two statues on the Rostra, "one representing him [Caesar] as the savior of the citizens and the other as the deliverer of the city from siege, and wearing the crowns customary for such achievements." More specific is Appian (*BC* 2.106) who says one of the statues was "crowned in oak as the savior of his country." The other statue was adorned in a grass wreath, the *corona obsidionalis*, which Caesar was awarded as the savior of Rome from siege. It was the highest of such accolades. Weinstock (pp. 148-152) discusses the conditions under which a person was awarded the *obsidionalis* and those so honored. A motion was put forward in the Senate in 63 that Cicero should be awarded a *corona civica* for saving Rome from the insurrection incited by Catiline and his comrades but, literally-speaking, there was no war, no battlefield, no soldier involved. Cicero was awarded instead the honorific *Parens Patriae* "Father of the Country." Weinstock (p. 167) says, "It is certainly not too bold to conclude that it was Cicero who inspired the Senate to grant Caesar in 45 the *corona civica* which should have been given to him [Cicero] in 63 B.C." Taylor (1957, p. 12) makes reference to the dissertation of her student Helen E. Russell (1950) who says, using Livy (23.23.6) as her source, that recipients of the *corona civica* were granted membership in the Senate by Sulla.

7... For a very long time Fortuna was a popular goddess among every class, rank, sex, and occupation in Rome and Italy. People sought to be favored by her. When they were, they experienced *felicitas*. Sulla was able to say his victories were not due to *virtus* but to his *felicitas*. Indeed, Cicero (*Imp* 28) shares that view saying that, among the four qualities a general needs to be successful, Felicitas has a place, that is, "luck grounded in divine support." It was ranked with *scientia rei militaris*. There are many examples of Caesar in his own writings calling upon, or making reference to Fortuna/Felicitas. In making a crossing in a boat during the civil war, he says (*BC* 3.26.4), "Our men profited from Fortune's kindness." In a show of piety, before leaving Rome in December 49 he was sure to offer sacrifice to the goddess. Velleius (2.55.1) says that luck (*felicitas*) was always with him which allowed him to overpower his enemies. Caesar viewed Fortuna as a kind of guardian angel, a *daimon* who was his divine companion. As Lydia Matthews has pointed out (p. 115), "during the Republic, men like Q. Lutatius Catulus, Fulvius Flaccus, and Sp. Carvilius Maximus advertised their relationships with fortuna by founding various cults to her."

In his wonderful exposition on the subject of the goddess (pp. 112-127), from which these notes were extracted, the late Hungarian-born classicist, Stefan Weinstock (1901-1971), says that Caesar (p. 127), "had already built a temple for Felicitas who was called outside Rome 'Felicitas Caesaris'... she was advertised on coins and realized, in a modified form, in the Fortuna Redux of Augustus. She was like the Tyche of kings and serves with these as the model of Fortuna Augusti of the emperors from Galba onwards." With respect to Galba, Suetonius in his life of the emperor (4.3) shows Galba's commitment to Fortuna, "When he assumed the gown of manhood, he dreamt that Fortune said that she was tired of standing before his door, and that unless she were quickly admitted, she would fall a prey to the first comer. When he awoke, opening the door of the hall, he found close by the threshold a bronze statue of Fortune more than a cubit [18 inches] high. This he carried in his arms to Tusculum, where he usually spent the summer, and consecrated it in a room of his house; and from that time on he honored it with monthly sacrifices and a yearly vigil."

8... Plutarch (*Caes* 32.7) says Pollio (65 BC-4 AD) was such a trusted friend of Caesar, that the general consulted him about the advisability of crossing the Rubicon in 49. He says, "For a long time, too, he discussed his perplexities with his friends who were present, among whom was Asinius Pollio, estimating the great evils for all mankind which would follow their passage of the river, and the wide fame of it which they would leave to posterity." Pollio was a renowned historian; his *Historiae* was used by both Appian and Plutarch in their accounts. After he retired from public political life, he devoted himself to the arts, rubbing elbows with the likes of the poet Catullus. He was said to be Rome's first true Renaissance man. Quintilian (*Inst* 6.3.110) described him as a man for all occasions (*omnium horarum*). He was the first to organize public recitations in public spaces and he himself is said to be the first Roman to read his own work in public. And the magnificent art collection he had put together he later made available to the public (See Morgan, p. 52).

The library that he established was situated in the *Atrium Libertatis*, the House of Freedom, where the offices and archive of the censors were located. Livy (34.44.5) says the building had been restored in 194 and then Pollio followed suit with a glorious restoration of his own. It was known that funds for the construction came from the spoils of his Parthian campaign. The library contained works of art including sculptures and portraits of artistic people such as Marcus Terentius Varro whom Caesar originally gave the task of overseeing the project. Thus, in addition to serving as a library the building was a public art museum of sorts. Ovid (*Tris* 3.1.71) says that at one time his books were banned from the library. Pliny the Elder's statement on the library (*HN* 35.2.14-17) is worth reading in full: "There is a new invention too, which we must not omit to notice. Not only do we consecrate in our libraries, in gold or silver, or at all events, in bronze, those whose immortal spirits hold converse with us in those places, but we even go so far as to reproduce the ideal of features, all remembrance of which has ceased to exist; and our regrets give existence to likenesses that have not been transmitted to us, as in the case of Homer, for example. And indeed, it is my opinion, that nothing can be a greater proof of having achieved success in life, than a lasting desire on the part of one's fellow men, to know what one's features were. This practice of grouping portraits was first introduced at Rome by Asinius Pollio, who was also the first to establish a public library, and so make the works of genius the property of the public. Whether the kings of Alexandria and of Pergamus, who had so energetically rivalled each other in forming libraries, had previously introduced this practice, I cannot so easily say.

"That a strong passion for portraits formerly existed, is attested both by Atticus, the friend of Cicero, who wrote a work on this subject, and by M. Varro, who conceived the very liberal idea of inserting, by some means or other, in his numerous volumes, the portraits of seven hundred individuals; as he could not bear the idea that all traces of their features should be lost, or that the lapse of centuries should get the better of mankind. Thus was he the inventor of a benefit to his fellow-men, that might have been envied by the gods themselves; for not only did he confer upon them immortality, but he transmitted them, too, to all parts of the earth; so that everywhere it might be possible for them to be present, and for each to occupy his niche. This service, too, Varro conferred upon persons who were no members of his own family."

9... Feeney provides (p. 295 n135) the genealogy of his thinking, giving credit to Neil Coffee for the suggestion and to John Dugan who pointed him in the direction of the work of Patrick Sinclair who spoke of "the systematizing and rationalizing approach to the *De Analogia* to language." See especially pp. 92-96.

10... In an effort to manage information-flow during his rule, Augustus discontinued the publication of the *acta senatus* but preserved the proceedings of the senate—which included the speeches of the senators and emperors—in the imperial archives (*tabularium*) or even in special departments of public libraries, to access which one had to get permission from the *praefectus urbi*. Suetonius quite simply says (*Aug* 36.1) that one of the innovations that Augustus made was that "the proceedings of the senate should not be published." The job of compiling and housing the information was given to a junior senator *de actis senatus*. There is evidence that the *acta* were consulted by many historians as primary sources. As a senator, the historian Tacitus had access to the archives which he used as a source in writing his *Annales*. He reveals (*Ann* 5.4) that, "There is in the Senate one Junius Rusticus, who having been appointed by the emperor to register its debates, was therefore supposed to have an insight into his secret purposes." Later (*Ann* 15.74) he refers to the *commentarii senatus* (the register of the senate) by which he means the *acta senatus*. In his *Panegyricus* (75) Pliny mentions the archives, "As if my speech could either contain, or my memory recollect, what you, my Lords, to rescue from all oblivion, have been pleased to insert in our public records, and preserve in more lasting inscriptions on brass." The aforementioned archivist, Junius Rusticus, appears to be the senator Quintus Junius Arulenus Rusticus (35-93 AD) whom Suetonius refers to as Junius Rusticus. As a Stoic he wrote a panegyric in honor of his beleaguered teacher, Paetus Thrasea, whom Pliny the Younger (*Epis* 8.22) describes as "one of the gentlest and therefore one of the noblest of men." Elsewhere (*Epis* 6.29) he quotes one of Paetus' favorite maxims, "that a pleader ought to undertake either the causes of his friends, or those which others refused to touch." For taking up the cause of his friend, he was put to death by Domitian.

11... Cicero (*Att* 1.12.5) also says that "loyalty to the Republic has caused him to hold one who was his friend guilty of treason." Dio (41.4.3-4) says, "One might feel surprise, now, that after having always been most highly honored by Caesar to the extent even of commanding all the legions beyond the Alps whenever the proconsul was in Italy, he should have done this. The reason was that when he had acquired wealth and fame he began to conduct himself more haughtily than his rank warranted, and Caesar, seeing that he put himself on the same level with his superior, ceased to be so fond of him. And so, as Labienus could not endure this change and was at the same time afraid of coming to some harm, he transferred his allegiance." Cicero suggests (*Att* 7.7.6) that Labienus' independence was due to his wealth. Theodor Mommsen (4, p. 435) says, "To all appearance Labienus was one of those persons who combine with military efficiency utter incapacity as statesmen, and who in consequence, if they unhappily choose or are compelled to take part in politics, are exposed to those strange paroxysms of giddiness, of which the history of Napoleon's marshals supplies so many tragicomic examples. He may probably have thought himself entitled to rank alongside of Caesar as a second chief of the democracy; and the rejection of this claim of his may have sent him over to the camp of his opponents." Caesar trusted Labienus to produce votes making him the governor of Cisalpine Gaul in 51 "that it might be won over to give stronger support to his candidature for the consulship." The lieutenant was killed at the Battle of Munda in March 45, then serving as the commander of Pompey's cavalry. Appian (*BC* 2.105.1) says Labienus' "head was brought to Caesar who gave orders for its burial." But the writer of the Spanish Civil War (*BH* 31.9) says that Labienus, along with Attius Varus, "were buried where they fell, and about three thousand Roman knights besides, some from Rome, some from the province."

12... Oppius was not only Caesar's personal secretary but also considered an intimate friend; the same was true for Cornelius Balbus. Both were in charge of Caesar's affairs when he was away from Rome, going so far as to issue ordinances—though Marcus Lepidus, as the *magister equituum*, was the general's official deputy. Cicero (*Fam* 6.8.1) says, "All that had happened . . . convinced me that whatever Balbus and Oppius had arranged in Caesar's absence was usually confirmed by him." Gellius (17.9.1) mentions volumes of Caesar's letters in Oppius' and Balbus' possession which were extant while Gellius was writing his "Attic Nights." In September 54 (*Fra* 3.1.8) Cicero mentions Oppius as the manager of Caesar's letters and refers to him often once the civil war broke out.

Oppius was a writer of sorts as well. He is credited with having written: a biography of Caesar; a biography of Scipio Africanus the elder; a life of Cassius; a life of Marius; and a life of Pompey. A number of these works are referenced by ancient authors but all are lost now. Both Suetonius and Plutarch used information from Oppius's life of Caesar in their histories. Townsend points to a number of instances where both historians relied on Oppius' biography for their respective narratives. As might be imagined, Oppius was an apologist for his boss. Plutarch in his *Pompey* (10.4-5) indicates, for example, that Oppius speaks ill of Pompey saying that he mistreated the Latin poet and grammarian, Quintus Valerius Soranus "with unnatural cruelty" and later had him executed. But, in fact, the poet seems to have been one of the victims of Sulla's proscription in 82. Thus Plutarch warns, "when Oppius discourses about the enemies and friends of Caesar, one must be very cautious about believing him."

For some time the histories of the Alexandrine, African, and Spanish wars were attributed to Oppius but Suetonius (*Div* 56.1) says they could easily be attributed to Hirtius. However, when the styles of Hirtius' Book 8 of *De Bello Gallico* and the history of the Alexandrine War are compared, it is clear that Hirtius was responsible for the latter. As might be expected, Oppius took up the cause of the young Octavian after the death of Caesar and urged Cicero to follow suit (cf. *Att* 16.15.3). Later the secretary—at the urging of Octavian?—wrote an apologia "proving" that Caesarion was not Caesar's son with Cleopatra. On this matter Suetonius (*Div* 52.2) says, "In fact, according to certain Greek writers, this child was very like Caesar in looks and carriage. Mark Antony declared to the senate that Caesar had really acknowledged the boy, and that Gaius Matius, Gaius Oppius, and other friends of Caesar knew this. Of these Gaius Oppius, as if admitting that the situation required apology and defense, published a book, to prove that the child whom Cleopatra fathered on Caesar was not his." Plutarch (*Ant* 81.2-82.1) says, "Caesarion, who was said to be Cleopatra's son by Julius Caesar, was sent by his mother, with much treasure, into India, by way of Ethiopia. There Rhodon, another tutor like Theodorus, persuaded him to go back, on the ground that Caesar invited him to take the kingdom. But while Caesar was deliberating on the matter, we are told that Areius [Arius Didymus] said, 'Not a good thing were a Caesar too many.' Caesarion, then . . . was afterwards put to death by Caesar [Augustus]—after the death of Cleopatra." Areius was playing on a line from the *Iliad* (2.204) "No good thing is a multitude of lords; let there be one lord." At the time the teenager, after his mother had taken her own life, was the sole king of Egypt. See Gray-Fow for details.

13... Plutarch (*Caes* 17.11) says Caesar gave Oppius the room "while he himself with the rest of his company slept on the porch." Suetonius (*Div* 72.1) adds that when Caesar was in power, "he advanced some of his friends to the highest positions, even though they were of the humblest origin, and when taken to task for it, flatly declared that if he had been helped in defending his honor by brigands and cut-throats, he would have requited even such men in the same way."

14... Toward the end of his time in the provinces, Caesar provided examples of singular cruelty. When the Carnute leader Gutruatus instigated a rebellion, he "was whipped to death, and his head cut off." (*BG* 8.38.5) The tribe had been accused of murdering the *negotiatores* at Genabum. And though the enemy surrendered and gave hostages as proof of their defeat, Caesar still responded with the whipping and mutilation.

15... For Caesar's campaign of terror during his proconsulship in Gaul and other nations, see Slonsky.

16... While the depiction of an aged man groveling at the feet of an imperious public official strikes a pathetic chord, the situation is aggravated all the more when we realize that Lucius Licinius Lucullus had been a consul in 74, and that he had been engaged, as a general, in warring against Mithridates for eight years. Caesar threatened him with prosecution because during that time Lucullus—working for the interests of his superior Sulla rather than for Rome's *imperium*—allowed Mithridates to escape thereby prolonging the war. Mithridates was later able to retake Pontus and Cappadocia. Moreover, as a general, Lucullus had shown a blatant disregard for the well-being of his soldiers such that they mutinied, refused to accept his orders on the spot. To his great disgrace before the eyes of Rome, Lucullus was superseded by Pompey in 66. For years there has been ill-will between the two supporters of Sulla that was aggravated when Sulla dedicated his memoirs to Lucullus and entrusted his son to him upon his death in 78. But there was more to Caesar's threat. Ideologically, Lucullus stood firmly in Cato's camp, indeed married—and later divorced—his "loose" sister Servilia. Thus, Lucullus was as much a thorn in the side of Caesar as was Cato.

But Lucullus also drew the ire of the establishment—the equestrian class as well as the triumvirate Caesar, Crassus, and Pompey—when he offered tax relief to cities in Asia. The tax farmers saw their portfolios shrink and avidly sought his recall. At one point Lucullus was accused of plotting against the life of Pompey in what came to be known as the Vettius Affair. Cicero (*Vat* 10; *Att* 2.24) more than hints at Caesar's implication in the scheme. Lily Ross Taylor (1950, p. 51) says, "Vettius was an agent of Caesar who was trying to bring Curio into bad repute and thus put an end to his campaign for the election of a magistrate unfriendly to Caesar." Lucullus was also the envy of many Romans because he had amassed tremendous wealth during his time in the provinces. Later, he lived a most lavish lifestyle, on one occasion having spent 50,000 denarii on one dinner. He built a great private library whose works he made available to scholars and generously patronized poets and philosophers. Indeed, he built a great park in the middle of Rome that came to be known as the Gardens of Lucullus. During his campaigns in Asia he was singular in his fair treatment of conquered enemies as well as their cities and provinces, as evidenced by his offering tax relief to those forced to pay outlandish tribute. In disposition he was said to be most like Cicero.

It is worth offering Plutarch's note (*Luc* 39. 1-5) on the life of Lucullus to fill out his profile, "And it is true that in the life of Lucullus, as in an ancient comedy, one reads in the first part of political measures and military commands, and in the latter part of drinking bouts, and banquets, and what might pass for revel-routs, and torch-races, and all manner of frivolity. For I must count as frivolity his costly edifices, his ambulatories and baths, and still more his paintings and statues (not to speak of his devotion to these arts), which he collected at enormous outlays, pouring out into such channels the vast and splendid wealth which he accumulated from his campaigns. Even now, when luxury has increased so much, the gardens of Lucullus are counted among the most costly of the imperial gardens. As for his works on the sea-shore and in the vicinity of Neapolis, where he suspended hills over vast tunnels, girdled his residences with zones of sea and with streams for the breeding of fish, and built dwellings in the sea, — when Tubero the Stoic saw them, he called him Xerxes in a toga. He had also country establishments near Tusculum, with observatories, and extensive open banqueting halls and cloisters. Pompey once visited these, and chided Lucullus because he had arranged his country seat in the best possible way for summer, but had made it uninhabitable in winter. Whereupon Lucullus burst out laughing and said: 'Do you suppose, then, that I have less sense than cranes and storks, and do not change residences according to the seasons?' A praetor was once making ambitious plans for a public spectacle, and asked of him some purple cloaks for the adornment of a chorus. Lucullus replied that he would investigate, and if he had any, would give them to him. The next day he asked the praetor how many he wanted, and on his replying that a hundred would suffice, bade him take twice that number. The poet Flaccus [Horace] alluded to this when he said that he did not regard a house as wealthy in which the treasures that were overlooked and unobserved were not more than those which met the eye."

17... Suetonius (*Div* 84.2) says that Antony read aloud "the oath with which all pledged themselves to watch over his personal safety."

18... As indicated, Caesar's account is filled with trigger words and images: the enemy were conspirators against the Roman people "*contra populum Romanum coniurare*" (*BG* 2.1.1.); unpredictable insurrectionists seeking regime change "*mobilitate et levitate animi novis imperiis studebant*" (*BG* 2.1.3); reeds blowing in the wind "*Gallorum infirmitate*;" (*BG* 4.13.3); full of trickery and deceit "*perfida et simulatione*" (*BG* 13.4).

19... Suetonius (*Div* 45.2) says, "his baldness was a disfigurement which troubled him greatly, since he found that it was often the subject of gibes of his detractors. Because of it, he used to comb forward his scanty locks from the crown of his head, and of all the honors voted him by the senate and the people there was none which he received or made use of more gladly than the privilege of wearing a laurel of wreath at all times." The Rijksmuseum van Oudheden in Leiden, Netherlands, has installed a permanent exhibit called "The Netherlands in Roman Times." Part of the exhibit includes a "new face" of Caesar which the National Museum of Antiquities constructed and unveiled in 2018. It affirms that Caesar was not only bald but also had a deformed skull caused at birth. Archaeologist Tom Bijtendorp in his *Caesar in de Lage Landen* (2018) (Caesar in the Low Countries) describes Caesar's campaigns in the Netherlands and offers a glimpse of the new head which shows Caesar almost totally bald. Information about the exhibit can be found at: "https://www.rmo.nl/en/exhibitions/permanent-exhibitions/netherlands-in-roman-times/.

CHAPTERS 1–15

20... To be fair, an increasing number of scholars have recently taken issue with Caesar's character with respect to his genocidal actions. A prime example is Kurt Raaflaub's 2021 article which I came upon several years after I began this project. I did not scan it until I was near done with the present manuscript.

21... Of course, traditionally, that is legally, a grand jury is not empowered to determine the guilt or innocence of a suspect, never mind what punishment should be meted out for the alleged crime(s). The jury is impaneled to hear evidence to determine whether the state should bring charges or an indictment against a potential defendant. And a unanimous decision is not needed to bring forth charges; a super majority of agreement is sufficient. And should the jury choose not to indict, the state may bring the defendant to trial when it otherwise deems sufficient evidence exists to bring a conviction.

22... Historians, ancient and modern, have associated the name of Julius Caesar with Alexander of Macedon because of the similar thrust and impact of their respective generalships. Numerous mentions are made of the relationship in the text. Alexander was hailed as *Magnus*, the Great One, and Caesar wanted to be in that club, as Pompey had come to be. Conferral of *Magnus* brought unparalled prestige to the holder so that even today, readers of history want to know what the person did to receive such a distinction.

But there is one story about the Caesar/Alexander relationship that ancient historians have shared which reveals much about the personality of Caesar. It's like having the results of a modern-day personality inventory. And, while the French historian Gérard Walter minimizes the story by calling it "romanticized," Christian Meier (p. 141) says it "is certainly not incredible" and that seems to be the case. And, while many Romans of the day, secretly and in public, sought to emulate Alexander, Julius Caesar harnessed the power necessary to make that dream a reality.

Pompey was given the title *Magnus* by his troops after shining in battle and was later called Great in public by the dictator Sulla—we can imagine Caesar's stomach turning with psychic pain. In 81, when Sulla gave Pompey a triumph, Plutarch says (*Pomp* 13.4), the dictator "went out and met him, and after giving him the warmest welcome, saluted him in a loud voice as *Magnus*, or *The Great*, and ordered those who were by to give him this surname." Pompey was 25 with a résumé; Caesar was turning 19 with little to his credit. And, when he had a chance to assess where he stood in relation to the great Macedonian, he became crestfallen and depressed. Suetonius (*Caes* 7. 1-2) says that, in 69, as Caesar was performing his job as quaestor in Spain, part of the job included going from city to city to conduct or oversee assizes courts, Rome's form of the administration of provincial justice. While at Gades (modern-day Cádiz), he visited the statue of

Alexander the Great in the temple of Hercules. When he saw that giant of history, "he heaved a sigh, and as if out of patience with his own incapacity in having as yet done nothing noteworthy at a time of life when Alexander had already brought the world to his feet, he straightway asked for his discharge to grasp the first opportunity for greater enterprises at Rome."

To discern what that entailed is interesting but more interesting is the dream Caesar had the following night when he dreamed he had sex with his mother. He got panicky and called upon the soothsayers, the interpreters of dreams, commanding them to tell him what was going on. The seers told him not to worry, it wasn't his birth mother, the mother in the dream was the earth, mother earth, and "he was destined to rule the world, since the mother whom he had seen in his power was none other than the earth, which is regarded as the common parent of all mankind." In his version of the story Plutarch says when Caesar was in *Hispania Ulterior* (Outer Iberia) as governor in 61 (*Caes* 11.5-6), one day while "at leisure [he] was reading from the history of Alexander, [and got] lost in thought for a long time, and then burst into tears. His friends were astonished and asked the reason for his tears. 'Do you not think,' said he, 'it is matter for sorrow that while Alexander, at my age, was already king of so many peoples, I have as yet achieved no brilliant success?'" All Dio (37.52.2) says about the matter is that during that quaestorship, Caesar "had dreamed of intercourse with his mother, and learned from seers that he should enjoy great power. Hence, on beholding there a likeness of Alexander dedicated to the temple of Hercules, he had groaned aloud, lamenting that he had performed no great deed as yet."

That Pompey was a *Magnus* ate at Caesar. Pompey was a great warrior who, however wrongly, was called *adulescentulus carnifex,* the boy butcher. In his biography of Pompey, John Leach (pp. 117-118) says that in and around 61 Pompey had built a great palace for himself; he bought land and laid plans for Gardens (the Portico of Pompey); he honored Minerva with a temple; he started on a great stone theatre which was done in 55. In September 61, at a public gathering to honor his achievements, he regaled people with stories about how he conquered all those barbarians; how he killed people on all three continents; and the amounts of money he brought back to Rome that nearly doubled the city's coffers."

And, as far as being one with Alexander, Appian (*Mith* 117) says the union was consummated the day Pompey was celebrating the aforementioned triumph not because he was being "borne in a chariot studded with gems" but because he was "wearing, it was said, a cloak of Alexander the Great, if anyone can believe that. This was supposed to have been found among the possessions of Mithridates that the inhabitants of Cos had received from Cleopatra." Your hero's clothes on your very skin.

On the other hand, in 61, Caesar, on the way to his assigned province, was in debt beyond belief; he had to borrow 830 talents from Rome's money man, Marcus Licinius Crassus, to get out of town—an enormous sum—and people said it was a fraction of what he owed. And the year before, just a few weeks into his praetorship, he was stripped of the standard that reflected the power of his office, his lictors; he took off the praetor's robes in disgrace, went home and sulked like Achilles until reinstated. Anyone who knows the nature of Caesar's drive, knows that the dream with Alexander was not only about the Macedonian but Pompey, Rome's Numero Uno, Rome's Mr. *Magnus*, so Caesar decided that that Alexander had to go and it was his job to make that happen, even if by means of a civil war. Finally, with respect to Caesar's lavish outlays of funds, subsequent debt, and borrowing, Plutarch (*Caes* 5.8-9) says, "He was unsparing in his outlays of money, and was thought to be purchasing a transient and short-lived fame at a great price, though in reality he was buying things of the highest value at a small price. We are told, accordingly, that before he entered upon any public office he was thirteen hundred talents in debt. Again, being appointed curator of the Appian Way, he expended upon it vast sums of his own money; and again, during his aedileship, he furnished three hundred and twenty pairs of gladiators, and by lavish provision besides for theatrical performances, processions, and public banquets, he washed away all memory of the ambitious efforts of his predecessors in the office. By these means he put the people in such a humor that every man of them was seeking out new offices and new honors with which to requite him."

23... Pliny (*HN* 7.25). Plutarch (Caes 15.3) says Caesar took 800 cities, subdued 300 nations, fought with three million people of which he killed a million, and took a million as prisoners. In his *Pompey* (67.6) Plutarch offers slightly different statistics. He says Caesar took by storm 1,000 cities, subdued more than 300 nations, fought with Germans and Gauls in more battles that could be numbered, took 100 times 10,000 prisoners, and slayed an equal number on the battlefield. The numbers that historians differ on are only part of the equation. We shall grapple with the numbers Caesar provides elsewhere in his Commentaries. The arguments of David Henige (1998), who has provided analyses of these numbers, will be taken up later in both text and notes.

24... Marcus Claudius Marcellus (c.268-208 BC) was elected consul five times, the last shortly after he had turned 60. His crowning achievement was the killing of Viridomarus (some sources say Britomartus) the king or leader of the Insubres in a one-on-one joust-like showdown at the Battle of Clastidium in 222. Polybius (*Hist* 2.17.45) says that so many details were offered about the encounter that a goodly number of historians look upon the facts with suspicion. Nevertheless, for his victory, Marcellus earned the *spolia opima*, the armor and arms a general stripped from the body of an opposing commander in a duel-like combat. It was regarded as the highest such award a general could earn. But Marcellus was also known and condemned for his intransigence and brutality. For example, in 225, before he assumed the consulship, the Insubres had surrendered to the presiding consuls, but Marcellus persuaded the Roman leaders to refuse their terms of surrender causing the Insubres to put together a fighting force of 30,000 warriors (Polybius 2.34). Thus, rather than negotiate a peace settlement Marcellus continued the war.

When he was assigned a command in Sicily in 214, he rampaged the city during the Siege of Syracuse (213-212), slaughtered many of the Syracusans, and enslaved thousands. During the battle, the famed inventor and polymath, Archimedes, in his late seventies, was killed. While Marcellus did spare some of the inhabitants, he summarily executed 2,000 Romans who had comprised part of the town's garrison. And although ancient historians (see Plutarch, *Marc* 20 and Cicero *In Verrem* 2.2; 4.52, 54) praised his clemency and moderation, reality provided contradictory evidence. That is, deputies from Sicilian cities traveled to Rome to lay before the Senate a myriad of accusations about Marcellus' not *clementia* but *saevitia*, his out-and-out cruelty.

The delegation found support among the senatorial ranks. And though the senate was not prepared to condemn the general outright, they switched his provincial duties from Sicily to a command in Italy to fight against Hannibal (See Livy, 26.22; 26, 29-32; and Plutarch (*Marc* 23). With respect to the facts of Marcellus' military endeavors, William Smith in his dictionary (Vol. 2, 927-931, 1870 edition) says, "There are few characters in Roman history of which the picture transmitted to us has been more disfigured by partiality than that of Marcellus. Almost the whole account of his military operations against Hannibal has been so perverted, that it is difficult now to arrive at the truth." (See Plutarch, *Comp Pelop*, c. *Marc* 1; and Polybius 15.11).

Smith suggests that many of the contradictions and distortions that surround the facts of Marcellus' life found their way into the canon of literature from statements that Marcellus' son made during his father's funeral oration. Thus, statements about his *clementia* and *humanitas* must be held in abeyance. It is impossible to push aside his cruel executions at Leontini and his approval of the massacre at Enna. Livy (26.29) describes what happened when the Sicilians came to Rome to make their case before the Senate. He says the delegates made "the rounds of the senators' houses in mourning garb, asserting that they would not only leave, each group of them, their native city, but all Sicily, if Marcellus should return again in command. For no fault of theirs he had before been merciless to them, what would he do when angry, knowing that Sicilians has come to Rome to complain about himself?" They ended with, "it was better for that island to be overwhelmed by the fires of Aetna or sunk in the strait than to be handed over" to the supposed command of Marcellus and his *clementia*.

25...   Harris, p. 7, was making reference to Claude Nicolet, "Armeé et société à Rome sous la république: à propos de l'ordre équestre" in *Jean-Paul Brisson, Problèmes de la guerre* à *Rome*. Rome, IT: Mouton & Co., 1969, p. 117.

26...   The situation was no different in the late Republic, as Katherine E. Welch (p. 10) points out, "By the late Republic, military prowess had become a self-conscious aspect of Rome's image of itself, as evidenced by Marius' famous rhetorical speech to the Roman people in which he criticizes the nobility for their effeminacy and boasts of his own battle scars." Plutarch (*Mar* 9.2) speaks of, "the boldly insolent and arrogant speeches with which he [Marius] vexed the nobles, crying out that he had carried off the consulship as spoil from the effeminacy of the rich and well-born, and that he had wounds upon his own person with which to vaunt himself before the people, not monuments of the dead nor likenesses of other men." For Marius's speech, see Sallust (Jug 85.1-50)

27... A considerable literature exists on the racial bias the Romans maintained, even celebrated, toward any culture not Roman, the *"externi."* Benjamin Isaac speaks of Rome's "invention of racism." "Foreigners" were depicted—and treated—as unruly, fickle, booty-loving, womanizing drunkards, to name just a few epithets found in the writings of the self-appointed ethnographers of old. Strabo (4.4.2) referred to all Gauls as "fighters by nature." Chapter Two of Polybius is filled with such debasing language. Cicero, a supposed man of learning, could not escape the moral- and cultural-superiority trap as well. In his *Pro Fonteio* (27) his Roman hubris allows him to query: "is one of the greatest of Gaul to be compared, not only with the highest men of our state, but with the lowest Roman citizen?" Diodorus Siculus (5.28.2) describes the Gauls as animals who pull their hair "back from the forehead to the top of the neck, with the result that their appearance is like that of Satyrs and Pans, since the treatment of their hair makes it so heavy and coarse that it differs in no respect from the mane of horses." Horses? Satyrs? Pans? Satyrs were animal-like beings: men with the ears, tail, legs, hooves, and horns of a goat; they were animalistic lovers of wine, women, song, dancing—beings out of control. Pans were described as similarly biologically-structured. When Velleius references the Germans he says (2.117.3) they are, "a people who were men only in limbs and voice." Dennis Bain Saddington (p. 92) notes that, "In military contexts *'gentes'* are often described as savage and wild: the tribes of Britain, for example, appear as *'gentes barbaras'* on a triumphal inscription of Claudius." The reference is I.L.S. 216: *Ti. Clau[(/!0 Drusi f. Caijsari | Augu[s/o Gemanijco pontiflc[j | maximo, trib potes]lat. XI', | cos. V, im[p. XX . . .^ patri pa]triai, senatus \)o[pulusque] Ro[manus, q]uod reges j Brit[annjai] XI [devictos^ sine] \ ulla iactur[a m dedilionem acceperit] gentesque b[arbaras trans Oceanum] primus in dici^onew populi Romani redegerit].* More about the cultural biases throughout the text.

28... The Swedish classical philologist Erik Wistrand (p. 29) notes that, "*Dignitas* is a notion akin to *gloria* . . . [it] connotes a man's rank and prestige in society [which can be] acquired through noble birth (*dignitas generis*) . . . and personal achievements (*res gestae, honores*)." Caesar says at times that his *dignitas* is his most important possession and feels wounded because some people are not paying him the respect due him. When he was recalled from Gaul, he said the Senate short-shrifted him in this regard. Thus, Wistrand adds that *dignitas* implies, "that you are worthy of something; that you deserve to obtain something; in other words it implies a claim." In his book on the civil war (1.77) Caesar urges his soldiers "to defend his reputation [*existimationem*] and *dignitas* against his enemies, after all, it was under his command and leadership that for nine years they had achieved the greatest deeds for the state . . . the soldiers . . . shouted their agreement: they were ready to defend their general and the tribunes of the plebs from the outrage they had suffered." Later in the work (*BC* 1.32.4) he says he was willing to make a deal with Pompey that they both disband their armies, even though he would suffer a loss of *dignitas* and prestige [*honor*]. Some writers, Cicero among them, list *dignitas* among the personal virtues or traits that every Roman should aspire to. For the Romans, however, *dignitas* was not exactly what we today would call human dignity but had more to do with one's standing in society, one's political, economic, and social worth. And it was the responsibility of every Roman man to maintain the *dignitas* his family had attained. *Existimatio* also means reputation, good name, and character which can be connected to the rumors about a person. Cicero links *existimatio* to wealth as well. In his *Pro Flacco* (52) he speaks of Maeandrius who is a "*homo egens, sordidua, sine honore, sine existimatione, sine censu.*" That is, "a needy, sordid man, without honor, without character, without income." For a list of personal as well as public virtues a Roman should embrace, see https://www2.hawaii.edu/~lanning/maximus.html.

29... After the famed Battle of Arausia, the shoe of the *magna copia* was on the other foot. Plutarch (*Mar* 21.3) says, "the people of Massalia fenced their vineyards round with the bones of the fallen, and that the soil, after the bodies had wasted away in it and the rains had fallen all winter upon it, grew so rich and became so full to its depths of the putrefied matter that sank into it, that it produced an exceeding great harvest after years, and confirmed the saying of Archilochus that 'fields are fattened' by such a process."

30... While the moniker *adolescentulus carnifex* has frequently been applied to Pompey by modern historians, especially by bright lights such as Theodor Mommsen and Ronald Syme, there is only a single source in ancient literature where the phrase can be found; in Book 6 (2.8) of the *Memorable Days and Sayings* of the first century Roman author, Valerius Maximus. The label was first applied in 55 during a speech Helvius Mancia gave in which he condemns Pompey for four notorious killings: (1) Gnaeus Papirius Carbo, in 82; (2) Gnaeus Domitius Ahenobarbus in 81; (3) Marcus Junius Brutus, in 77; and (4) Marcus Perperna Vento, in 72. The original text reads, "*quod indemnati sub te adolescento carnifice occidissent.*" That is, "that they should be killed without trial under a young executioner as you." Gaius Oppius, Caesar's friend and secretary, was to mention Pompey's cruelty in his execution of Quintus Valerius Soranus, poet, grammarian, and tribune of the people, which also took place during war in 82.

First of all, Pompey born in 106, was hardly an *adolescens* in 82, never mind 10 years later. Secondly, in Plutarch's life of Pompey (10.5), we find a different take, that is, while, "Pompey was compelled to punish those enemies of Sulla who were most eminent, and whose capture was notorious; but as to the rest, he suffered as many as possible to escape detection, and even helped to send some out of the country." And though Cicero was engaged in a kind of Pompeian encomium in his speech defending the Manilian Law—designed to give Pompey, in addition to the command he already possessed, unlimited power in Bithynia, Pontus, and Armenia, for the purpose of conducting the war against Mithridates—he does say (*Imp* 21.61) that Pompey, when dealing with the Sicilian cities and Africa "conducted himself in these provinces with singular blamelessness, dignity, and valor." It is worth quoting at length the conclusion of the Dutch classicist, Alexander Todd in his Master's thesis dealing with the labeling of Pompey by his adversaries, "When taken out of the context of Valerius Maximus' work, Helvius Mancia's speech and the *adulescentulus carnifex* label expressed within it, paint a far more negative image of Pompeius than the majority of ancient sources portray and serves to distort the modern perception of his early character and career accomplishments. The narrative constructed by Helvius was clearly meant to amplify the negative reputation surrounding Pompeius' role in the civil war, alongside his enacting of Sulla's proscriptions against the dictator's enemies . . . The result of this adversarial quip by the son of a freedman from Formiae was far more devastating than even Helvius could initially have imagined, as almost every modern work pertaining to this period in and around Pompeius' early career makes reference to his reputation as the *adulescentulus carnifex*. These negative opinions of Pompeius can be seen exhibited in the works of influential scholars such as Theodor Mommsen and Ronald Syme, whose own opinions have trickled down to infiltrate more modern works of scholarship that cover a diverse range of literary styles, further cementing a tradition that is unfairly biased against Pompeius." University of Glascow classicist Catherine Steel (2013) also offers an analysis of how Helvius Mancia's speech affected history's perception of Pompey.

31... Even a well-traveled and worldly man like Cicero says he never heard of the nation whose people he was about to slaughter and enslave. It didn't matter, they had no human identity, were nobodies. He tells Atticus (*Att* 5.20.1), "On the morning of the Saturnalia (17th December) the Pindenissetae surrendered to me, on the fifty-seventh day from the beginning of our investment of them. 'Who the mischief are your Pindenissetae? who are they?' you will say: 'I never heard their name.' Well, what am I to do?"

32... The Suebi were originally from the Elbe region which is part of present-day Germany and the Czech Republic. By the time of Caesar's governorship they had settled in the region on the east side of the Rhine—east of the Ubii— where the city of Cologne stands today. What is referred to as the Suebi is really an extensive confederation of clans living east of the Elbe, each with its own name and distinct cultural qualities. Among them are the Hermundari, the Marcomanni, Quedi, Lombards, and Semnones whom Tacitus (*Germ* 29) described as "the most ancient and renowned branch of the Suevi." Harry Mountain (Vol 1, pp. 224-225) says, "Every year half the tribe would leave the territory to go warring while the other . . . stayed home and supplied the food. The next year the warriors would trade positions. The Suebi did not cultivate much land and believed that a tribe's prestige was demonstrated by the amount of wilderness it contained. They believed that to become domesticated or drink wine like the Gauls would weaken the spirit and body. Because of this they only allowed traders into their land to purchase their booty, and not to trade for luxuries." Henri Hubert (p. 114) says, "On coming into contact with Gaul, they [the Suebi] were induced, between 72 and 62, to take sides in one of the squabbles for hegemony in which the Sequani and Aedui engaged." He adds (p. 116) that, "The encroachments of the Suebi and Dacians on the frontiers, old and new, of the Celts, by creating a pressure in the border districts, caused the last migrations of the continental Celts, that of Helvetii and Boii." The Ubii, after being attacked by the Suebi and forced to pay tribute, called upon the Romans for aid.

33... As Susan Mattern says, the Romans—whether during the Republic or empire—sought to instill an indisputable, non-ambiguous respect for the boundaries they set through fear. That is, the Romans came to see that fear of annihilation was a greater deterrent to any potential marauder than any river or mountain range could be. She says (p. 194) that, "Rome was willing to do whatever it took to retain its territory ... crucial were issues of psychology, the emotions of terror and awe that they hoped to produce in the enemy; and the moral and status issues, such as the need to repress *superbia*, avenge *iniuriae*, and maintain the honor or *decus* of the empire. It was on these things that, as they believed, their security depended; it was for these that they fought."

34... Cicero in his *De officiis* (1.11. 33-37; 12.38) addresses the requirements for engaging in a war that is considered just. He says, "Again, there are certain duties that we owe even to those who have wronged us. For there is a limit to retribution and to punishment; or rather, I am inclined to think, it is sufficient that the aggressor should be brought to repent of his wrong-doing, in order that he may not repeat the offence and that others may be deterred from doing wrong." That is, there are limits to the counter-violence an aggrieved person or nation can inflict on another. When the offender repents and says he will not do such harm again, the goal of the inflicted pain has been achieved. He goes on to say, "Then, too, in the case of a state in its external relations, the rights of war must be strictly observed. For since there are two ways of settling a dispute: first, by discussion; second; by physical force; and since the former is characteristic of man, the latter of the brute, we must resort to force only in case we may not avail ourselves of discussion. The only excuse, therefore, for going to war is that we may live in peace unharmed; and when the victory is won, we should spare those who have not been blood-thirsty and barbarous in their warfare . . . In my opinion, at least, we should always strive to secure a peace that shall not admit of guile. And if my advice had been heeded on this point, we should still have at least some sort of constitutional government, if not the best in the world, whereas, as it is, we have none at all." Thus, the only criterion for going to war is to prevent one's peaceful life from being interrupted by violence or other means.

And, when it comes to dealing with those who have been subjugated through warful means, the barrister says, "Not only must we show consideration for those whom we have conquered by force of arms but we must also ensure protection to those who lay down their arms and throw themselves upon the mercy of our generals, even though the battering-ram has hammered at their walls. And among our countrymen justice has been observed so conscientiously in this direction, that those who have given promise of protection to states or nations subdued in war become, after the custom of our forefathers, the patrons of those states." Cicero wrote his *De Officiis* in 44 so perhaps he had Julius Caesar in mind when he spoke about the duty of protecting those who have laid down their arms. Indeed, so grave is engaging in war that those who make such decisions must see it as the will of the gods. Cicero continues, "As for war, humane laws touching it are drawn up in the fetial code of the Roman People under all the guarantees of religion; and from this it may be gathered that no war is just, unless it is entered upon after an official demand for satisfaction has been submitted or warning has been given and a formal declaration made . . ."

Even those who engage in war to pad their résumés are bound by the same rules, he says, for, even "when a war is fought out for supremacy and when glory is the object of war, it must still not fail to start from the same motives which I said a moment ago were the only righteous grounds for going to war. But those wars which have glory for their end must be carried on with less bitterness." In his *De republica* (2.23.35), written seven years earlier, he laid out the principles governing those who are considering war as a means to an end. He says, "Those wars are unjust which are undertaken without provocation. For only a war waged for revenge or defense can actually be just … No war is considered just unless it has been proclaimed and declared or unless reparation has first been demanded."

35… The Treveri inhabited the lower valley of the Moselle, a left bank tributary of the Rhine, in an area known as the Ardennes Forest. That area today extends through Luxembourg, southeastern Belgium and western Germany. Its main city Trier takes its name from the tribe. Tacitus (*Germ* 28) says, "The Treveri and Nervii are even eager in their claims of a German origin, thinking that the glory of this descent distinguishes them from the uniform level of Gallic effeminacy." Mountain (1, p. 233) says the Treveri, "had the largest complement of horse warriors in Gaul and in 57 they contributed horse warriors to help Caesar against the Nervii." For a full discussion of the Treveri, see Edith M. Wightman, 1970.

36… The Menapii were a sea-faring nation like their neighbors, the Morini and Ambiani. As early as the sixth century they settled near the mouths of the Rhine and Waal where they were surrounded by swamps, marshlands, and forests. (Mountain, p. 196) Cassel was the chief city of the tribe (*civitas Menapiorum*). In the Table of Peutinger it is listed as *Castellum Menapiorum*, the tribe's oppidum. To be more specific, they were located in what today is the southwestern Netherlands around the Rhine and Maas estuaries between Antwerp and Rotterdam on both sides of the Scaldis, the modern River Scheldt. To the northeast of the Menapii were the Batavi and Canninetates, to their east and south were the Paemani and Eburones; to the south were the Nervii, and west the Morini.

Mountain (p. 196) reports that, in 57, the tribe contributed 100,000 warriors to fight under Galba, the head chieftain of the Suessiones, against the invading Romans. In 56 they aided the Veneti when Caesar invaded their territory, one of the last tribes to suffer defeat. The invasion of the Usipetes and Tencteri is described in the text. Later in 55, when Caesar was invading Britain, he sent two legions with a part of his army against the Menapii and Morini to keep them under control (*BG* 4.22). When the natives fled to the woods, the Romans burned their buildings and crops (*BG* 4.38). In 53 the Menapii, Aduatuci, and Nervii invited German forces to join them in defeating the Romans, without success. Ultimately Caesar had to send five legions to subdue them (*BG* 6.2-6).

Dio (39.44) describes the difficulty Caesar had tracking down the Menappi and Morini and eventually subduing them because of the landscape. He says Caesar "made a campaign against the Morini and Menapii, their neighbors, hoping to terrify them by what he had already accomplished and capture them easily. He failed, however, to subdue any of them, for having no cities, and living only in huts, they conveyed their chief treasures to the most densely wooded parts of the mountains, so that they did the attacking parties of the Romans much more harm than they themselves suffered. Caesar attempted by cutting down the forests to make his way into the mountains themselves, but renounced his plan on account of their size and the nearness of winter, and retired."

37... Deterring nations from joining in the fray against Rome through tactics of annihilation was part of Rome's governing ideology. In a letter to Porcius Cato in January 50, Cicero (*Fam* 15.4.10) shares how he terrorized a nation. "Having completed these operations, I led the army away to Pindenissus, a town of the Eleutherocilices. And since this town was situated on a very lofty and strongly fortified spot, and was inhabited by men who have never submitted even to the kings, and since they were offering harborage to deserters, and were eagerly expecting the arrival of the Parthians, I thought it of importance to the prestige of the empire to suppress their audacity, in order that there might be less difficulty in breaking the spirits of all such as were anywhere disaffected to our rule." Resistance was defined as audacity which reflected a rebellious spirit that needed to be eradicated from the nation.

38... The Ubii inhabited lands on the east side of the Rhine south of the Sugambri, opposite the Treveri who lived in Gaul. As mentioned, the Suebi had been pressing the Ubii such that the latter felt compelled to seek relief from Caesar. They gave him hostages and offered him boats for crossing the river. (*BG* 4.16) Many decades later the Ubii, because of their conflict with the Catti, received Rome's protection, this time under Marcus Agrippa; they were assigned lands on the west side of the river to serve as a defense against threatening German tribes. Tacitus (*Germ* 100.28) says of the Ubii, "although they have been thought worthy of being made a Roman colony, and are pleased in bearing the name Agrippinenses from their founder, [do not] blush to acknowledge their origin from

Germany; where they formerly migrated, and for their approved fidelity were settled on the bank of the Rhine, not that they might be guarded themselves, but that they might serve as a guard against invaders."

Agrippina, wife of Claudius, and mother of Nero, was born among them while her father commanded troops in those parts so that the colony was called Colonia Agrippina and the people Agrippinenses which caused the Germans east of the Rhine to despise them. With their new name they were condemned as traitors. Suetonius (*Aug* 21) says that the emperor forced German tribes to the farther side of the river Albis, "with the exception of the Suebi and Sigambri, who submitted to him and were taken into Gaul and settled in lands near the Rhine." Tacitus (*Ann* 12.27) says, "To demonstrate her power to the allied people, as well, Agrippina successfully petitioned for a colony of veterans—its title was derived from her own name—to be established in the chief town of the Ubii, in which she had been born. And it so happened that this was the tribe that her grandfather Agrippa had taken under Roman protection when it crossed the Rhine."

39... Not to put too fine a point on the grammar, but Caesar uses the verb *impero* as in "to order," consistent with his power as a commanding general. He was reflecting Ariovistus' statement that, "It was the right of war that conquerors dictated as they pleased to the conquered." (*Ius esse belli, ut qui vicissent eis, quos vicissent, quem ad modum vellent imperarent* . . .") To ask Rome for help was to submit as a conquered nation.

40... See *Dig.* 26 tit. 8 s5 "*Sed si per interpositam personam rem pupilli emerit, in ea causa est, ut emptio nullius momenti sit, quia non bona fide videtur rem gessisse* . . ." Cicero *De officiis*, 1.23 says, "The foundation of justice, moreover, is good faith—that is, truth and fidelity to promises and agreements. And therefore we may follow the Stoics, who diligently investigate the etymology of words; and we may accept their statement that 'good faith' is so called because what is promised is 'made good.'"

41... In describing the skirmish between the Usipetes and Tencteri horse soldiers and the Roman troops, Caesar engages in one of the most salient features of propaganda to tug on the heart strings of his audiences back home. That is, he delineated between who was and who was not a worthy victim. Whose life was worth more? He says that (*BG* 4.12.3-6) among the 74 horse soldiers who were killed, was a certain "Piso, an Aquitanian, a most valiant man, and descended from a very illustrious family; whose grandfather had held the sovereignty of his state, and had been styled friend by our senate. He, while he was endeavoring to render assistance to his brother who was surrounded by the enemy, and whom he rescued from danger, was himself thrown from his horse, which was wounded under him, but still opposed [his antagonists] with the greatest intrepidity, as long as he was able to maintain the conflict. When at length he fell, surrounded on all sides and after receiving many wounds, and his brother, who had then retired from the fight, observed it from a distance, he spurred on his horse, threw himself upon the enemy, and was killed." The grandfather in question was King Ollovico of the Nitiobroges who ruled around 70 BC and on whom the Senate had conferred the title of *amicus*. The soldier's courage to save his brother is highlighted in bold while the hundreds of thousands of Usipetes and Tencteri who would be killed, essentially moments later, are treated as worthless detritus. Caesar was manufacturing consent to his dastardly deed from the politicos back home.

The political scientists, Ed Herman and Noam Chomsky, spoke about using weighted affective language to emphasize the distinction between worthy and unworthy victims in their 1988 classic *Manufacturing Consent: The Political Economy of the Mass Media* (p. 35). They hypothesized "that worthy victims will be featured prominently and dramatically, that they will be humanized, and that their victimization will receive the detail and context in story construction that will generate reader interest and sympathetic emotion. In contrast, unworthy victims will merit only slight detail, minimal humanization, and little context that will excite and enrage." How can a brother, who loses his own life trying to save the life of a brother, they being two soldiers whose grandfather was a king, and not just any king but a king Rome had raised to the level of friend: is not their life worth more than a band of ruffian barbarians threatening the life of every Roman even though Rome was 500 miles away?

The Nitiobroges did remain friends of Rome until 52 when they sent 5,000 of their soldiers to join the confederation of Vercingetorix under the leadership of

Ollovico's son King Teutomatus. (*BG* 7.31.5) Apparently the king was close to the front because Caesar says he was able to escape a surprise attack of the Roman army. As the Roman soldiers were taking charge of the enemy's camps, he says, (*BG* 7.46.5) "so great was their activity in taking the camps, that Teutomarus, the king of the Nitiobriges, being suddenly surprised in his tent, as he had gone to rest at noon, with difficulty escaped from the hands of the plunderers, with the upper part of his person naked, and his horse wounded." Exit the king from history. Aginnum (Agen), first the capital of the Nitiobroges, was superseded by the *Civitas Aginnensis* in 27 AD by Augustus, and the Nitiobroges were assimilated. Aginnum was on the road from Burdigala to Argentomagus. According to the *Notitia provinciarum*, by the 4th c. the prosperous Aginnum, served by several major routes, had become the second city of *Aquitania Secunda*.

42... The truth about the truce comes only from what we get from Caesar and the more one reads between the lines (*intellegere*), the more one is convinced that Caesar is running something like a three-card-Monte scam on historical fact. As is discussed throughout the text, many scholars consider him a propagandist of the first order. To add a note to the note: it will never be known who caused the initial skirmish between the two rival cavalries. Caesar could have collected his cavalry irregulars from the Eburones who bordered the Menapii on the south and were itching to teach the two invading tribes a lesson for taking over lands on their side of the Rhine. Or perhaps they wanted to show off their own prowess as horsemen to tribes noted for their horsemanship. The Tencteri, although their numbers were temporarily diminished, would have been most confident to have faced down their supposed Gallic inferiors. As Tacitus (*Germ* 32) notes, "The Tencteri enjoy the usual high reputation of Germans as warriors, and in particular are distinguished for the excellence of their cavalry, whose reputation is equal to that of the infantry of the [German tribe] Chatti. In this they do not follow the example set them by their forefathers. Horsemanship among them is the amusement of children and the passion of youth, while even the old persist in keeping it up. Horses pass by inheritance as well as slaves and household goods and other property to which there are rights of succession; but primogeniture gives no preferential claim to them as it does to the rest; the son who gets the horses gets them as being a bold warrior and the better man." It is unlikely that they would easily be spooked by a glaring enemy; indeed, their diminished number did leave 74 Romans dead.

43... With respect to his slaughter of the Usipetes and Tencteri women and children, Caesar ends Chapter 14 of Book 4 with, "*ad quos consectandos Caesar equitatum misit.*" Edwards in the Loeb edition of *De Bello Gallico* (p. 197) translates this as, "and Caesar dispatched the cavalry in pursuit." T. Rice Holmes in a bit bolder statement says, "Caesar sent his cavalry to hunt them down." See Holmes, 1908, p. 107. Much is made about how bold the general is in revealing that he sent his horsemen to mow down women and children. Lee, p. 100, says that Caesar does not deny the massacre—it would have been impossible to do so—but his "description of the affair is by no means 'straight.'" He says, "The words *ad quos consectandos Caesar equitatum misit* have been singled out for their "tremendous frankness'" making reference to Holmes' *De Bello Gallico* (Oxford, 1914), p. 140. But we find Holmes in his *Caesar's Conquest of Gaul* (p. 190) issuing forth a robust apologia for his generalissimo. He says that, even if Caesar's "robust conscience was ill at ease. I do not believe it ever occurred to him to gloze over his misdeeds; for if so, why did he make the following almost brutally candid avowal. . ." offering the *ad quos* phrase in question.

Holmes, a great apologist for Caesar, and others in that league, miss the point totally of the massacre of women and children. There was no need to gloss over anything. Caesar's non-admission admission is a dog whistle blown like a trumpet from the highest ramparts of his cunning mind. The slaughter of women and children was for him not a source of disgrace but genuine pride. By slaughtering the kids, he had rid Rome of the tribes' future; there would be no one left in immediate future generations to come after him and the people of Rome. And by destroying the women he was destroying the biological fields in which all future Germanic-warrior offspring would find life. In short, for Caesar the slaughter was a cause for celebration; he wanted his readers in Rome and its provincial satellites to know about his military acuity, that is, that he had saved Rome from a triple threat: (1) the armed warriors of the Usipetes and Tencteri he had slaughtered; (2) the youth who would grow up and become a source of future incursions upon the *maiestas* of Rome; and (3) the women who would bring forth still future generations. Elsewhere we talk about women, children, and the aged being fair game for slaughter during the Republic.

44... *Fides* means reliability, as in the trust that exists between two parties because the parties are keeping their word or oath. In Latin we see the phrase *bona fides* especially among jurists which means good faith, the opposite of *mala fides* or *dolus malus*. *Bona fides* is sometimes equated with *aequum* (equitable conduct toward others) or *justum* (uprightness), qualities that were especially important when oral contracts were made. The violation of *fides* had religious as well as legal consequences because it personified the goddess *Fides*. The Temple of Fides was located on the Capitoline Hill, west of the Temple of Jupiter. It was also referred to as *Fides Publica* or *Fides Publica Populi Romani*. It was dedicated in 254 during the consulship of Aulus Atilius Calatinus; its symbol was a pair of covered hands representing agreement. *Fides* appears on a number of Roman coins. In one instance she is shown standing with a bowl of fruits in one hand and a couple of ears of wheat or barley hanging from the other. In another, on the reverse side of a silver denarius of Vespasian, there is a pair of hands clasped around a caduceus and some corn and poppy stems, symbolizing trade and the annual corn supply. There are also a billion antoninianus [coin worth two denarii] of Victorinus depicting *Fides Militum*, symbolizing the loyalty of the army, she holding military standards. There is still another depiction with priests being borne on a chariot with their heads covered and their right hands wrapped up to the fingers indicating a devotion to her and a commitment to trust. All the descriptions noted above and others can be found on the website: forumancientcoins.com.

The establishment of devotion to *Fides* has been traced to the reign of the second king of Rome Numa Pompilius (r. 715-673 B.C.). Livy (1.21) says Numa, "instituted a yearly sacrifice to the goddess Fides and ordered that the Flamens should ride to her temple in a hooded chariot, and should perform the service with their hands covered as far as the fingers, to signify that Faith must be sheltered and that her seat is holy even when it is holy in men's right hands." See also Plutarch (*Numa* 16) who mentions "just dealing" and Dionysius (2.75) who says the construction of a temple instituting sacrifice in her name meant that "the attitude of good faith and constancy on the part of the State toward all men would in the course of time render the behavior of the individual citizens similar . . . so revered and inviolable a thing was good faith in their estimation, that the greatest oath a man could take was by his own faith . . . And if there was any dispute between one man and another concerning a contract entered into without witness, the faith of either of the parties was sufficient to decide the controversy and prevent it from going any farther." On the walls of the *Aedes Fidei* were fastened tables on which international agreements were inscribed. For this, see *Annali dell'Instituto di Corrispondenza Archeologica*, 1858, p. 198ff. Pliny (*HN* 35.100) says there was also on view in the temple of *Fides* on the Capitol a picture of Aristides of Thebes showing an old man with a lyre giving lessons to a boy. For the connection between loyalty and the lyre, see Littlewood, pp. 267-285.

45... While Cato's life in many ways appears complex, and sometimes contradictory, his relationship with Julius Caesar was unfailingly straightforward, the two differing radically on personal, political, social, and ethical matters. With respect for Cato, it is worth spending a moment describing who the man was. To Caesar and other ideological opponents—Pompey and Crassus to name two—Cato was a political thorn-in-the-side, in modern terms a pain-in-the-ass. That was in part because he walked the straight-and-narrow, living a life of stoical simplicity. It was not uncommon for fellow citizens to see him walking around the streets of Rome, Gandhi-like, unashamedly without shoes and tunic. Nevertheless, from his earliest days, Cato seemed destined to live a life of service to others and later, upon entering the political arena, to bolster the stanchions of the Roman Republic which were increasingly eroding—in large part because of the invasively despotic acts of Julius Caesar. Cato's sense of fairness and wanting to make things right manifested itself early in life. At a birthday party, when he was a boy, the kids started playing a game that involved judges in court meting out sentences. When one of the younger boys was sentenced to prison and was locked in a room, the panicked soul cried out for help; Cato pushed aside the boys who were guarding the "prison" and freed the prisoner. Although a youth himself, he took the boy home accompanied by a band of sympathizers.

When he was 14 his tutor, Sarpedon, took him to see a friend of his father, none other than the dictator Lucius Cornelius Sulla. It was during the time Sulla had instituted his proscriptions, in 82. When the boy saw the heads of noted citizens of Rome paraded before Sulla, he was repulsed especially upon hearing the groans of disgust from others present. He asked his teacher, Plutarch (*Cat Min* 2.3-4) says, "Why does no one kill that tyrant?" He was told because "men fear him [Sulla] more than they hate him." Straightaway the boy demanded a sword so that he "might put him to death, and restore my country to freedom." From that point forward the teacher kept a close eye on the boy lest the young man follow through with his threats. In 67, when he was given the command of a legion in Macedonia under Marcus Rubrius—though he was ill-suited for military life—he was highly esteemed by his men. He treated them, as Smith (1, p. 646) says, "as rational beings, not as mere machines, and he preserved order without harsh punishments or lavish bribes." Upon his return to Rome, he brought with him the Stoic philosopher Athenodorus (Cordylion) who had been in charge of the library of Pergamon. Cato studied daily with his teacher who lived with him for the rest of his life. Friends and opponents alike said Cato seemed better suited for a life of contemplation and philosophy than for politics.

Upon being considered for the job of quaestor in 65, Cato said he would not take the position until he knew all that was entailed. He assiduously studied every aspect of the job and, when his tenure as questor began, he uncovered much fraud and other forms of abuse such as the falsification of decrees—which he put a stop to. And, although his going-by-the-book intransigence offended many at first, his work soon garnered considerable admiration. At the end of his tenure he had replenished the treasury. Because of his ethical stance on matters, over the years friends and opponents alike described him as: independent, stubborn, argumentative, honest, uncompromising, and even rigid. His greatest failure in the eyes of some was that he lacked political vision. Understandably, an unscrupulous political animal like Julius Caesar rubbed Cato's ethical constitution the wrong way. Their enmity was intensified when the senate was discussing how to respond to supporters of Catiline who sought to overthrow the government in 63. Plutarch (*Caes* 8.1-2; *Cic.* 21.4) says Cato sought the death penalty for the insurrectionists while Caesar argued only for imprisonment. Cato's position won the day, the Stoic all along insisting that Caesar was indirectly involved in the conspiracy.

Understandably as well, as a supporter of the Republic, Cato was vehemently opposed to the formation of the first triumvirate by Caesar, Crassus, and Pompey, viewing the privatized centralization of power as detrimental to the life of his country. When, as consul in 59, Caesar was trying to get an agrarian bill passed in the senate, he became so annoyed with Cato's filibustering stubbornness that he had lictors drag his (non-resisting) political opponent out of the senate and temporarily imprisoned. When one of the senators, Marcus Petreius, followed Cato to the prison, he was, Dio (38.3) says, "rebuked by Caesar because he was taking his departure before the senate was yet dismissed." His response to Caesar was, "I prefer to be with Cato in prison than here with you." Shaken by the reply Caesar released Cato and adjourned the senate. Cato also opposed Caesar's five-year appointment to Illyria and Cisalpine Gaul for his proconsulship. And, when Caesar massacred hundreds of thousands of Germans from the Usipetes and Tencteri tribes in 55, as is noted in the text, Cato called for him to be handed over to the tribes to be prosecuted in their system of justice. In 49, he argued before the senate, and with success, that Caesar finally be relieved of his command.

In several of his writings Cicero shows admiration for Cato, calling him (*Att* 2.5.1) a friend, "who is as good as a hundred thousand in my eyes." The barrister also called attention to Cato's studiousness (*Tusc disp* 5.4) and "voracious appetite for reading" (*Fin* 2.7). And while Cicero (*Off* 3.8) called attention to his intransigence, he also noted (*Att* 1.18.7) that "There is one man who does take some trouble [to concern himself with the Republic], with consistency and honesty." When the civil war was in full swing, Cato was forced to side with Pompey though his mistrust of the general was almost as great as that he had for Caesar. When Pompey was assassinated in 48, he took flight to Campania and later to Utica in Africa, the only city that had not submitted to Caesar. Seeing that the cause of the Republic was gone, he took his own life by stabbing in 46 BC, only 49 years old. Caesar, having been alerted that something like this might occur, rushed to Utica with the intent of forgiving the traitor and winning him over to his cause. Obviously, Cato did not allow Caesar to have such satisfaction, as Plutarch (*Cat Min* 72.2) says, "if Cato had consented to have his life spared by Caesar, he would not be thought to have defiled his own fair name, but rather to have adorned that of Caesar." Caesar's response to Cato's death was, Plutarch continues (*Cat Min* 72.2), "O, Cato, I begrudge you your death because you begrudged me the chance to spare your life." Elsewhere the historian quotes Cato as saying (*Cat Min* 66.2), "if I were willing to be saved by the grace of Caesar, I ought to go to him in person and see him alone; but I am unwilling to be under obligation to the tyrant for his illegal acts, And he acts illegally in saving, as if their master, those over whom he has no right at all to be the lord."

Shortly after Cato's death, Cicero produced a panegyric in the form of a dialogue called "Cato" which caused Caesar to respond with an "Anti-Cato" polemic, the text of which has not survived. Regardless of Caesar's criticism, many saw Cato as the personification of godlike virtue. Indeed, the life of Cato written by Plutarch reads much like one of the gospels of the New Testament and, although he does call attention to the Stoic's faults, he causes the reader to reflect deeply on who exactly the man was. While Cato's life was treated by many as hagiography after his death—the reader must be astute in his assessment—there appears to be little excuse for the pejorative book-length assessment of Drogula (p. 5) who says that "Cato's efforts to protect the Republic unintentionally but directly contributed to the collapse of the Republic." He follows with the outlandish condemnation of Cato as one (p. 6), "who fought to save his vision of the Republic, and who—as much as Caesar or Pompey—contributed to the collapse of that Republic." Plutarch in his life of Cato (43.1-5) provides a valuable snapshot of the character of the man when arguments were being made to distribute provinces to Pompey and Crassus in 55:

And now Caius Trebonius proposed a law for the assignment of provinces to the consuls, whereby one of them was to have Spain and Africa under him, the other Syria and Egypt, and both were to wage war on whom they pleased, and attack and subdue them with land and sea forces. The rest of the opposition were weary of their efforts to prevent such things, and forbore even to speak against the measure; but Cato mounted the rostra before the vote was taken, expressed a wish to speak, with difficulty gained permission, and spoke for two hours. After he had consumed this time in long arguments, expositions, and prophecies, he was not allowed to speak any longer, but an official went up to him as he sought to continue, and pulled him down from the rostra. But even from where he stood below the rostra he kept shouting, and found men to listen to him and share his indignation. So the official once more laid hands on him, led him away, and put him out of the forum. Then, the instant that he was released, he turned back and strove to reach the rostra, shouting, and commanding the citizens to help him. This was repeated several times, until Trebonius, in a passion, ordered him to be led to prison; but a crowd followed listening to what he said as he went along, so that Trebonius took fright and let him go.

In this manner Cato consumed that day; but during the days that followed his adversaries intimidated some of the citizens, won over others by bribes and favours, with armed men prevented one of the tribunes, Aquillius, from leaving the senate-chamber, cast Cato himself out of the forum when he cried out that there had been thunder, and after a few of the citizens had been wounded and some actually slain, forced the passage of the law. Consequently, many banded together and wrathfully pelted the statues of Pompey. But Cato came up and stopped this. However, when once more a law was introduced concerning Caesar's provinces and armies, Cato no longer addressed himself to the people, but to Pompey himself, solemnly assuring and warning him that he was now, without knowing it, taking Caesar upon his own shoulders, and that when he began to feel the burden and to be overcome by it, he would neither have the power to put it away nor the strength to bear it longer, 6 and would therefore precipitate himself, burden and all, upon the city; then he would call to mind the exhortations of Cato, and see that they had sought no less the interests of Pompey than honour and justice. Pompey heard these counsels repeatedly, but ignored and put them by; he did not believe that Caesar would change, because he trusted in his own good fortune and power.

And when Cato—joined by the famed jurist Sulpicius Rufus—prosecuted Lucius Licinius Murena for electoral bribery in 63, their opponent was Cicero himself. In his argumentation for his client, Cicero (*Mur* 35.74) says of his stoical opponent:

But I must change my tone for Cato argues with me on rigid and stoic principles. He says that it is not true that good-will is conciliated by food. He says that men's judgments, in the important business of electing to magistracies, ought not to be corrupted by pleasures. Therefore, if any one, to promote his canvass, invites another to supper, he must be condemned. "Shall you," says he, "seek to obtain supreme power, supreme authority, and the helm of the republic, by encouraging men's sensual appetites, by soothing their minds, by tendering luxuries to them? Are you asking employment as a pimp from a band of luxurious youths, or the sovereignty of the world from the Roman people?" An extraordinary sort of speech! but our usages, our way of living, our manners, and the constitution itself rejects it. For the Lacedaemonians, the original authors of that way of living and of that sort of language, men who lie at their daily meals on hard oak benches, and the Cretans, of whom no one ever lies down to eat at all, have neither of them preserved their political constitutions or their power better than the Romans, who set apart times for pleasure as well as times for labour; for one of those nations was destroyed by a single invasion of our army, the other only preserves its discipline and its laws by means of the protection afforded to it by our supremacy.

With a smile Cato supposedly said to a bystander (Plutarch, *Cat Min* 21), "My friends, what a comic fellow our consul is!" In his "Divine Comedy" Dante does not send Cato to hell as he does with other non-Christians but gives him an administrative role welcoming new souls on the shore of Purgatory. He is recognized for his efforts to save the Republic by standing up to the corruption of Caesar. Dante said he was the embodiment of the four cardinal virtues: Prudence, Justice, Fortitude, and Temperance. And in *The Theory of Moral Sentiments* published in 1759, Adam Smith (1.59) offered his assessment of the moralist:

Cato, surrounded on all sides by his enemies, unable to resist them, disdaining to submit to them, and reduced, by the proud maxims of that age, to the necessity of destroying himself; yet never shrinking from his misfortunes, never supplicating with the lamentable voice of wretchedness ... but on the contrary, arming himself with manly fortitude, and the moment before he executes his fatal resolution, giving with his usual tranquillity, all necessary orders for the safety of his friend; appears to Seneca, that great preacher of insensibility, a spectacle which even the gods might behold with pleasure and admiration.

In the Louvre there is a life-size sculpture of Cato of Utica created by French sculptor Jean-Baptiste Roman—finished in 1832 by François Rude upon Roman's death—depicting Cato contemplating suicide reading the "Phaedo" of Plato on the death of Socrates.

Finally, with respect to Cato's love for the fruit of the grape, Plutarch (*Cat Min* 6.1-2) says, "At suppers, he would throw dice for the choice of portions; and if he lost, and his friends bade him choose first, he would say it was not right, since Venus was unwilling. At first, also, he would drink once after supper and then leave the table; but as time went on he would allow himself to drink very generously, so that he often tarried at his wine till early morning. His friends used to say that the cause of this was his civic and public activities; he was occupied with these all day, and so prevented from literary pursuits, wherefore he would hold intercourse with the philosophers at night and over the cups. For this reason, too, when a certain Memmius remarked in company that Cato spent his entire nights in drinking, Cicero answered him by saying: 'Thou shouldst add that he spends his entire days in throwing dice.'"

46... The *ius gentium* was a concept of international law which the Romans subscribed to (at least in theory). The codex was not written down per se but fitted into the realm of what is described as customary law. For example, a Roman who was exiled might lose the rights that came with his citizenship but would be protected under the umbrella of *ius gentium*. The international code also protected the rights of persons during war especially foreign ambassadors engaged in negotiations. To violate these rights, especially during a truce, was considered an offense against religion and was certain to bring the wrath of the gods on the perpetrator. In his commentary on the civil law (*ius civile*) of Quintus Mucius Scaevola (140-82 BC, a Pontifex Maximus as well as an authority on Roman law), the second-century jurist Sextus Pomponius clarifies that, "If someone strikes an ambassador of the enemy (*legatus hostium*), he is regarded as having acted against the law of nations (*ius gentium*), because ambassadors are regarded as sacred (*sanctus*)." How odd or ironical that a priest who explained the conditions for the safe conduct of officials in international relations, should find a "contract" put out on him by Marius' son in 82. Scaevola, having learned that he and several "unreliable" senators were to be murdered in the senate house by the henchmen of Lucius Junius Brutus Damasippus, fled to the Temple of Vesta but was tracked down and was murdered in the vestibule of the temple. His body, and those of the three senators who had been murdered, were tossed into the Tiber. (Appian, *BC* 1.88; Livy, *Per* 86.6) How odd as well that Caesar himself recognized that attacking an opponent during a *colloquium* during a time of truce was a violation of the *ius gentium*. (*BC* 1.85.3;1.46.5)

47... The cavalry of the two nations who were out scouting for food (Caesar adds booty) must have been shocked upon their return to camp or upon hearing the news of the massacre while still afield. They crossed the Rhine and joined the Sugambri for security. Caesar sent messengers to the Sugambri demanding that they hand over the remnant of the two tribes. Caesar says (*BG* 4.16-3-4) the Sugambri's response was, "the Roman empire ended at the Rhine. If Caesar thought that it was not right for the Germans to cross over into Gaul against his wishes, why was he claiming any form of rule or power on the other side of the Rhine?"

48... The *supplicatio* in this case called for a public celebration of gratitude to the gods for helping Rome achieve a military victory. On other occasions the city celebrated with a supplication of expiation when the city, suffering from distress or danger, sought to peremptorily avert the wrath of the gods. Livy (3.7;10.23; 31.9; 37.3) offers several instances of this practice. In the case of a *supplicatio* recognizing a military victory, the senate would decree a certain number of days for the public acknowledgment of the event. Early on, the celebration might last a day or perhaps even four or five but, over time, the Senate increased the length of the celebration to satisfy a general's ego. When Pompey returned to the city from his victory over Mithradates in 65, the Senate issued a decree for a 10-day *supplicatio* (Cicero, *Pro Con* 11). When Caesar defeated the Belgae, he was honored with a celebration of 15 days which he acknowledged was the longest *supplicatio* decreed up to that time (*BG* 2.35). In his slaughter of the Upisetes and Tencteri, as was the case when he defeated Vercingetorix (*BG* 7.90), he was granted a supplication of 20 days. During the Empire a celebration might extend to 40 days as Cicero points out (*Phil* 14.14), and even as long as 60 days (Dio,

40.50). Livy (3.63) provides an example of a one-day *supplicatio* which the citizenry spontaneously extended for a second day without senatorial approbation, noting that, "this unauthorized thanksgiving was celebrated with almost greater enthusiasm than the former." It should be noted that the longer celebrations did not necessarily constitute an extended holiday for the populace and that, while often enough a *supplicatio* was followed by a triumph, it was not necessarily so. (Cicero, *Fam* 15.5) It is also worth noting that, after Cicero's defeat of Catiline in the courts, he was honored with a *supplicatio* for his efforts, the first time a private citizen was so honored, a fact the barrister was not bashful in reminding his fellow citizens of from time to time. (*Cat* 3.6.10; *Pis* 3.6 and *Phil* 2.6.13) The above information was garnered from William Smith, *A Dictionary of Greek and Roman Antiquities*, London: UK: John Murray, 1890, pp. 729-730.

49... Caesar engages in playing the "worthy victim" against the "unworthy victim" to justify his actions whenever the opportunity arises. Vassar College classicist, Robert Brown (pp. 391-392n2) provides the names of 18 men serving in the Roman army who were killed in battle. They all get an obituary, if you will, because in one way or another, they are men of rank and importance. In Book 1 (*BG* 58.5-7) Caesar provides the prototype of the worthy/unworthy dichotomy. He tells of the plight of Gaius Valerius Procillus, "a young man of outstanding courage and culture" (*BG* 1.47.4 *summa virtute et humanitate adulescentem*), with a father who had become a Roman citizen, who had been "dragged by his guards [the enemy] in the fight, bound with a triple chain" when Caesar came upon him as he was "pursuing the enemy with his cavalry." About this stroke of luck Caesar says Fortuna, "afforded him no less pleasure than the victory itself; because he saw a man of the first rank in the province of Gaul, his intimate acquaintance and friend, rescued from the hand of the enemy, and restored to him, and that fortune had not diminished aught of the joy and exultation [of that day] by his destruction."

Of his ordeal Procillus himself relates the superstition-based cruelty of the barbarians in that "in his own presence, the lots had been thrice consulted respecting him, whether he should immediately be put to death by fire, or be reserved for another time: that by the favor of the lots he was uninjured." As Brown notes, "The *humanitas* of Procillus ... marks him out as a Gaul who has outgrown the native flaws of a barbarian and 'acquired cultural competence in Roman standards.'" He (p. 400) adds, "Piso is cut from the same cloth as Procillus: highly-born, descended from a family loyal to Rome, courageous, dutiful, and human—and perhaps, like him, a Roman citizen." On the other hand, Caesar describes the losses of the unworthy enemy with scant detail, especially the fate of the wives and daughters of Ariovistus, a king, *rex Germanorum*. He says, "Ariovistus had two wives, one a Suevan by nation, whom he brought with him from home; the other a Norican, the sister of king Vocion, whom he had married in Gaul, she having been sent [thither for that purpose] by her brother. Both perished in their flight. Of their two daughters, one was slain, the other captured." Nothing more is said about how the three women were killed and whether the king's daughter was dragged off in chains; the obituary of the three who died scarcely receive a headline. As Herman and Chomsky (p. 35) say about an enemy's losses, "unworthy victims will merit only slight detail, minimal humanization, and little context that will excite and enrage."

50... *Deditio* involved the surrendering of a Roman citizen to a foreign tribe or country which had been harmed through a breach, shall we say, of the religious etiquette of law. It was a way to purge or expiate the sin committed. Rich (p. 197) describes it as the City's responsibility to compensate a victim based on the principle of "noxial liability." Historians list five cases when Rome was faced with dealing with a breach that required a governmental response, three of which involved the handing over of the person deemed responsible for the harm in question. In each case the purpose of the *deditio* was to remove the sacrilegious burden the City felt saddled with because of the infidel's acts; in the cases that follow the breach was due to a treaty that a commander had effected with a foreign nation or tribe.

Perhaps the most famous or most often-cited case involved the consuls of 321 BC, Titus Veturius Calvinus and Spurius Postumius Albinus Caudinus. They had engaged the Samnites in battle but Postumius was defeated at the Battle of Caudine Forks that year. He was forced to accept surrender under disgraceful conditions, his army having been, as Livy (9.1-6) says, "put under the yoke."

Having defiled the *fides publica* and been removed from office, the consuls proposed that they be stripped and bound in chains and handed over to the enemy. They were brought to the enemy but Gaius Pontius, the commander of the Second Samnite War, refused to accept them. He viewed the humiliation as reason enough for annulling the treaty that had been made. It is worth recounting how Livy described the situation, "The fetials [priests] went on in advance, and on arriving at the city gate they ordered the garment to be stripped off from those who had made the capitulation and their arms to be tied behind their backs. As the apparitor, out of respect for Postumius' rank, was binding his cords loosely. Why do you not, he asked, draw the cord tight that the surrender may be made in due form? When they had entered the council chamber and reached the tribunal where Pontius was seated, the fetial addressed him thus: Forasmuch as their men have, without being ordered thereto by the Roman people, the Quirites, given their promise and oath that a treaty shall be concluded and have thereby been guilty of a high crime and misdemeanor, I do herewith make surrender to you of these men, to the end that the Roman people may be absolved from the guilt of a heinous and detestable act. As the fetial said this Postumius struck him as hard as he could with his knee, and in a loud voice declared that he was a Samnite citizen, that he had violated the law of nations in maltreating the fetial who, as herald, was inviolable and that after this the Romans would be all the more justified in prosecuting the war."

A second case of *deditio* involved the consul of 137 BC, Gaius Hostilius Mancinus who was in charge of the war against Numantia. Appian (*Hist* 83) says he was defeated by the Numantines because of cowardice. To save his skin, he negotiated a peace treaty. Refusing to recognize his authority to make such an agreement, the Romans handed him over to the enemy bound and naked via the fetiales. When the enemy refused to accept him, he returned to Rome where a great debate took place over whether he had forfeited his rights (cf. Cicero, *Orat* 1.40). They were most likely restored because Aurelius Victor (*Vir Illus* 69) says he was later elected to the position of praetor. Cicero, (*Caec* 98), writing between 71 and 69 describes the process of expiation as well as the restoration of rights: "So that the city might be released from religious pollution, a Roman citizen is surrendered; and when he is accepted, he then belongs to those men to whom he was surrendered. If they refuse to accept him, as the people of Numantia did in the case of Mancinus, he then retains his original rights of citizenship unimpaired."

The third case of *deditio* involved Marcus Claudius Clineas who had been sent to Corsica with troops by Claudius Licinius Varus in 236. Claudius had effected a peace treaty with the enemy which he had no authority to do. Varus disregarded the agreement and fought the Corsicans until they were subjugated. To expiate the breach of *fides* that had been committed and thereby avoid the wrath of the gods, the Romans offered Claudius to the Corsicans as compensation. When they refused to accept him, he was sent into exile. See Dio (12.18). There were two other cases of *deditio* which involved injuries to ambassadors which Rich (p. 196n48) discusses.

51... Pliny has a story that addresses the earliest relationship between the Helvetii and the Romans. He says (*HN* 12.2) that, "the Gauls, separated from us as they were by the Alps, which then formed an almost unsurmountable bulwark, had as their chief motive for invading Italy, its dried figs, its grapes, its oil, and its wine, samples of which had been brought back to them by Helico, a citizen of the Helvetii, who has been staying at Rome, to practice there as an artisan. We may offer some excuse, then, for them, when we know that they came in quest of these various productions, though at the price even of war." Strabo (7.2.2), using Posidonius as a source, says that the Helvetii, early on, were "a rich and peaceful people" but that when they saw other tribes—the Teutones, Cimbri and Ambrones —engaged in spoils-producing raids, decided to associate themselves with their expeditions. Tacitus (*Germ* 28.2) says earlier they were settled between the Rhine, Main, and the Hercynian forest.

52... For a discussion of what passing under the yoke means and entails, see W. Warde Fowler, 1913. The Swiss are still reminded of the event through "*Les Romains passant sous le joug*" ("The Romans Passing under the Yoke") a painting done by the Swiss artist Charles Gleyre in 1858. Gleyre depicts the Romans walking with the yoke of oxen bearing down on their shoulders as the young Helvetian chief Divico waves his sword in victory. See the graphic on the cover of this book. See also Wickham, Chapter Two; Pompeius Trogus (*Phil Hist* 38.4.12) says that, "many states of Italy, armies of the Romans had been cut off by the sword, and by others, with a new species of insult, sent under the yoke." The earliest instance of passing under the yoke mentioned by Livy was when the Aequi were made to pass under three spears by the Roman Commander Cincinnatus in 457 BC. Livy (3.28. 10-11) says, "When they were bid by the consul to go to the dictator, he, incensed against them, added ignominy (to defeat). He orders Gracchus Cloelius, their general, and other leaders to be brought to him in chains, and that they should evacuate the town of Corbio; 'that he wanted not the blood of the Aequans: that they were allowed to depart; but that the confession may be at length extorted, that their nation was defeated and subdued, that they should pass under the yoke.' The yoke is formed with three spears, two fixed in the ground, and one tied across between the upper ends of them. Under this yoke the dictator sent the Aequans." On p. 35 of his dissertation, Wickham speaks about how passing under the yoke was also a rite of purification for those who had murdered.

53... Rome's collective memory of injuries done to its sovereignty never seemed to abate. Livy, writing during the Augustan Age, refers to an event back in 169 BC when a braggadocio Rhodian embassy enumerated "the services they had rendered to Rome, and practically claimed the greater share in the victory over Antiochus at all events." He says, "I am quite certain that even today such language cannot be read or heard without a deep feeling of indignation." And it has been suggested that Caesar had plans in 45 to wage war against Parthia, in part to avenge the killing of Crassus in 53 but, shortly before sending his mobilized troops into action in 44, he was assassinated.

Plutarch relates (*Cras* 32.1-3) that the Parthian general Surena, "took the head and hand of Crassus and sent them to Hyrodes in Armenia, but he himself sent word by messengers to Seleucia that he was bringing Crassus there alive, and prepared a laughable sort of procession which he insultingly called a triumph. That one of his captives who bore the greatest likeness to Crassus, Caius Paccianus, put on a woman's royal robe, and under instructions to answer to the name of Crassus and the title of Imperator when so addressed, was conducted along on horseback. Before him rode trumpeters and a few lictors borne on camels; from the fasces of the lictors purses were suspended, and to their axes were fastened Roman heads newly cut off; behind these followed courtesans of Seleucia, musicians, who sang many scurrilous and ridiculous songs about the effeminacy and cowardice of Crassus; and these things were for all to see."

54... See Timothy Joseph, pp. 150-161.

55... The legates mentioned are: Quintus Caecilius Metellus Creticus; Gnaeus Cornelius Lentulus Clodianus; and Lucius Valerius Flaccus who had been governor of *Gallia Transalpina* and most likely *Gallia Cisalpina* in the mid-80's.

56... The same was true for the Boii when they left their homeland in Bohemia; they left behind the "Desert of the Boii" which Strabo (7.1.5) makes mention of, "The country of the Rhaeti adjoins the lake for only a short distance, whereas that of the Helvetii and the Vindelici, and also the desert of the Boii, adjoin the greater part of it." Pliny (*HN* 3.146) refers to "*deserta Boiorum.*" Both Tacitus and Dio refer to desert lands as "uninhabited zones" or "empty fields." In some instances the Romans sought to keep some zones or fields free from settlers and, at other times, wanted the space filled with inhabitants as in the case of the Helvetii, Caesar telling them to go back whence they came and fill the space their departure left empty. As Potter (p. 269) clearly points out, using Tacitus (*Ann* 13.54.1) as a source, the Romans removed Frisian settlers who had moved into their "empty lands" near Cologne, only to find the German tribe, the Ampsivarii, moving in right after them, saying they had been driven from their homeland by the Chauci. In hopes of staying there, they made the argument that, if they returned to their homeland, unfriendly German peoples might move in the space and present problems for Rome. The Romans would not have it; they kicked the Ampsivarii out. At other times the Romans preferred to maintain a "neutral zone." And tribes who moved into such zones uninvited did not do so unwittingly. The Romans set up markers, such as boundary stones, at different junctures to let travelers know they were trespassing on Roman property. Potter (p. 272) says there could have been as well watchtowers erected, manned by soldiers, to let tribes know they had just entered Roman territory. The empty zones were large enough for a small tribe such as the Frisians to subsist on and must have been partially arable to allow the tribe to eke out an existence without clearing land from scratch. In the case of the German tribe, the Marcomani, Dio (71.15) says, they saw "restored to them one-half of the neutral zone along their frontier" but "grudgingly and reluctantly" by Marcus Aurelius who then "established the places and the days for their trading." In this case, the management of a neutral zone was related to controlling the trade that took place between Romans and tribal members. Marcus Aurelius was engaged in warfare with the Marcomani that began in 166 and lasted for more than three years.

57... Hubert (1, pp. 153-154) says the Santones came from Germany and not Gaul. More specifically Mountain (p. 214) says they came from the area between the Main and Neckar rivers in Germany and that, around the ninth century, a portion of the tribe moved to lands bordered by the Bay of Biscayne, and the Girone, Isle, and Vienne rivers. The province was Saintonge whose capital city was Saintes, which became the first Roman capital of Aquitane. In Roman times the city was known as *Mediolanum Santorum* which means the Center of the Santones. In addition to mentioning the Helvetii migrating to settle among them in 58 (*BG* 1.10.1, 1.11.6), Caesar lists them among the tribes which joined Vercingetorix's confederation in 52 (*BG* 7.73.3). Emeritus professor of ancient history at the University of Poitiers, Jean Hiernard, has examined the question *Pourquoi le Santons?* That is, why did the Helvetii pick them to settle among. Through numismatic, archaeological, and literary research he found that the two peoples were neighbors long before their respective migrations. For an enlightening and most interesting overview, see Tranoy, http://www.cervantesvirtual.com/bib/portal/simulacraromae/libro/c12.pdf.

58... With respect to the numbers Caesar uses to make his case about the extent of his war-making massacres, it is surprising that few historians over time challenged them, or more accurately, him. Perhaps the numbers did raise doubts in their minds and even in the minds of everyday readers of Caesar, but there is no body of evidence delineating those challenges. In his encyclopedia-style 1998 article, historian and bibliographer David Henige has done his best to gather the existing evidence of the records of ancient and modern historians who took issue with Caesar's numbers on several fronts. He and others have remarked that the first modern historian to question the statistics Caesar offers regarding the size of the massacre of the Helvetii is French historian and medievalist, Ferdinand Lot (1866-1952). One does not have to read between the lines to hear Lot chide his fellow historians for accepting Caesar's numbers uncritically. With respect to the number of Helvetii involved in the caravan and slaughter, he says, (p. 57) "L'assertion que les Helvètes et leurs alliés auraient perdu 226.000 personnes (compte tenu des Boïes qui furent recueillis par les Hédues) est si invraisemblable qu'on peut s'étonner qu'il y ait des historiens qui l'acceptent." That is, "The assertion that the Helvetii and their allies would have lost 226,000 people (taking into account the Boii who were taken in by the Aedui) is so implausible that one can be surprised that there are historians who accept it." He goes after Caesar as well, "It is surprising that Caesar did not sense the improbability of his story. It would not be impossible for a figure of 110,000 to represent the real number of emigrants, a figure which would have to be increased by the unknown figure of losses, and that, without guarantee, of the Boii. If we admit for emigration a third of the total number put forward by Caesar, we would perhaps not be far from reality." And, with a little bit of frustration, he challenges the reader of Caesar, professional and amateur alike, "Is it necessary to point out that here again Caesar is abusing the credulity of his reader? Most of the Usipetes and Tencteres, who were certainly infinitely less numerous, crossed the Rhine again." Ancient historians adjusted the figures as well. Plutarch says (*Caes* 18.1) the Helvetii were "three hundred thousand in all, of whom one hundred and ninety thousand were fighting men." And Orosius, writing in the fifth century and following the lost books of Livy, says (6.7.5) that the caravan, "counting both sexes amounted to one hundred and fifty-seven thousand. Of these, forty-seven thousand fell in battle, the rest were sent back to their own lands." And Dio Cassius, while not giving specific numbers, says (38.33.5-6) that only one group "came to terms with him, and going back again to their native lands, whence they had set out, they rebuilt and occupied their cities there." And the group "who refused to surrender their arms . . . set out for the Rhine; but being few in numbers and laboring under a defeat, they were easily annihilated by the allies of the Romans through whose territory they passed." Strabo (4.3.3) raises the stakes by saying 400,000 were killed, "by their war against the Deified Caesar, in which about 400,000 were destroyed, although

Caesar allowed the rest of them, about eight thousand, to escape, so as not to abandon the country, destitute of inhabitants, to the Germans whose territory bordered on theirs." The modern historian, C. E. Stevens, siding with Orosius (p. 168) says Livy's numbers via Orosius "are surely much more likely" but that "the migration *en masse* must be untrue."

To account for the numbers Caesar offers in his war against the Usipetes and Tencteri, the French historian and geographer Ernest Desjardins (1823-1886) (2, p. 652) says the inconsistencies and exaggerations must have been due to a transcription error: "The total number of the two Germanic tribes, the Tencteri and the Usipetes, which would have thus been exterminated en masse, would not have been less than 430,000! - always the same exaggeration and the same inconsistency in the figures of the *Commentaries* (4, H-15). Unless the manuscripts, instead of ccccxxx, mistakenly carry xxxxiii." Henige lays out in great detail—and to whom I am indebted for the data presented here—what historians said the caravan must have looked like, if we take Caesar's numbers at face value, that is, if we accept the number of Helvetii as 368,000. In his life of Caesar, Napoleon (2, p. 63) says that, even if every traveler were allotted a meagre supply of daily grain, about 8,500 wagons would be required and these would in turn require 34,000 draft animals. If forced to move ahead in single file, the caravan would have stretched 32 leagues, close to 110 miles. Hans Delbruck (1, pp. 487-489) says such a caravan would have gone on for 180 miles. He concludes (1, p. 475) that a more realistic assessment of the facts would require us to accept the number of migrants at about 20,000. Why then the inflated numbers? Bergier (p. 12) says the exaggeration was "designed to enhance the military talent of Caesar and to justify the considerable expense" his incessant operations were costing Rome.

59... It is worth listening to what Henige (p. 217) has to say about the tables that were reportedly found. "Why record the names of all the members of the tribe, if indeed that was the case? For that matter, how would it have been possible to do this for so many? And why Greek letters, and by whom? When had this been done and how were names removed? Furthermore, if these were actually 'tablets,' as Caesar's term suggests, where could they have been stored in transit? Presumably they would have been of wood or stone, and their sheer number and weight would have rendered them virtually untransportable. And how was access to them gained? And how long would it have taken for them to be prepared—no matter by whom—before the migrants left home?" He adds (p. 232, n11) that, "Modern telephone directories typically have about 250 to 300 names per page, written much smaller than these tables could have been. This means that it would require about 350 directory pages to list 92,000 names, and 1400 such pages to encompass 368,000 names, at four columns to the page. The Helvetian tables would be tantamount to listing every inhabitant of Nice or Bologna or Edinburgh."

60... Though there is no way of knowing for certain, it is likely that the Helvetii brought with them the gold they had mined and refined for years. Strabo (7.2.2) described them as "rich in gold" as well as "peaceful." Athenaus of Naucratis (fl. c. 200 A.D.), using Posidonius (c. 135-51 BC) as a source, says (6.233d), "In the most remote parts of the world there are certain small rivers which contain gold nuggets. These are sieved out of the sand by women and physically weak men, and then brought in for smelting as, according to my informant Poseidonius, was common amongst the Helvetii and some other tribes." See Jaffé (1982), Giukio Morteani and Jeremy P. Northover, and Jaffé (1989).

61... It shall be recalled that Dumnorix, along with Orgetorix, had entered upon an agreement with Casticus, the son of the king Catamantaloedes, who had ruled the tribe for many years; at some point the Roman senate declared the king a friend. (*BG* 1.3.3); Strabo (4.3.2.) describes the relationship between the Aedui and Sequani as follows, "But across the Arar dwell the Sequani, who, for a long time, in fact, had been at variance with the Romans as well as with the Aedui. This was because they often joined forces with the Germans in their attacks upon Italy; aye, and they demonstrated that theirs was no ordinary power: they made the Germans strong when they took part with them and weak when they stood aloof. As regards the Aedui, not only were the Sequani at variance with them for the same reasons, but their hostility was intensified by the strife about the river that separates them, since each tribe claimed that the Arar was its private property and that the transportation tolls belonged to itself. Now, however, everything is subject to the Romans."

62... Heinrich Kloevekorn says that a three-month supply of flour would require a wagon train of 8,000 carts long. Andres Furger-Gunti (p. 104) says that, even taking into account reduced numbers, the baggage train would have stretched at least 40 km, even as much as 100 km. Colonel Stoffel (Vol 2, p. 451) says the train would have extended for 15 miles.

63... The Charente is a river in southwestern France situated in the Saintonge region—in ancient times part of the Roman province of Gallia Aquitania and later a province of France. Its capital was the town of Saintes which, during the early Empire was known as *Mediolanum Santorum* which translates to the Center of the Santones or Santini, the tribe the Helvetians had made arrangements with to settle near. In the first century BC Strabo (4.2.1) says, "Mediolanium is the capital of the Santoni."

64... Sands (p. 11) says "that a king was styled '*socius*' by Rome even where no treaty existed at all; that where a treaty existed, its terms stipulated no more than friendship, and made no provision for active alliance; that requests for aid were made to and answered by Rome in such terms as plainly indicate the absence of any definite conditions of alliance" and perhaps more importantly "that Rome only granted such requests when her own interests were involved, and moreover herself sometimes solicited help only in the name of goodwill or friendship." When the sovereignty of a king was recognized by Rome, he was greeted with one of three titles: "*rex*," "*amicus*," or "*socius atque amicus*" and the terms of the agreement might describe the relationship as, "friendship," or "alliance" or even "friendship and alliance." Whatever term was applicable, the inequality of the relationship was one of protector and client. As Sands says, "The protector used them as compliments in return for services which the client out of gratitude, fear, or hope of reward had already rendered, and to accustom the client to such voluntary service; the client desired the title 'ally of Rome' as a moral support against his neighbours, even though Rome rarely vouchsafed him active support. Practically the client's relation to Rome was simply one of friendship."

Matthaei says (pp. 185-186), "But whatever delicate degrees of difference there may be in the use of the current, popular, and wide *amicus* or the official title *amicus et socius*, it is indisputable that *amicus* and *amicus et socius* are applied to the same persons in one and the same decree: hence we are driven to the conclusion that there is a single class of allies, called indifferently *amici* or *amici et socii*, not one class of *amici* and a second of *amici et socii.*" However, there was a difference in what was expected of the client, as Matthaei continues, "The position was this: the *socius* was obliged to send year in, year out, a fixed contingent to the Roman army: *the amicus* was never obliged to do so: he might, however, if he liked, give voluntary military assistance to Rome during any particular war. This for him was supposed to be a privilege, and hence arose the phrase *socius et amicus*, originally a title of honour, then simply the official designation for the friend who gave voluntary military help." In the case of Philip V of Macedon, for example, he describes himself as "*socius atque amicus*" of Rome. But, as Livy (39.28.1) notes, Philip says he received no fair treatment from the Romans, he was treated as a *hostis* rather than an *amicus*. Sands adds (pp.154-155), "Rome consulted her own interests first and last . . . It would not be hard to deduce from the number of occasions upon which Rome overlooked wrongful aggression against her clients, or neglected to take decisive action, that her willingness to intervene did not spring from a sense of the 'iniuria,' and the desire to right the wrong committed, but depended upon the degree in which her own interests were affected."

65... The first we hear of the Aedui is as a member of six tribes who were involved in a great movement of expansion into Italy when Tarquinius Priscus was king of Rome (r. 616 to 579). Livy (5.34.1-6) says that Bellovesus, the nephew of Ambigatus, the legendary king of the Bituriges, journeyed into northern Italy with members of the Averni, the Senones, the Aedui, the Ambarri, the Carnutes, and the Aulerci. The reason for the migration was that, during the reign of Ambigatus, "harvests were so abundant and the population increased so rapidly in Gaul that the government of such vast numbers seemed almost impossible." Then an old man, Ambigatus was "anxious to relieve his realm from the burden of over-population. With this view he signified his intention of sending his sister's sons Bellovesus and Segovesus, both enterprising young men, to settle in whatever locality the gods should by augury assign to them." With the surplus population of six tribes Bellovesus was told "to invite as many as wished to accompany them, sufficient to prevent any nation from repelling their approach."

That is, to be armed for any dangers that might arise. "Starting with an enormous force of horse and foot," the caravan crossed "the Alps by the passes of the Taurini and the valley of the Douro." There, Livy continues (5.34.9), "they defeated the Tuscans in battle not far from the Ticinus, and when they learned that the country in which they had settled belonged to the Insubres, a name also borne by a canton of the Haedui, they accepted the omen of the place and built a city which they called Mediolanum." (Milan) By 121 they were fully settled between the Saône and Loire rivers.

It was at that time that the Aedui were granted the title of *fratres populi Romani* by Rome and it seems the offer was made by the Romans with an ulterior motive, that is, so they would be able to attack the Allobroges with impunity. The Roman proconsul Gnaeus Domitius Ahenobarbus engaged the Allobroges in war because they had offered sanctuary to Teutomalius, King of the Salluvii who had laid waste to the territory of the Aedui, an ally of the Roman people—though it has been suggested that the underlying reason for the war was to create a secure route to Roman provinces in Spain through Gaul. Domitius and Quintus Fabius Maximus Allobrogicus, consul in 121, defeated the Allobroges and their ally, Bituitus, king of the Arverni, at the Battle of Vindalium, a town located at the confluence of the Rhône and Durance rivers in Southern France. Tacitus (*Ann* 11.25) says, "The Aedui became the first to acquire senatorial rights in the capitol: a concession to a long-standing treaty and to their position as the only Gallic community enjoying the title of brothers of the Roman people." Strabo (4.3.2) adds that, "The Aedui were not only called kinsmen of the Romans, but they were also the first of the peoples in that country to apply for their friendship and alliance." And Livy (*Epit* 61.3) mentions the Aedui as "an ally of the Roman people," a status they enjoyed as far back as the Gracchan period.

Before Caesar's time, the Sequani had joined with the Arverni to war against the powerful Aedui and, being unsuccessful, in 71 sought the help of German mercenaries under the leadership of Ariovistus. When the Sequani coalition defeated the Aedui at the Battle of Magetobriga in 63, the defeated tribe sent their druid leader Diviciacus to Rome to ask the Roman Senate for assistance but the effort seems to have met with little success. Strabo (4.3.2) says that the hostility between the Aedui and Sequani had "intensified by the strife about the river that separates them, since each tribe claimed that the Arar was its private property and that the transportation tolls belonged to itself." See also Jullian (2. 222ff). So the basis of war between the tribes was a turf battle based in a claim about economic sovereignty. When Caesar arrived in Gaul in 58, he restored the Aedui to their original independent status, however, in his *Commentaries* he reports (*BG* 7.42) that they sent warriors to join the Gallic federation led by Vercingetorix against him in 52. When Vercingetorix was defeated in the Battle of Alesia, the Aedui returned to their *socius populi Romani* relationship, but with their trust diminished. Then, as Tacitus (*Ann* 3.40ff.) indicates, in 21 AD we find the leader of the Aedui, Julius Sacrovir and Julius Florus, leader of the Treveri—both of whom had received Roman citizenship for their services—leading a revolt against the Romans because Rome had prohibited the practice of Gallic druidism and because the tribes were in dire economic straits. Florus, cornered by the troops of the governor of *Germania inferior*, Gaius Visellius Varro, at the Ardennes Forest, took his own life. Sacrovir, after raising an army of more than forty thousand to take back the city of Augustodunum (Autun), the capital of the Aeduan tribe, saw his army defeated by the governor of *Germania superior*, Gaius Silius. Sacrovir and his companions, taking refuge in a house and refusing to yield to the enemy, killed each other after setting fire to the house, which served as their funeral pyre.

Despite the uprising against Rome in 48 AD, members of the Aedui became the first Gauls to whom the Emperor Claudius (r. Jan 41- to Oct 54) granted the distinction of *jus honorum*, that is, being allowed to serve as Roman senators. Claudius had been interested in extending Senate vacancies to all areas of the Empire. Tacitus reports (*Ann* 11.25) that, "The emperor's speech was followed by a decree of the Senate, and the Aedui were the first to obtain the right of becoming senators at Rome. This compliment was paid to their ancient alliance, and to the fact that they alone of the Gauls cling to the name of brothers of the Roman people." During the speech, Claudius was not beyond reinforcing Roman propaganda begun before but intensified by Caesar. He said that some citizens will be against sharing this honor with the Gauls because "Gaul sustained a war against the divine Julius for ten years."

66... The Tigurini, as noted elsewhere, were one of the four *pagi*—rural tribal subddivisions, of a tribal territory—comprising the Helvetii "nation." Caesar says (*BG* 1.12.4) "*nam omnis civitas Helvetia in quattuor pagos divisa est*" ("for the Helvetian nation as a whole was divided into four cantons").

67... Liscus says there were "certain persons, of paramount influence with the common folk [who had] more power in their private capacity than the actual magistrates. These persons by seditions and insolent language, were intimidating the population against the collection of corn as required . . ." He added that this faction were saying, "it was better for the Aedui, if they could not now enjoy the primacy of Gaul, to submit to the commands of Gauls rather than of the Romans." The reason given was that "they did not doubt that if the Romans overcame the Helvetii, they meant to deprive the Aedui of liberty, in common with the rest of Gaul." Indeed, the group informed the Helvetii of what the Roman army was doing.

68... Caesar says (*BG* 1.18.1-10), and it is worth reading in full, that he kept, "Liscus back, and questioned him separately on his statement in the assembly. Liscus now spoke with greater freedom and boldness. Caesar questioned others privately upon the same matters, and found that it was so—that Dumnorix was the man who, unequalled in boldness, and strong in the influence that his generosity gave him over the common folk, desired a revolution. For several years, it was said, he had contracted at a low price for the customs and all the rest of the Aeduan taxes, for the simple reason that when he made a bid none dared bid against him. By this means he had at once increased his own property and acquired ample resources for bribery; he maintained a considerable body of horses permanently at his own charges, and kept them about his person; not only in his own but even in neighbouring states his power was extensive. To secure this power he had given his mother in marriage to the noblest and most powerful man among the Bituriges, he had taken himself a wife from the Helvetii, and had married his half-sister and his female relations to men of other states. This connection made him a zealous supporter of the Helvetii; moreover, he hated Caesar and the Romans on his own account, because their arrival had diminished his power and restored his brother Diviciacus to his ancient place of influence and honour. If anything should happen to the Romans, he entertained the most confident hope of securing the kingship by means of the Helvetii: it was the empire of the Roman people which caused him to despair not only of the kingship, but even of the influence he now possessed. Caesar discovered also in the course of his questioning, as concerning the unsuccessful cavalry engagement of a few days before, that Dumnorix and his horsemen (he was commander of the body of cavalry sent by the Aedui to the aid of Caesar) had started the retreat, and that by their retreat the remainder of the horse had been stricken with panic."

69... When Caesar veered from the road the Helvetii were taking on their way to Bribacte, they were informed of the change by deserters of the troop of Lucius Emelius, a decurion in the auxiliary cavalry. It is no great assumption that they were Aedui and part of Dumnorix's faction. (*BG* 1.23.2)

70... Caesar says (*BG* 5. 5-7) that when he went to Port Itius with his legions, he discovered that 40 of his ships, after being been driven back by a storm, returned to port. There he gathered the cavalry of the whole of Gaul, numbering 4,000, as well as the chief persons of all the states. He let a few stay behind in Gaul whom he had come to trust; he took the rest as hostages because he feared that they would start trouble if left behind. Among those going with him was Dumnorix "because he had discovered him to be fond of change, fond of power, possessing great resolution, and great influence among the Gauls," in other words was dangerous. Indeed, Dumnorix told an assembly of Aeduans that Caesar had now put him in charge which Caesar had learned from his own personal friends.

Dumnorix said he should not go on the trip because, being unaccustomed to sailing, he feared the sea; plus he said, the omens advised against him sailing. When he saw that his plea was having no effect on the general, he called the chief persons of the Gauls and, one by one, exhorted them to remain on the continent; to agitate them with fear saying that Caesar planned to strip Gaul of all her nobility, nay more, that Caesar planned to bring the leaders over to Britain and murder them there in sight of the Gallic peoples. Dumnorix pledged himself to the common cause, asking the others to swear that they would collectively do what was best for Gaul.

Caesar, having been informed of this harangue, determined to restrain Dumnorix in any way he could, because he was getting increasingly dangerous. He had his spies watching. When a favorable wind came after 25 days, he ordered the foot soldiers and horsemen to board the ships. While this was taking place, Dumnorix escaped from the camp with his Aeduan cavalry unbeknownst to Caesar. Infuriated, the general sent his cavalry after him, ordering them to bring him back but, if there was resistance of any sort, they were to kill him. When the cavalry caught up with Dumnorix, he resisted and defended himself with his weapons, exclaiming that "he was free and the subject of a free state." Caesar's soldiers surrounded him and killed him on the spot, the leaderless Aeduan contingent returning to rejoin the ranks of Caesar. Exit Dumnorix and the leader of great anti-Roman sentiment in the Aeduan nation.

71... In the ancient Greek and Roman world, war was for the most part an all-out annihilation activity so that anyone who got in the way of an invading army was at risk of losing his life. In Greece, for example, non-combatants had no recourse to protection from harm. A victorious army would kill women and children as if they were warriors. Women were often subject to rape by the soldiers. And while Adriaan Lanni (p. 481) says it was rare for women to be killed, "The victorious army was permitted according to custom to kill the men and enslave the women and children, or to enslave the entire population. References to rape, enslavement, and others ill-treatment of women are common in literary sources." Thucydides (*Hist* 3.36-48) records a debate in the Athenian Assembly over whether to kill the entire male population of Mytilene and then provides a detailed account of Thracians in 413—fighting on the side of the Athenians—killing women and children in the city of Mycalessus. The historian called it one of the greatest calamities any city ever suffered. Issues of mercy and compassion were subordinated to the army's aim to deter other states from ever thinking of getting involved in the fray. But there did appear a norm that did not allow generals and their armies to desecrate sacred buildings and objects. This is what he says about the genocidal slaughter of the women and children in Mycalessus (*Hist* 7.29.4-5): "The Thracians dashed into the town, sacked the houses and temples, and slaughtered the inhabitants. They spared neither old nor young, but cut down, one after another, all whom they met, the women and children, the very beasts of burden, and every living thing which they saw. For the Thracians, when they dare, can be as bloody as the worst barbarians. There in Mycalessus the wildest panic ensued, and destruction in every form was rife. They even fell upon a boys' school, the largest in the place, which the children had just entered, and massacred every one of them. No calamity could be worse than this, touching as it did the whole city, none was ever so sudden or so terrible." Roman generals and their armies followed the same ethic, Caesar telling his men to chase down women and children who were escaping the slaughter and kill them on the spot.

72... Holmes (pp. 224-225) offers these numbers in his account of the losses to the caravan. The records say the original number of travelers was 386,000. The population of the Tigurini, one of the four sub-tribes who were slaughtered, was given as 110,000, which leaves the remaining host at 276,000. Holmes offers that because the caravan included women, children, and the aged, about 2000 of whom died during the two-month trip. He adds that the Verbigeni (*BG* 28.1) were killed or sold as slaves which brings the number to 268,000 and the Boii, 32,000 strong, were allowed to settle among the Aedui (*BG* 28.5) bringing the number to 236,000. If 110,000 returned, it means that about 126,000 were killed in the battles. Colonel Stoffel (1890 p. 77) says that, counting the women and children who were killed, the death toll was about 150,000.

73... After slaughtering the vast majority of the Helvetii, Caesar says (*BG* 1.29.3) that he sent 110,000 back home to repeople the Helvetian desert. He says he knows that that was the number of returnees because he had his men take a census.

74... As Caesar tells us (*BG* 1.5. 2-3) before leaving their homeland the Helvetii had "set fire to all their strongholds . . . their villages . . . and the rest of their private dwellings." And with respect to their food supply, "they burnt up all their corn . . ." that is, what they did not take with them. And though, after their defeat, the general "required the Allobroges to give them a supply of corn" (*BG* 1.28.3), he had disarmed the tribe thereby rendering them helpless against potential marauders they might encounter on the way home. On July 6, he (*BG* 1.27-28) ordered them, "to restore with their own hands the towns and villages which they had burnt." They were to resettle their excellent farmlands so as to keep the Germans from moving further west and south.

Some historians have surmised that not all the Helvetii had been part of the great migration, that some stayed back, but extant records do not say anything to move such thinking beyond conjecture. Nevertheless, it would seem that the Helvetii were heading toward oblivion, but not exactly. For one thing, Cicero says in his speech *Pro Balbo*, delivered in 56, two years after the great slaughter, that the Helvetii among several tribes had existing treaties with Rome which seems strange. Why would the Romans make a treaty with a nation they just tried to destroy? The barrister says (14.32), "there are in existence certain treaties, such as those concluded with the Cenomani, the Insubres, the Helvetii and the Iapudes, and also with some of the barbarians in Gaul, and in their treaties there is a saving clause that none of their people may be admitted by us to citizenship."

Theodor Mommsen (1881) says that the treaty Cicero was talking about was concluded in 58 but now such an assessment seems far-fetched. First of all, nowhere does Caesar provide information about Rome's legal relationship with subjugated tribes. Secondly, given Caesar's *memoria tenebat* ethic of retribution, we would not expect him to throw a bone, so to speak, to a tribe that he recently deemed threatening to Rome's interests and which in the past had caused destruction to Rome's protective agency, her army. We might also keep in mind that in 65, when Caesar was aedile, he made a dramatic point of reminding Rome that its citizens ought never forget their victories over marauding German foes. At that time, Suetonius says (*Div* 11), Caesar, "restored the trophies commemorating the victories of Gaius Marius over Jugurtha and the Cimbri and Teuroni, which Sulla had long since demolished." He was not a man to forget.

And in 58, Caesar believed that the Helvetii were continuing the aggression of the Cimbri and Teutoni when they "engaged in laying waste their [the Aedui's] land." (*BG* 1.11.1) They had ill-treated not only the Aedui but "the Ambarri, [and] the Allobroges" (*BG* 1.14.3) as well. Best and Benjamin argue that, if we accept Cicero's argument that the Helvetii had become *foederati* in 58, it would fly in the face of Rome's policy at the time which was to rarely grant such a status to communities outside Italy. Sherwin-White, (pp. 174ff.) sheds light on this policy. Indeed, only in the winter of 51-50 does Caesar make any mention of tribes being afforded an honored status. Then he addressed, "the states in terms of honor, by bestowing ample presents upon the chiefs, by imposing no new burdens." He thereby, "easily kept Gaul at peace after the exhaustion of so many defeats, under improved conditions of obedience." *Quidquid id est timeo Romanos et dona ferentes.*

But in 58, even if Caesar were disposed to make such a treaty, he did not have the authority to do so whether the tribes were conquered or not. That was a power reserved for the Senate. Caesar's power was limited to accepting conditional surrender known as *"deditio."* Thus, in 58 when the Helvetii capitulated, they remained *dediticii*, subject to paying some sort of tribute. So when Cicero refers to treaties made with the Helvetii and other tribes as in effect *foedera extant*—he was referring to treaties that had been made long before and which were still in effect. This was true not only for the Helvetii but also for the Cenomanni, the Insubres, and Iapydes. The treaty referred to with the Helvetii, therefore, goes back to 107. When Caesar and Divico speak about the relationship between Rome and the Helvetii, the reference is to what had happened in 107, when Gaius Publius was handed over to the Tigurini.

In his telling of the story, Orosius (*Hist* 15. 23-24) refers to the deal made as a *"turpissimus foedus,"* a treaty of the most disgraceful proportions. When the Helvetii handed over hostages, their weapons, and the slaves who had come to them in 58, the disgraceful part of that treaty had been expunged. And when the Helvetii came back to help Vercingetorix in 52, supplying him with 8,000 men, whatever treaty once existed was vitiated. What then of the Helvetii's future? Tacitus (*Hist* 1.67) notes that, upon their return home, the Helvetii had created a garrison at some point which they maintained at their own expense—and this freedom, if you will, cannot be viewed as Rome extending favorable conditions to a despised tribe but as a way for Rome to keep the Germans from encroaching on Rome's provincial outposts. But that was not sufficient surety for Rome. The empire began to make settlements to ensure that their own people were present to discourage encroachment. Thus, between 46 and 44 AD, Rome established the

Colonia Julia Equestris at the site of the Helvetii's settlement Noviodunum (modern-day Nyon). The take-over was achieved through a land distribution program for veterans.

At the same time, the city of Aventicum arose which became the capitol of the re-invented Helvetii nation, the *caput gentis*. The new settlement was later incorporated into the Roman province of *Gallia Belgica*. What is interesting to note is that records show that the Helvetii maintained their long-time tribal structure of four *pagi*, the Tigurini mentioned as one of the four. (*CIL* 13, 5076). It appears as well that the Helvetii enjoyed a certain degree of autonomy in maintaining their security through such strongholds. We gain some insight into this in 68 AD upon the death of Nero and it turns out to be the last time we hear of the Helvetii.

That is, in 68, the Roman general Aulus Caecina Alienaus was appointed by Galba, who became emperor in June of that year—the first emperor of the Year of Four Emperors—to take command of affairs in upper Germany. Caecina was somewhat of a loose cannon. Tacitus describes (*Hist* 1.67) him as one who "reveled more freely in plunder and blood shed" and who was "provoked by the Helvetii" because of their lack of information about current events. That is, after the death of Nero the *civitas Helvetiorum* did not know that Galba had been murdered and rejected the authority of Vitellius—unaware as well that Otho had even ascended to the throne before him. Tacitus (*Hist* 1.67) says a war "originated in the rapacity and impatience of the 21st legion, who had seized some money sent to pay the garrison of a fortress, which the Helvetii had long held with their own troops and at their own expense." The fortress was situated at Vindonissa, between the Aare and Reuss rivers, the area that comprises modern-day Windisch. A small guard post had been established there as early as 15 BC and in the mid-forties AD, the 21st legion replaced the *Legio XIII Gemina*, one of Caesar's key divisions in Gaul and the army he crossed the Rubicon with. In response to the aggression of the Roman army, Tacitus continues, the Helvetii, "intercepted some letters written in the name of the army of Germany . . . and detained the centurion and some of his soldiers in custody." Caecina, ready to pounce at every opportunity, "ravaged a place, which during a long period of peace had grown up into something like a town, and which was much resorted to as an agreeable watering-hole." He had his Rhaetian auxiliaries prepare a rear-end attack on the Helvetii while he engaged the "enemy" up front. And though the Helvetii had chosen Claudius Severus as their leader, whatever skill he had as a leader was of little use.

That is, the Helvetii, according to Tacitus (*Hist* 1.68) did not know "how to use their arms, to keep in their ranks, or to act in concert." They were no longer a warrior nation. They were in a state of panic, "Wandering to and fro between the two armies ... [they] threw aside their arms, and with a large portion of wounded and stragglers fled for refuse to Mount Vocetius." (Today's Bözberg Pass which is situated between Vindonissa and Augusta Raurica.) But they were pursued there, "by the Germans and Rhaetians ... cut down in their forests and even in their hiding places. Thousands were put to the sword, thousands more were sold into slavery." Then the army headed to Aventicum, the capital of the Helvetii. A contingent of Helvetii came forward from the city to surrender. One of their leaders, a certain Julius Alpinus, was executed by Caecina, the rest "left to the mercy or severity of Vitellius." It is hard to believe that that mercy would be kinder than the soldiers who kept shouting "exterminate the race" as they brandished their weapons in the face of the envoys. It was said that Vitellius himself engaged in such words and gestures, until one of the envoys, Claudius Cossus, a man known for his eloquence, "soothed the rage of the soldiers" who then began to show pity on the Helvetii and "procured pardon and protection for the state." Tacitus ends by saying (*Hist* 1.70) that Caecina halted "for a few days in the Helvetian territory, till he could learn the decision of Vitellius. . . ." Assuredly, Vitellius would give great counsel to what Caecina said because the general, along with Fabius Valens, was responsible for the emperor's ascendancy to the throne. It was the second slaughter of the Helvetii, nearly a century after Caesar dashed their hopes of resettlement among the Santones. The general could smile from his grave; Caecina had put the final nail in the coffin he had built. *Roma memoria tenebat.*

75... In his "Introduction" to *Massacre in History*, Mark Levene (pp. 5-6) says, "If the dictionary, therefore, sidesteps the issue of numbers, either of perpetrators or victims, it also fails to spell out other critical ingredients. One surely is the relationship at the point of delivery between those killing and those being killed. A massacre is when a group of animals or people lacking in self-defense, at least at that given moment, are killed—usually by another group . . . who have the physical means, the power with which to undertake the killing without physical danger to themselves. A massacre is unquestionably a one-sided affair and those slaughtered are usually thus perceived of as victims, even as innocents . . . All this assumes quite specific spatial and temporal dimensions. Massacre implies an event which takes place in a limited, though not defined geographical arena, as well as in a limited, though again not clearly defined time period." See below in the text for additional definitional information regarding massacre and genocide but as well for now the "Introduction" (p. 4) of Sémelin and Schoch's *Purify and Destroy* where the authors view "the notion of 'massacre' as a minimal term of reference or the smallest common denominator." Thus, for starters they offer "an empirical, typically sociological definition of massacre as a form of action that is most often collective and aimed at destroying non-combatants."

76... See Camille Jullian, *Histoire de La Gaule III*, p. 323 and Michel Rambaud, *L'art de la deformation historique dans les commentaires de César*, p. 118.

77... Yale University historian, Ben Kiernan, says that the first Roman genocide occurred in 146 when Rome destroyed Carthage at the end of the Third Punic War. Carthage, not a military threat to Rome in any way, was ordered to surrender the city's arms which it did: 200,000 sets of armor and 2000 catapults; and its warships were burned in the harbor of Utica. In an assault that lasted six days the Romans entered the residential part of the city and killed every human being encountered and then set the city's buildings on fire. It is estimated that 150,000 Carthaginians were killed and 54,000 taken prisoner to be sold off as slaves. Rome had destroyed an entire culture. Submission and disarmament were not sufficient; it was an ancient version of carpet-bombing. Appian (8.20.135) says, "The Senate sent ten of the noblest of their own number as deputies to arrange the affairs of Africa . . . [decreeing] that if anything was still left of Carthage, Scipio should obliterate it and that nobody should be allowed to live there. Direful threats were leveled against anyone who should disobey . . . The towns that had allied themselves with the enemy it was decided to destroy, to the last one."

78... As is well known by high-achieving high school Latin students, "Caesar" was added to the 2012-2013 AP syllabus. Raaflaub asks why should students devote time and energy to a text that celebrates, or at least does not question, the ethics of genocide? Should Homer's *Iliad* be purged from high school and college curricula? He says (p. 69), "Would it not be better to help our students enhance their critical thinking through insights gained from discussing this seminal and deeply humane work not least, but emphatically, against the inhuman aspects of its content?" Thus the importance of this grand jury testimony.

79... The word "genocide" was coined by the Polish lawyer Raphaël Lemkin in 1942. See *Axis Rule in Occupied Europe,* pp. 79-95; he defined genocide (p. 79) as, "the destruction of a nation or of an ethnic group. This new word, coined by the author to denote an old practice in its modern development, is made from the ancient Greek word genos (race, tribe) and the Latin cide (killing) . . . Generally speaking, genocide does not necessarily mean the immediate destruction of a nation, except when accomplished by mass killings of all members of a nation. It is intended rather to signify a coordinated plan of different actions aiming at the destruction of essential foundations of the life of national groups, with the aim of annihilating the groups themselves. Genocide is directed against the national group as an entity, and the actions involved are directed against individuals, not in their individual capacity, but as members of the national group."

80... The Eburones, under the leadership of two chiefs, Ambiorix and Catuvolcus, led an attack on the Roman army under the leadership of Quintus Titurius Sabinus and Lucius Aurunculeius Cotta in 54. Their two armies were settling down for winter among the Eburones (*BG* 5.24.5) whose grain crop had suffered because of a drought during the growing season. Caesar says, "*quod eo anno frumentum in Gallia propter siccitates angustius provenerat.*" Not long after the armies had settled down, he adds (*BG* 5.26.1), "*initium repentini tumultus ac defectionis ortum est.*" That is, "the beginning of a sudden insurrection and revolt arose [from Ambiorix and Cativolcus]." With food in short supply, the demands of the Roman armies were taking food out of the mouths of the tribe's children, thus the two leaders organized to put a stop to the assault—which Caesar and other writers call a "rebellion," a dangerously-loaded catch phrase that projects the Romans to be the besieged nation. Whenever the word is used, it must be translated into metaphors that reflect the reality of a tribe's taking action to defend itself. Nevertheless, as Caesar began to slaughter the nation, Cativolcus saw only one exit; Caesar says (*BG* 6.31.5) he "was old and worn, and finding that he could not endure the effort of war or fight, cursed Ambiorix and all his gods for suggesting such a project, and hanged himself to a yew tree, of which there are a great many in Gaul and Germany." His fellow chief (*BG* 43.4-6), "stole away from covert or glade and hidden by night, made for other districts or territories, which no more escort of horsemen than four troopers, to whom alone he dared to entrust his entire life." Did he make it to safety and live? Hirtius in Book 8 of *De Bello* (8.24.4) picks up on the story saying Caesar had lost hope of "being able to bring the frightened fugitive into his power, he deemed it the best thing, out of regard for his own prestige [*dignitas*] to strip his territory of citizens, buildings, and cattle so as to make Ambiorix hated by any of his subjects who might change to survive, and to leave him no return to the state on account of the destruction delivered to it." Dio's version of the story is worth noting as well (40.32.1-5), "Many escaped even as it was, but Caesar took no account of these, except in the case of Ambiorix. This man, by escaping now to one place and now to another and doing much injury, caused Caesar trouble in seeking and pursuing him. When he was unable to catch him in any way, he made an expedition against the Germans, alleging that they had wished to help the Treveri. On this occasion likewise he accomplished nothing, but retired rapidly through fear of the Suebi; yet he gained the reputation of having crossed the Rhine again . . . Then, in anger at the successful flight of Ambiorix, he permitted that chieftain's country, although it had been guilty of no rebellion, to be plundered by any who wished. He gave public notice of this in advance, so that as many as possible might assemble hence many Gauls and many Sugambri came for the plunder. Now it did not enough for the Sugambri to make spoil of Gallic territory, but they even attacked the Romans themselves. They watched until the Romans were absent securing provisions and then made an attempt upon their camp; and when the soldiers, perceiving it, came to the rescue, they killed a good many of these. Then, becoming afraid of Caesar as a result of this affair, they hurriedly withdrew homeward; but he inflicted no punishment upon any of them because of the winter and the turmoil in Rome, but after dismissing the soldiers to their winter-quarters, went himself to

Italy on the plea of looking after Cisalpine Gaul, but really in order that he might watch from close at hand the events that were taking place in the city."

81... The Latin text reads, "*Non hos palus in bello latrociniisque natos, non silvae morantur.*" H. J. Edwards in his translation for the Loeb series renders "*in bello latrociniisque natos*" as "children of war and brigandage." W. A. McDevitte and W. S. Bohn in their 1869 translation of the *De Bello* say, "born amid war and depredations." "*Latrociniis*" is translated as brigandage and depredations. I humbly suggest it be translated as "born for war and fleecing" people of their homes and belongings and women and children, like a farmer would fleece a sheep, stripping the animal of what protects him from the elements that threaten survival.

82... Edith Mary Wightman, (1985 p. 53).

83... In Rome's history there were earlier noted examples of large numbers of foreign citizens being sold off as slaves. During the Third Macedonian War, Molossia sided with Macedonia against Rome. In 167 Lucius Aemilius Paullus Macedonicus (cos 182, 168) led an assault on the Epirotes comprised mostly of Molossians. He took over 70 cities and then turned 150,000 Molossians into slaves, the largest such enterprise in the history of Roman imperialism. As Adam Ziolkowski points out, it was the Senate who ordered the slaves to be brought to Italy to bolster the City's workforce. Plutarch (*Aem* 29.1-5) speaks of Paullus' crushing blow to the Epirotes, "When he [Paullus] had put everything in good order, had bidden the Greeks farewell, and had exhorted the Macedonians to be mindful of the freedom bestowed upon them by the Romans and preserve it by good order and concord, he marched against Epirus, having an order from the senate to give the soldiers who had fought with him the battle against Perseus the privilege of pillaging the cities there. Wishing to set upon the inhabitants all at once and suddenly, when no one expected it, he sent for the ten principal men of each city, and ordered them to bring in on a fixed day whatever silver and gold they had in their houses and temples. He also sent with each of these bodies, as if for this very purpose, a guard of soldiers and an officer, who pretended to search for and receive the money. But when the appointed day came, at one and the same time these all set out to overrun and pillage the cities, so that in a single hour a hundred and fifty thousand persons were made slaves, and seventy cities were sacked; and yet from all this destruction and utter ruin each soldier received no more than eleven drachmas as his share, and all men shuddered at the issue of the war, when the division of a whole nation's substance resulted in so slight a gain and profit for each soldier."

Another famed example of the mass enslavement of captives can be found in the work of Quintus Fabius Maximus Verrucosus, aka Cunctator, who served as consul five times and dictator twice; he came to be known as "The Shield of Rome" and heralded as the inventor of guerilla warfare by his delay tactics. During his third consulship in 209, Orosius (4.18.5) says, "The consul Fabius Maximus . . . stormed Tarentum a second time and captured the city, which had withdrawn from its alliance with Rome. On that occasion he destroyed huge numbers of Hannibal's army and also killed their general Carthalo. He sold thirty thousand of the captives and remitted the proceeds of the sale to the state treasury." Livy's (27.16) take is that, "After the carnage followed the sack of the city. It is said that 30,000 slaves were captured together with an enormous quantity of silver plate and bullion, 83 pounds' weight of gold and a collection of statues and pictures almost equal to that which had adorned Syracuse. Fabius, however, showed a nobler spirit than Marcellus had exhibited in Sicily; he kept his hands off that kind of spoil. When his secretary asked him what he wished to have done with some colossal statues—they were deities, each represented in his appropriate dress and in a fighting attitude—he ordered them to be left to the Tarentines who had felt their wrath. The wall which separated the city from the citadel was completely demolished." Save the deities but not human life.

84... As an educated man with a sense of history—cf. *memoria tenebat*—one wonders whether Caesar, in mentioning 53,000 captives sold as slaves, was not competing with the 50,000 Carthaginians sold at the end of the Third Punic War. That is, Caesar was seeking to out-Scipio Publius Cornelius Scipio Africanus Aemilianus, the commanding Roman general during the war—in the same way he sought to outstrip Alexander and Pompey in their successes. But it needs to be pointed out that there are diverse opinions on how many captives were sold as slaves or whether the remnant were sold at all. Appian (*Pun* 131) says after the city was devastated, "there came out 50,000 men and women together, a narrow gate in the wall opened, and a guard was furnished for them." Wickham (p. 136 n222) says the guard was furnished to protect the captives from abuse by the soldiers. With respect to the numbers in question Orosius (4.23.3) says, "First a line of women came down—a wretched enough sight—and following them a still more miserable looking body of men. Tradition says that there were twenty-five thousand women and thirty thousand men." In (4.23.2) he says, "They begged that the survivors of the disastrous battle might be permitted to become slaves." And while Livy provides only a few insignificant facts (*Per* 51.1-7), Zonarus (*Zon* 9.30) says only a few of the captive nobles were sold while others died during their incarceration. Florus (*Epit* 1.31.16) says there were 36,000 captives involved but there is no mention of enslavement, "When the position finally became hopeless, 36,000 men led—though it is scarcely credible—by Hasdrubal surrendered themselves." Appian, who seems to provide the most detailed account of the horror, describes the end-time for the Carthaginians and it seems worthwhile to point out what he says took place (App 129-134) during what has been described as Rome's first great genocide. Appian says (133), "Carthage being destroyed, Scipio gave the soldiers a certain number of days for plunder, reserving the gold, silver, and temple gifts. He also gave prizes to all who had distinguished themselves for bravery, except those who had violated the shrine of Apollo. Probably the Carthaginian god that is called Apollo was Rešef. He sent a swift ship, embellished with spoils, to Rome to announce the victory. He also sent word to Sicily that whatever temple gifts they could identify as taken from them by the Carthaginians in former wars they might come and take away. Thus, he endeared himself to the people as one who united clemency with power. He sold the rest of the spoils, and, in sacrificial cincture, burned the arms, engines, and useless ships as an offering to Mars and Minerva, according to the Roman custom." Clearly, once again, we see Rome's confusion of immeasurable destruction with clemency.

Appian (134) goes on to say that, "When the people of Rome saw the ship and heard of the victory early in the evening, they poured into the streets and spent the whole night congratulating and embracing each other like people just now delivered from some great fear, just now confirmed in their worldwide supremacy, just now assured of the permanence of their own city, and winners of such a victory as never before. Many brilliant deeds of their own, many more of their ancestors, in Macedonia and Spain and lately against Antiochus the Great, and in Italy itself, had they celebrated; but no other war had so terrified them at their own gates as the Punic wars, which ever brought peril to them by reason of the perseverance, skill, and courage, as well as the bad faith of those enemies. They recalled what they had suffered from the Carthaginians in Sicily and Spain, and in Italy itself for sixteen years, during which Hannibal destroyed 400 towns and killed 300,000 of their men in battles alone, more than once marching up to the city and putting it in extreme peril.

"Pondering on these things, they were so excited over this victory that they could hardly believe it, and they asked each other over and over again whether it was really true that Carthage was destroyed. And so they gabbed the whole night, telling how the arms of the Carthaginians got away from them and how, contrary to expectation, they supplied themselves with others; how they lost their ships and built a great fleet out of old material; how the mouth of their harbor was closed, yet they managed to open another in a few days. They talked about the height of the walls, and the size of the stones, and the fires that so often destroyed the engines. They pictured to each other the whole war, as though it were just taking place under their own eyes, suiting the action to the word; and they seemed to see Scipio on the ladders, on shipboard, at the gates, in the battles, and darting hither and thither. In this way the people of Rome passed the night. And, as in the cases with Caesar's massacres, Rome celebrated as if the enemy involved were fallen pieces of wood." Appian (135) adds, "The next day there were sacrifices and solemn processions to the gods by tribes, also games and spectacles of various kinds. The Senate sent ten of the noblest of their own number as deputies to arrange the affairs of Africa in conjunction with Scipio, to the advantage of Rome. They decreed that if anything was still left of Carthage, Scipio should obliterate it and that nobody should be allowed to live there. Direful threats were leveled against any who should disobey and chiefly against the rebuilding of Byrsa or Megara, but it was not forbidden to go upon the ground."

85... Calls for the annihilation of anything that moves can also be found in the Hebrew scriptures. Hans Van Wees (pp. 241-242) alerts us to the extremes of annihilation found in the Book of Deuteronomy (20.16-20) when Moses tells the Israelites that God is on their side and, to show their appreciation for such support, they are to "save nothing that breathes." They are to wipe out all infidel nations because, "If you allow them to live, they will persuade you to worship their disgusting gods." But, the leader cautions, "don't chop down the fruit trees . . . Fruit trees are not your enemies." Plus, they are a source of food. In other passages in the Hebrew scriptures, women and children and animals are all fodder for the slashing sword of the righteous. In Saul's destruction of Amalek, the writer of the Book of Samuel says (1 *Samuel* 15.3) God's people are to destroy "all that they [the Amalekites] have. Do not spare them, but kill both man and woman, child and infant, ox and sheep, camel and donkey." It was the same message Moses sent: kill everything that breathes. But Van Wees cautions (p. 242) that, "The genocidal campaigns claimed for the early Israelites, however, were largely fictional . . . [but that] even if the events were not historical, the ideology of legitimate genocides which underlies these stories did exist, and may occasionally have been put into practice."

86... See Simon James, pp. 98-115.

87... *De Provinciis Consularibus* 33; see as well Cicero's *Pisonem* (81-82) where he says, "I could not feel otherwise than friendly towards a man who had performed and was daily performing such mighty actions. Now that he is in command, I no longer oppose and array the rampart of the Alps against the ascent and crossing of the Gauls, nor the channel of the Rhine, foaming with its vast whirlpools, to those most savage nations of the Germans. Caesar has brought things to such a pass, that even if the mountains were to sink down, and the rivers to be dried up, we should still have Italy fortified, not indeed, by the bulwarks of nature, but by his victory and great exploits."

88... See Jane Bellemore, pp. 38-49. In his *Histories*, Polybius in one speech in his own voice, and two in the voice of projected others, calls the Romans "barbarians," [βάρβαροι] an uncivilized savage people.

89... Pliny (*HN* 29.14): *Iurarunt inter se barbaros necare omnis medicina, sed hoc ipsum mercede faciunt, ut fides iis sit et facile disperdant. Nos quoque dictitant barbarous et spurcius nosquam alios Opicon appelatione foedant. Interdixi tibe de medicis."* See Plutarch (*Cat Mai* 23) as well as Craige Champion, especially p. 426 n4 and n5.

90... Cicero expressed great dissatisfaction with his appointment to Cilicia saying that his talents were being wasted there. Thus, he began to scheme how to turn his time there into successful "triumph-hunting." In a letter to the barrister in August 51, Marcus Caelius Rufus speaks of that scheme directly (*Fam* 8.5.1), "If we could only manage to make the development of the war correspond to the strength of your forces and win just so much success as was requisite for a laurel wreath and a triumph and avoid the dangerous and decisive engagement you apprehend, nothing could be so desirable." Then on November 14, 51, Cicero responds (*Fam* 2.10.2), "It is just as you desired; for you say you could wish that I should be put to only just so much trouble as to secure me a laurel." Cicero had already become an eraser-in-chief himself; he tells Cato (*Fam* 15.4-9), "We pitched camp for four days near the Altars of Alexander in the foothills of Amanus, spending all our time erasing the last traces of Amanus and the lands on that part of the mountain that is in our province." Erasing? Yes, because, as he tells Cato, the pirate-spawning Cilicians are our eternal enemies, *perpetuum hostem* (he tells Caelius they were *hostes sempiternos)*. In mid- to late-December 51, he shares the news with Atticus (*Att* 5.20.1), "I arrived at Tarsus on the 5th of October. Thence I pressed on to Mount Amanus, which divides Syria from Cilicia by the line of its watershed—a mountain full of immemorial enemies. Here, on the 13th of October, we cut a large number of the enemy to pieces. We took some very strongly fortified posts by a night attack of Pomptinus's, and by one led by myself in the morning, and burnt them. I was greeted as imperator by the soldiers. For a few days we were encamped on the very spot which Alexander had occupied against Darius at Issus, a commander not a little superior to either you or me! Having stayed there five days, and having ravaged and devastated Amanus, we evacuated that place."

He says he continued with the slaughter elsewhere and assumed the role of a *mango*, slave-trader (*Att* 5.20.3), "I was at Pindenissus, the most strongly fortified town of Eleutherocilicia, never peaceful within living memory. The people were fierce and brave, and furnished with everything necessary for standing a siege.

We surrounded it with stockade and ditch, with a huge earthwork, penthouses, an exceedingly lofty tower, a great supply of artillery, a large body of archers. After great labor and preparation, I finished the business without loss to my army, though with a large number of wounded. I am spending a merry Saturnalia, and so are my soldiers, to whom I have given up all spoil except captives: the captives were sold on the third day of the Saturnalia (I 9th December), the day on which I write this. The sum realized at the tribunal is 12,000 *sestertia* (about £ 96,000)."

91... Because the losses of the Nervii were so great—scarcely a remnant existed—Caesar says he was moved to show mercy [*misericordia*] toward the tribe. He tells the remnant (*BG* 2.28.3), "to enjoy their own territories and towns, and commanded their neighbors to restrain themselves and their dependents from causing any injury or outrage to them."

92... Gabriel Baker (pp. 99, 100) gives an example of the Roman strategy of beheading a society of its leaders by beheading the leaders themselves. He says in Capua during the Second Punic War, the Capuans, in a show of surrender, opened their gates to the Roman army under the leadership of Appius Claudius Pulcher and Quintus Fulvius Flaccus. Fulvius had the leaders of the town tied to a stake, beaten with rods, and beheaded in the view of all the citizens. Some of the leading aristocrats who saw what was forthcoming took their own lives. Baker says (p. 100) that, "By pursuing defector communities and their leaders in highly visible ways, Roman commanders sought to make an example of them that would deter further defections." Livy's touching account (26.13.1-18) is worth spending the time to read in full: "The sight of so merciless a punishment broke the spirit of the Capuans. a gathering of the people before the Senate House compelled Loesius to summon the senate. And they openly threatened the leading citizens, who for a long time had been absent from public deliberations, that if they did not come into the senate, they would make the rounds of their homes and forcibly bring them all out into the streets. The fear of that gave the magistrate a full session of the senate. there, while all the rest were speaking of sending legates to the Roman generals, Vibius Virrius, who had proposed rebellion from Rome … on being asked for his opinion, said that the men who were speaking of embassies and of peace and surrender did not recall either what they would have done, if they had had the Romans in their power, or what they themselves must suffer. 'Tell me,' he said, 'do you suppose it will be the same kind of surrender as that under which we once gave up ourselves and all our possessions to the Romans, that we might obtain their aid against the Samnites? Have you already forgotten in what a critical moment and in what a situation for the Roman people we have revolted from them? Have you already forgotten how at the time of our revolt we with torture and as an insult put to death a garrison which we might have let go? Or how often and with what bitterness we have made a sally against the besiegers, have beset their camps, have called in Hannibal to overpower them? Or how —this the most recent occurrence —we have sent him away to lay siege to Rome? And now for the other side, recall what have been their acts of hostility towards us, that by so doing you may know what you have to expect. When a foreign enemy—was in Italy, and that enemy Hannibal, and when everywhere were the flames of war, neglecting everything, neglecting even Hannibal, they sent both consuls and two consular armies to besiege Capua. How for the second year they are wasting us away by starvation, shut up inside their contravallation, while they too like ourselves have endured the utmost dangers and most serious hardships, have been slain, many of them, about their earthworks and trenches, and have at last had their camp almost taken. But I pass over these things; to suffer hardships and dangers in besieging a city of the enemy is an old and familiar story. I proceed to proof of anger and hatred that are unspeakable. Hannibal with immense forces of infantry and cavalry besieged and partly captured their camp: by such danger they were not moved at all to give up the siege. setting out across the Volturnus he ravaged the territory of Cales with fire: by such a disaster to allies they were in no wise called away. he ordered his hostile standards to be carried to the city of Rome itself: that impending storm also they scorned. Crossing the Anio, he pitched camp three miles from the city, finally came close to the very walls and gates, showed that unless they should leave Capua he would take Rome away from them: they did not leave Capua. wild beasts, though excited by blind impulse and fury, can be diverted to bring help to their young, if one goes towards their lairs and their whelps. As for the Romans, the siege of Rome, their wives and children, whose wailing could almost be heard from here, their altars and hearths, the shrines of their gods, the desecrated and profaned tombs of their ancestors did not divert them from Capua. Such is their ardor in demanding punishment, such their thirst to drink our blood. And perhaps not without reason; we too should have done the same, had the chance been given us. Therefore, since the immortal gods have made a contrary decision, inasmuch as I ought under no circumstances to refuse death, I, while free and my own master, can escape tortures and insults which the enemy is preparing, by a death which is not only honorable, but also gentle. I shall not see Appius Claudius and Quintus Fulvius, emboldened by their insolent victory, nor shall I be dragged in chains through the city of Rome as a spectacle in a triumph, so that I may then breathe my last in the prison, or else, bound to a stake, with my back mangled by rods, may submit my neck to the Roman axe. Nor shall I see my native city destroyed and burned, nor Capuan matrons and maidens and free-born boys carried off to be dishonored. Alba, from which they had themselves sprung, they levelled with its foundations, that their stock, that the memory of their origin, might not survive; much less am I to believe that they will spare Capua, to which they are more hostile than to Carthage. Accordingly, as many of you as are minded to yield to fate before they see all these sights that are so bitter, for such in my house a feast is spread and in readiness today. When we have had our fill of wine and food, the same cup which has been served to me shall be carried round. That draught will defend the body from torture, the mind from insults, eyes and ears from seeing and hearing all the bitter and unseemly things which await the vanquished. men will be ready to light a great pyre in the court of the house and throw our lifeless bodies upon."

93...   Caesar spoke about how this tribe came to be, "upon their march into our Province and Italy, [the Cimbri and Teutones] set down such of their stock and stuff as they could not drive or carry with them on the near (i.e. west) side of the Rhine, and left six thousand men of their company therewith as guard and garrison. This party, after the destruction of the others, were harassed for many years by their neighbors, and fought sometimes on the offensive, sometimes on the defensive; then by general agreement among them peace was made, and they chose this place to be their habitation." Edith Wightman (1985, p. 30) says, "Eastwards beyond the Nervii were . . . the Aduatuci, the last supposedly descended from 6,000 wandering Teutones who had stayed behind in the north. These last are generally supposed to have occupied the middle Meuse valley, perhaps rightly, though the reasoning is suspect." At the Battle of Vercellae, also known as the

Battle of the Raudine Plain, a confederation of Germanic-Celtic tribes under the leadership of the Cimbrian chief, Boiorix, was defeated by Roman troops under the command of the famed Gaius Marius and Quintus Lutatius Catulus. It was another *memoria tenebat* event in that it was the Cimbrian king Boiorix —joined by the Teutoni under the leadership of Teutobod—who had handily defeated a Roman army—under the leadership of consul Gnaeus Mallius Maximus and proconsul Quintus Servilius Caepio—in October 105 at the Battle of Arausio. At Vercellae, Boiorix was killed along with Lugius another Cimbrian leader. The Roman victory followed on the heels of Marius' victory over the Teutoni in 102 at the Battle of Aquae Sextae. During that war Livy says (68.3) that, "200,000 enemies were killed and 90,000 captured." Some historians say the two victories put an end to the Germanic threat to Rome's stability for some time.

94... Turquin offers conclusive proof that the Battle of Sabis [also known as the Battle of the Sambre or Battle against the Nervians] took place at Saulzoir.

95... See https://en.wikipedia.org/wiki/Atuatuci#/media/File:Les_Aduatiques_Vendus_à_l'Encan_(détail).jpg

96... "Mango" was a pejorative term. Generically it means "dealer" but it carried the weight of hustler, huckster, someone who adorns the slaves he was offering for sale to inflate the market price. Martial (9.5(6).4-5) quips about a boy "no longer mutilated by the art of the greedy dealer (*arte mangonis*), to mourn the loss of his manly rights." Seneca (*Epis* 9.80.9) says that, "Slave-dealers (*mangones*) hide under some sort of finery any defect which may give offence, and for that reason the very trappings arouse the suspicion of the buyer. If you catch sight of a leg or an arm that is bound up in cloths, you demand that it be stripped and that the body itself be revealed to you." And Quintilian (2.15.25) says that, "the art of the slave-dealer, a flattery of gymnastic, for they produce a false complexion by the use of paint and a false robustness by puffing them out with fat."

With respect to the 53,000 captives sold off as slaves, it is difficult to see how the camp followers or sutlers managed such a large amount of product. When the general in command shared such human booty with his troops, Livy (10.17.9) says the troops were forced to dispose of great amounts of booty to traders. Elsewhere he says (10.17.6) that the soldiers who "sell prizes with hope of gain lure the traders on to follow your column." And the amounts could be large. Caesar says (*BG* 7.90.3) he was returning 20,000 captives to the Aedui and Arverni. Such prizes might even come from as far away as Britain, as Cicero says (*Att* 4.11.6) in October 54. The sutlers, as well as other merchants, were part of the camp as it moved from place to place. Sallust (*Jug* 44.5.7) says the camp-followers mingled with the soldiers "*lixae permixti cum militibus.*" That these traders were part of the daily mix of camp life Livy (28.22.3) says the inhabitants of the City of Astapa (modern-day Estepa, in Roman times called Ostippo) took delight in plunder making "excursions into the neighboring lands belonging to the allies of the Romans, and to intercept such Roman soldiers, sutlers, and merchants as they found ranging about." As part of the camp the sutlers moved from place to place with the army. Caesar (*BG* 6.37) describes one surprise attack when, "the sutlers who had their booths under the rampart had not an opportunity of retreating within the camp." Does that mean they were slaughtered without protection? Elsewhere he mentions their far-ranging presence (*BG* 1.39.1; 3.1.2; 4.3.3; 4.5.2; 4.20.4)

There are many words to describe the traders who were associated with the armies: *lixae, mercatores, negotiatores, publicani,* even *socii*. Wickham (p. 138n38) describes the nuances of each and his whole discussion of the slave trade is worth perusing. For now, suffice it to say that the merchants who contracted to supply the army "were known as *publicani* or classified as *socii* . . . [and] *Mercatores* and *negotiatores* were not necessarily the same as the sutlers (*lixae*) who followed the army and occupied a number of supplementary and auxiliary roles . . . *lixae* differed from private merchants and camp followers in that they were recognized and to a certain degree, employed by the army as 'licensed purveyors.'" Tacitus generally associated *lixae* with servants (*Hist* 1.49; 2.87; 3.20; 3.33) who seemed "to be free men, though of lowly origin."

Of course, there is the whole matter of the morality of trading in slaves whether in and around the camps or in distant markets to which war captives were transported. Using Livy as a starting point, Wickham (p. 15) says that, "the justification of slavery came from the universally recognized 'laws of war' which essentially gave the victor the right to do as pleased with those conquered . . .

Both the Greeks and the Romans observed that it was the right of the victor to take from the enemy whatever was desired." Livy himself (9.15; 33.13.8) used the justificatory phrase "laws of war." In Roman law, a captive was considered a slave by default and the slave was a *res* that could be managed or disposed of in any way the owner wished. For Caesar, as with other generals, moving the slaves was a cattle drive. And, legally speaking, since the general was an agent of the state doing the state's business, war-captives were considered the property of the state and proceeds from selling captives as slaves were expected to be forwarded to the state's treasury. But the law be damned; field commanders dealt with their human spoils as they saw fit. As we know, some enslaved captives were "saved" so they might be paraded before a jeering crowd during a triumph.

97... To commemorate the destruction of the Aduatuci, we recommend that the serious student read Caesar's account (*BG* 2. 29-33) in full: "(29) The Aduatuci, of whom I have written above, were coming with all their forces to the assistance of the Nervii, but upon report of this battle they left their march and returned home; and, abandoning all their towns and forts, they gathered all their stuff in one stronghold, which was admirably fortified by Nature. On every side of its circumference it looked down over the steepest rocks, and on one side only was left a gently sloping approach, not more than two hundred feet in breadth. This place they had fortified with a double wall of great height, and at this time they were setting stones of great weight and sharpened beams upon the wall. The tribe was descended from the Cimbri and Teutoni, who, upon their march into our Province and Italy, set down such of their stock and stuff as they could not drive or carry with them on the near (*i.e.* west) side of the Rhine, and left six thousand men of their company therewith as guard and garrison. This party, after the destruction of the others, were harassed for many years by their neighbours, and fought sometimes on the offensive, sometimes on the defensive; then by general agreement among them peace was made, and they chose this place to be their habitation.

"(30) And now, upon the first arrival of our army, they made frequent sallies from the stronghold, and engaged in petty encounters with our troops. Afterwards, when they had round them a fortified rampart of fifteen thousand feet in circumference, with forts at close interval, they kept within the town. When our mantlets had been pushed up and a ramp constructed, and they saw a tower set up in the distance, they first of all laughed at us from the wall, and loudly railed upon us for erecting so great an engine at so great a distance. By what handiwork, said they, by what strength could men, especially of so puny a stature (for, as a rule, our stature, short by comparison with their own huge physique, is despised of the Gauls), hope to set so heavy a tower on the wall?

"(31) But when they saw that it was moving and approaching the walls, they were alarmed at the novel and extraordinary sight, and sent deputies to Caesar to treat of peace, who spoke after this fashion: They supposed that the Romans did not wage war without divine aid, inasmuch as they could move forward at so great a speed engines of so great a height; they therefore submitted themselves and all they had to the power of Rome. In one matter only did they seek indulgence: that if perchance, agreeable to his mercy and kindness, whereof they heard from others, Caesar decided to save the Aduatuci alive, he would not despoil them of their arms. Almost all their neighbours were at enmity with them and envied their courage; and from such, if they delivered up their arms, they could not defend themselves. If they were to be brought into such case, it were better for them to suffer any fortune at the hand of Rome than to be tortured and slain by men among whom they were accustomed to hold mastery.

"(32) To this Caesar replied that he would save their state alive rather because it was his custom than for any desert on their part, if they surrendered before the batteringram touched the wall; but there could be no terms of surrender save upon delivery of arms. He would do, he said, what he had done in the case of the Nervii, and command the neighbours to do no outrage to the surrendered subjects of Rome. They reported this to their tribesmen, and agreed to perform his commands. A great quantity of arms was cast from the wall into the trench which was before the town, so that the heaps of weapons were well-nigh level with the top of the wall and the height of the ramp; and for all this about a third part, as was afterwards seen, was concealed and kept back in the town. So they threw open their gates, and on that day enjoyed the benefit of peace. (33) At eventide Caesar ordered the gates to be closed and the troops to leave the town, in order that the townsfolk might suffer no outrage at their hands in the night. In the belief that after the surrender our troops would withdraw their posts or would at least look after them less carefully, the townsfolk, it appeared, had previously formed a plan. Part of them had the weapons which they had kept back and concealed, part had shields made of bark or plaited osiers and hastily (as the shortness of time necessitated) spread over with hides. In the third watch they made a sudden sally from the town in full force, on the side where the ascent to our field-works seemed least steep. Speedily, as Caesar had ordered beforehand, the signal was given by flares, and the detachments from the nearest forts doubled in to the point. The enemy fought fiercely, as was to be expected of brave men in desperate case, where all hope of safety lay in valour alone, contending on unfavourable ground against troops who could hurl missiles at them from rampart and towers. Some four thousand men were slain, and the rest were flung back into the town. On the morrow the gates were broken open, for there was no more defense, and our troops were sent in; then Caesar sold as one lot the booty of the town. The purchasers furnished a return to him of three-andfifty thousand persons."

98... Numismatist Melinda Mays (1981) says there is enough archaeological evidence to pinpoint Hengistbury Head, Dorset as the site of the trading post. And the Oxford archaeologist, Barry Cunliffe (1978), says amphorae-remains suggest that Hengistbury Head was the main point of entry for the Roman wine trade. With respect to the lucrative nature of the trade with Britain, Cunliffe (1982, p. 42) makes reference to Cicero's *Pro Fonteio* where the barrister alludes to the fortunes that could be made by controlling the export of wine to the barbarian west through the levying of unofficial (illegal) taxes along the way. He says (*Fon* 9) that Fonteius had hatched a taxation scheme before he went to Gaul whereby, "at Tolosa, Titurius exacted four denarii per amphora of wine as a duty, at Crodunum, Porcius and Munius exacted three and a half, at Vulchalo, Servaeus took two and a half and that, in these places, duty was exacted by these men if anyone, not wishing to go to Tolosa, turned out at Cobiomagus (a town between Tolosa and Narbo) and that at Elesioduli, Gaius Annius exacted six denarii from those who were carrying wine to the enemy." A twenty-first century ferry from Roscoff (a department in Finistère) to Plymouth, England takes at least five hours. With respect to the composition of the ships themselves, see Weatherhill (1985).

99... However, Dio (39.31.2) refers to him as ὑπεστρατήγει which translates into Latin as *legatus*.

100... Crassus' soldiers, wintering among the Andes, were an occupying army. The leader of the tribe was a certain Dumnacus who headed a strong anti-Roman faction in the tribe. What we do know is that four years later, in 52 after Vercingetorix was defeated at Alesia, the chieftain kept taking the fight to Rome. In Book 8 of the Gallic War (8.26-31) Aulus Hirtius says Dumnacus laid siege on Limonum (modern-day Poitiers), an oppidum of the neighboring Pictones (oppidum Lemonum), where two legions of Gaius Caninius Revilus' army were stationed. The Roman army had forced a retreat and then pursued the Andes killing more than 12,000 in battle. Dumnacus, Hirtius says, "expelled from his own territories, wandering and skulking about, was forced to seek refuge by himself in the remote parts of Gaul." It is not the last we hear of the Andes. Tacitus, in his *Annals* (3.40-41), says in 21 AD, Gallic communities rose up because they were greatly in debt, in part due to provincial mismanagement and in part due to extortion which had been aggravated by the exactions of Germanicus (*Ann* 2.5). The first tribe to erupt, he adds (3.41.1), were the Andecavi (Andes) and the Turoni, the former being crushed by Gaius Calpurnius Acilius Aviola, the governor of Gallia Lugdunensis, who had "called out a cohort on garrison duty at Lugdunum." The territory where the Andes had lived for eons emerged during the medieval period as the Diocese of Angers in Anjou, both names derivatives of the Andes tribe.

101... Rambaud (1965, p. 273) says the economics behind the sale were due in part to the general having to pay for the rowers, seamen, and steersmen.

102... The decapitation of the ruling class of a society—alluded to earlier—happened in at least one other occasion, when tribes executed a senate that opposed their plans for making war. When Caesar sent Quintus Titurius Sabinus to the Venelli, he discovered that, "in the last few days the Aulerci, Eburovices, and the Lexovii, after putting their senate to death because they refused to approve the war, closed their gates and joined Viridovix." (*BG* 3.17.3)

103... See, for example, David Wardle, Catherine Steel (2009), Jeremy Paterson, and Elaine Fantham.

104... See Erich S. Gruen (2009), Jane F. Gardner (2009), and Ronald Syme (2017).

105... For an overview of Caesar's time in Gaul, see John T. Ramsey.

106... Not to jump ahead of ourselves in a footnote but allow me to state that, when Cicero mentions Caesar's *commentarii* in his Brutus in 46, the people of Rome had access to the text years before that. But we know of no extant manuscript of *De Bello Gallico* before the ninth century though, as Kraus points out "one branch has colophons naming late-antiquity readers or correctors." See Christina S. Kraus, p. 160; Michael Winterbottom, pp. 35-36; and Max Radin (1918).

107... Fantham (p. 143) says that gossip abounded that the general "used to quote the tyrant Eteocles from Euripedes' *Phoenissae*, to the effect that power was the only thing important enough to warrant behaving unjustly." That assessment comes from Suetonius (*Div* 30.5) "Some think that habit had given him a love of power, and that weighing the strength of his adversaries against his own, he grasped the opportunity of usurping the despotism which had been his heart's desire from early youth." Cicero too was seemingly of this opinion, when he wrote in the third book of his *De Officiis* (3.82) that Caesar ever had upon his lips these lines of Euripedes, (*Phoenissae*, 542ff.) of which Cicero himself adds a version:

> If wrong may e'er be right, for a throne's sake
> Were wrong most right: be God in all else feared!

108... The first line of Ode 1, Book 3 of Horace reads: *Odi profanum vulgus et arceo*.

109... Aulus Hirtius (90-43 BC) was a personal as well as political friend of Caesar. He was named a lieutenant (*legatus*) in the war on Gaul in 58 (Cicero, *Fam* 16.27) but his skills as a negotiator were deemed more valuable than his abilities as a soldier. He was in the innermost circle of Caesar's friends which included Oppius and Balbus. In 45, Hirtius received Belgic Gaul as his province but he governed via a deputy because he was called to attend to Caesar's business in Rome. In 44, his candidacy for consul was supported by Caesar, thus in 43 he, with Gaius Vibius Pansa, was elected consul. During that year Hirtius, with Pansa, was called upon to engage Antony in battle; both were killed in combat in the Battle of Mutina. But, because his troops devolved to Augustus, the emperor-to-be was said to have killed him (and Pansa). Suetonius (*Aug* 11.1) said it occurred "amid the confusion of battle." Dio (46.39.1) says so Augustus "might succeed to the office," and Tacitus (*Ann* 1.10) says so that he might take control of the armies of the two consuls. Tacitus says Pansa's wound was treated with poison and that Hirtius was killed by his own soldiers.

Hirtius authored Book 8 of the *De Bello Gallico* and was thought to have at least edited the *De Bello Alexandrino*, *De Bello Africo*, and *De Bello Hispaniensi*. And though he differed with Cicero politically, nine books of their correspondence were published but are since lost. Cicero has him as an interlocutor in his treatise on Fate and free will, *De Fato*. Suetonius (*Aug* 68.1) says the young Augustus "had given himself to Aulus Hirtius in Spain for three hundred thousand sesterces." Hirtius was a frequent enough dining companion of Cicero (*Fam* 9.16; 18; 20) and was known for extravagant dinners (*Att* 12.2). At the time he was taking lessons in oratory from Cicero; Suetonius (*Clar Rhet*) says Cicero called "the future consuls Hirtius and Pansa ... 'his pupils and his big boys.'" Two months after Caesar's death (May 17, 44) Cicero refers to (*Att* 14.22), "my pupil, who dines with me today, is much devoted to the victim of Brutus's dagger."

The late English journalist and librarian, William Bodham Donne (1807-1882), who wrote the entry for Hirtius in *Smith's Dictionary* (1870, Vol 2, p. 498) sums up his life thusly: "The character of Hirtius is easy to delineate. A revolution brought him into notice, ordinary times would have left him in obscurity. He was a good officer, without military genius—for his last campaign with Antony shows nothing beyond secondary talent, and a skillful negotiator when the terms were prescribed. But Hirtius merits without abatement the praise of unwavering loyalty to his patron, of moderation in political prosperity, and of using his influence with Caesar unselfishly. A staunch Caesarian, he protected the Pompeians, and while he deplored his benefactor's murder, he opposed the lawless and prodigal ambition of Antony." He adds that, "Caesar, when he commissioned him to answer the *Cato* of Cicero, must have thought highly of his literary attainments." And with respect to Hirtius' gustatory bent, Donne says, "Cicero frequently mentions his addiction to the pleasures of the table (*Fam* 9. 16; 18; 20; *Att* 12.2; xvi.1) and Q. Cicero describes him as a licentious reveler (*Fam* 16.17). Both charges were probably exaggerated, in the one case by political, in the other by personal dislike."

110... Kurt Raaflaub reminds us (2017, p. 205) that Caesar was: (1) a leading intellectual of his day; (2) a great literary talent; (3) a master of rhetoric; (4) well-versed in the Latin style; and (5) a poet with some credibility.

111... For an early example of such an assessment, see Stevens, pp. 165-179.

112... Michael Kulikowski, "A Very Bad Man," *London Review of Books*, 42 June 18, 2020.

113... Marincola, p. 197. In note 104 he quotes Edward Norden, *Agnostos Theos, Untersuchungen zur Formengeschichte religiöser Rede* (Leipzig and Berlin: Verlag B.G. TEÜBNER, 1913) as saying that Caesar never composed in the first person.

114... See Francis W. Kelsey, pp. 211-238. It should be pointed out that some believe that Suetonius wrote *De Bello Gallico*, the historian Orosius among them. He says (6.7.2), "*Hanc historiam (de Caesaris bello Gallico) Suetonius Tranquillus plenissime explicuit, cuius nos competentes portiunculas decerpsimus.*"

115... Michel Rambaud, p. 365.

116... See Stimson and Powell in particular.

117... To call attention to the times, Caesar uses *bellum* or *bella* in *De Bello Gallico*, Kelsey (p. 229) provides a listing. The examples are: (1) *bellum Helvetiorum* (1.30.1); (2) *Ariovisti bellum* (5.55.2); (3) *duo maxima bella* (1.54.2); (4) *bellum Venetorum* (3.16.1); (5) *veneticum bellum* (3.18.6; 4.21.4); (6) *Germanicum bellum* (4.16.1); (7) *Britannicum Bellum* (5.4.1); (8) *bellum Treverorum et Ambiorigis* (6.5.1); (9) *bellum Ambiorgis* (6.29.4); and (10) *Gallica bella* (4.20.1).

118... See Gruen (2017) where he says the line between the legitimacy and illegitimacy of Caesar's campaigns was quite gray even when the general went beyond the bounds of the Roman provinces. Two points are especially worth noting. The first (p. 34) that, "Caesar himself had promulgated a measure as consul, expanding a law of Sulla that prohibited provincial governors from leaving their provinces, leading an army beyond their borders, and waging war on their own initiative." The second (p. 36) summarily says, "In his report in the *Gallic War* he [Caesar] spoke freely of ignoring provincial boundaries, conducting aggressive warfare, extending imperial holdings, violating truces, and even cutting down women and children. Indeed, Caesar regularly credited Gauls with resisting Romans because they fought for their liberty and sought to avoid Roman slavery. Caesar, the victorious general, did not need to suppress facts, let along apologize for them. The *Gallic War* served to proclaim achievements rather than to rationalize them."

119... That Hirtius dined with Caesar that fateful night is often quoted but always prefaced with "it is said." The source for the gathering is given in Dando-Collins, p. 67. It says that Caesar "had dined at Ravenna with his staff officers [among whom were] ...the thirty-six-year-old Sallust ... the blindly loyal Hirtius ... Oppius ... the Spaniard Lucius Balbus ... And Sulpicius Rufus, whom Caesar would make a general the following year." But Dando-Collins offers no ancient sources for his assertion.

120... Caesar mentions on several occasions that, when his army went to their winter quarters, he traveled about the province to fulfill his duty as the overseer and administrator of the court of assizes. It was not an unfamiliar part of his assigned duties since he had served in that capacity in western Spain in 61; he traveled to the major towns and heard cases as a circuit judge. In the *De Bello Gallico* he (and Hirtius in Book 8) mentions his work as an assizes court judge. In (*BG* 1.54) he says, "Caesar having concluded two very important wars in one campaign, conducted his army into winter quarters among the Sequani, a little earlier than the season of the year required. He appointed Labienus over the winter-quarters, and set out in person for Hither Gaul to hold the assizes." In (5.1) he says, "He himself, on the assizes of Hither Gaul being concluded, proceeds into Illyricum, because he heard that the part of the province nearest them was being laid waste by the incursions of the Pirustae;" and in (5.2), "These things being finished, and the assizes being concluded, he returns into Hither Gaul, and proceeds thence to the army." In 6.44, he says, "having provided corn for the army, he set out for Italy, as he had determined, to hold the assizes." And in (7.1) he says, "Gaul being tranquil, Caesar, as he had determined, sets out for Italy to hold the provincial assizes." Hirtius (8.23) says, "For the year before, while Caesar was holding the assizes in Hither Gaul, Titus Labienus, having discovered that Comius was tampering with the state, and raising a conspiracy against Caesar, thought he might punish his infidelity without perfidy; but judging that he would not come to his camp at his invitation, and unwilling to put him on his guard by the attempt, he sent Caius Volusenus Quadratus, with orders to have him put to death under pretense of conference." And in (8.46) we have, "Having spent a few days in the province, he quickly ran through all the business of the assizes, settled all public disputes, and distributed rewards to the most deserving; for he had a good opportunity of learning how every person was disposed toward the republic during the general revolt of Gaul, which he had withstood by the fidelity and assistance of the Province."

Assizes in Latin is *conventus*, and Caesar says at the end of Book 1 (54.3) "*ipse in citeriorem Galliam ad conventus agendos prefectus est.*" "He set out in person for Hither Gaul to hold the assizes." And, while he never mentions the locations where he oversaw the administration of the court during his assizes-tour, he assuredly brought with him a contingent of soldiers to maintain order. The town would have been flooded with people jostling in a crowded courtroom waiting for their hearing. Thus, the jurist Ulpian advises (*Digest* 1. 16.8. 2-4), "The Proconsul must hear the advocates with patience and also with discernment, lest he appear contemptible; nor ought he to dissimulate if he ascertains that parties have trumped up cases or purchased the right to litigation; and he should only suffer those to institute proceedings who are permitted to do so by his Edict." In terms of managing the plaintiffs and defendants, "The Proconsul has power to dispose of the following matters extrajudicially; he can order persons to show proper respect to their parents, and freedmen to their patrons and the children of the latter; he can also threaten and severely menace a son brought before him by his father and who is said not to be living as he should. He can, in like manner, correct an impudent freedman either by reproof or by castigation." And the law says everybody should get a hearing, "Hence he should be careful to have a certain order prevail in legal procedure, namely, that the petitions of all persons shall be heard; lest it may happen that if the rank of some is favored, or attention is paid to others as are not worthy, those of moderate pretensions who have no one to appear for them, or having employed advocates of small experience or no standing, may not be able to properly present their claims."

Clearly the governor had clerks as assistants who kept some kind of records over the years as well as facilitated the timely and orderly management of the docket. It is likely that the proconsul, after his term was complete, took his records (*commentarii*), or a copy of same, with him—as well as the fees collected. Pliny (*Epis* 6. 22. 4) describes the case of an adviser of a proconsul who had tampered with records, "For it transpired that he had bribed the slave of Bruttianus's secretary, intercepted the diaries (*commentarii*) and cut out passages therefrom, thus, by a piece of shameful wickedness, making capital out of his own offences against his friend." In addition to adjudicating civil and criminal cases, the governor might look into the financial records of the town and other records having to do with the administration of daily affairs. He might oversee the water supply of the jurisdiction which might entail constructing aqueducts and even visiting springs that serve as the region's water supply. Roman law says, (*Dig* 1.16.7), "He should visit the temples and public monuments, for the purpose of inspecting them, and ascertaining whether they are in good condition, and properly cared for, or whether they need any repairs, and provide for the completion of such as have been begun, as far as the resources of the government permit; and he should appoint with the proper formalities superintendents who are diligent in their work, and also detail soldiers for the purpose of assisting the superintendents, if this should be necessary."

121... See Hermann Peter. *Historicorum Romanorum Reliquiae*, p. cclxxviii, *in aedibus* B.G. Teubneri, Lipsiae, 1870 and 1914.

122... Krebs says (p. 210) that in a true history we expect to see a preface (proem) in which the author situates the work in some kind of historical context. And he says, in the case of Caesar's work, the general presents his narrative as if he witnessed everything he wrote about which is not the case. As has been pointed out, Suetonius (*Div* 56.4) says Asinius Pollio, a respected historian himself, says the commentaries do not meet the standards of history-making because they show "too little diligence and too little concern for the 'truth,'" and he thinks that Caesar would have rewritten and corrected them. Krebs (p. 212) agrees, adding that the commentaries do not meet the standards of modern history. "They have been found inadequate," he says, "for their narrow range of interests, for their lack of any real detail, and above all for their tendentiousness as effected by distortion, omission, and falsification."

123...   See Debra L. Nousek, pp. 97, 108 and Andrew M. Riggsby, pp. 133-155.

124...   See Christian Meier, *Caesar: A Biography* and Mattias Gelzer, *Caesar: Politician and Statesman.*

125...   The Nervii came from what today is Belgium, including Brussels; their territory stretched into French Hainaut which got its name from the River Haine. It was said of them: (1) they were the most powerful of the Belgic tribes; (2) they were the most warlike of the Belgae; (3) their code of conduct was considered Spartan in nature; they drank no alcohol, they eschewed luxury; (4) they did not allow merchants into their territory and had no merchant class, believing that the cultural influences that came with trade weakened social cohesion. Caesar says (*BG* 5.39) that the Nervii had under their sway the Centrones, Grudii, Levaci, Pleumoxii, and Geidumni.

126...   Peter Wiseman, p. 2.

127...   *Litterae* are mentioned in *BG* 2.35.4; 4.38.5; and 7.90.8; see Sheldon, p. 94ff.; Gichon, p. 157ff.; and Ezov, pp. 64-94; Cicero mentions *litterae* (dispatches) in *Att* 5.20; and *Fam* 15.4. *Omni Gallia pacata* is found in *BG* at 2.1, 2.34, 3.26, and *parte Galliae pacata* at 6.5; Book 7 begins with *quieta Gallia*. See Latimer, pp. 98-113.

128...   See Gellius (*NA* 1.10.4) and Macrobius in *Saturnalia* (1.5.) also quoted the much-relished phrase, "*ego enim id quod a C. Caesare, excellentis ingenii ac prudentiae viro, in primo Analogiae libro scriptum est habeo semper in memoria atque in pectore, ut 'tamquam scopulum, sic fugiam infrequens atque insolens verbum.'"* That is, "Indeed, I myself always bear in mind and heart the precept of Julius Caesar, a man of approved genius and wisdom, who wrote in his book *De Analogia*, 'I would flee a rare and uncustomary word as though it were a rocky cliff.'" Andreas Willi (p. 229) says Caesar showed "linguistic self-discipline" by restricting the range of his vocabulary, using fewer than 1,300 lexemes, suggesting that his language was close to the conversational language (*cottidianus sermo*) in use during the Republic. He says (*Ibid*) that "Caesar might even be called the most colloquial of Latin authors: there is little in his writings which could not also have been said, without much stylistic effect, in a standard upper-class conversation at the time." Even more astounding is his insight (p. 235) referencing Patrick Sinclair, that "Caesar had observed in his court-hearings how the provincials struggled to master a 'Ciceronian' elite language based on Roman upper-class *consuetudo*. In order to win the support of these groups, he decided to remove the barrier to their social advancement by propagating a 'democratic grammatical agenda'. . ." He then adds that, "the Latin of the *Bellum Gallicum*, is primarily to be seen as directed against foreign, especially Greek, influences: it is nationalist rather populist." See Willi, pp. 229-242 and Sinclair, pp. 92-109.

129... The active reader who wishes to examine "*clementia*" in relation to other virtues the Romans embraced might look at Frears, 1980.

130... The goddess *Clementia* personified mercy and compassion. Dio (44.6.4) says, in describing the honors granted Caesar in 44, "finally they addressed him outright as Jupiter Julius and ordered a temple to be consecrated to him and to Clemency." Appian (*BC* 2. 106.1) says, "Many temples were decreed to him as to a god, and one was dedicated to him and the goddess Clemency, who were represented as clasping hands." Plutarch's view (*Caes* 57.4-5) is, "it is thought not inappropriate that the temple of Clemency was decreed as a thank-offering in view of his [Caesar's] mildness. For he pardoned many of those who had fought against him." And while there is no archaeological evidence that such a temple was ever built, the building is depicted in tetrastyle fashion on the reverse of a coin minted by Sepullius Macer, one of Rome's four moneyers in 44

BC. An example of the coin, once offered at Christie's for sale, can be found at: https://www.christies.com/en/lot/lot-2014963. The text accompanying the coin says: Roman Republic, Julius Caesar, Rome, P Sepullius Macer (44 B.C.), CLEMENTIAE CAESARIS, tetrastyle temple, *rev.* horseman galloping right, second horse behind (Cr 480/21; Syd 1076; RCV 1421). See Illustration in the present text. In 28 AD Tiberius was celebrated as a man of *clementia*. Suetonius (*Tib* 53.1) relates, "He even allowed a decree to be passed in recognition of this remarkable clemency, in which thanks were offered him and a golden gift was consecrated to Jupiter of the Capitol." *Clementia* appears on the coinage of Tiberius with the kindred virtue *moderatio*.

131... Curio, like his father, was a distinguished orator and earlier in life was an opponent of Caesar. When he underwent an about-face—it is said because Caesar paid off his heavy debts—Caesar gave him an army to go against Pompey's forces under the joint command of Publius Attius Varus and King Juba 1 of Numidia. On August 24, 49 Caesar's forces, under Curio's command, were defeated and Curio was killed. He had had an opportunity to escape with his life but chose to fight until the end, himself unable to face Caesar for having lost his army. Caesar himself says (*BC* 2.42), "Curio declares that he will never again present himself again before the eyes of Caesar after losing his army that he had received from him as a trust, and so he dies fighting."

132... Caesar uses "*clementia*" twice in *BG* (2.14 and 2.32) and once in *BC* (3.20) not in reference to himself but Trebonius "But through the equitable decrees and humanity of [Gaius] Trebonius, who was of opinion that in this crisis law should be administered with clemency and moderation." In Book 8 of *BG* Hirtius uses the word twice (*BG* 8.3; 8.21). Caesar also uses *mansuetudo* twice (paired with *clementia*) (*BG* 2.14, 31) *lenitas* once (referring to a river) (*BG* 1.12); (and *misericordia* four times (*BG* 2.28; 7.15, 26, 28). See Angel, p. 46 notes 4 and 5.

133... In his legal speeches, delivered before the civil war, Cicero uses the word *clementia* sparingly, fewer than a handful of times. But in 46 and 45 he delivered three monumental speeches known as the Caesarinae, that collectively mention *clementia* 13 times. He was asking Caesar to show clemency toward people who had opposed him in battle and otherwise and thus, in Caesar's eyes, deserved considerable punishment. The *Pro Marcello* and *Pro Ligario* were delivered in 46 and the *Pro Rege Deiotaro* in 45. In all three cases Caesar acted as judge; in the case of the *Pro Rege*, he heard Cicero's appeal for his client in his own home.

Marcus Claudius Marcellus, whom Cicero defended in his famous speech, had served as consul in 51. He not only opposed Caesar's attempts to settle a colony at Comum but was involved in scourging a Roman magistrate there—Caesar's turf, if you will—a punishment which the *Lex Porcia* forbade. Cicero reports (*Att* 13.10) that Marcellus, on his return to Rome in 45, had been murdered by one of his attendants Publius Magius Chilo near Athens. At the trial the year before, Cicero praised Caesar's *clementia, mansuetudo, sapientia,* and *misericordia* and asked the dictator to transcend feelings of anger and vengeance. In the very first section of the speech (1.1) he begins, "For so great humanity, so unusual and unheard of clemency, so great restraint of all affairs in the highest position of authority, and finally such unbelievable and almost divine wisdom, I am in no wise able to pass over in silence." With respect to Marcellus' murder, Cicero tells Atticus in June 45, "who would have feared this? Such a thing never happened before and it did not seem as though nature could allow such things to happen. So one may fear anything."

The *Pro Ligario* was delivered on behalf of Quintus Ligarius who fought against Caesar in Africa in 46. At the Battle of Thapsus, when Pompey's side was defeated, Ligarius was taken prisoner and, although Caesar spared his life, he did not permit him to return to Rome, so he was essentially banished. When friends failed to make headway in securing Ligarius' return, Cicero took up the case at the urging of Ligarius' brothers. It took some doing. In a letter to Ligarius he says (*Fam* 6.14.2), "On November 26 [46], at your brothers' request I paid a visit to Caesar early in the morning. And, while I was suffering every kind of humiliation and annoyance trying to approach him for an interview, your brothers and relatives were prostrating themselves at his feet, and when I had stated all that the case and your critical position demanded, the impression left upon my mind when I left—not only by Caesar's speech, mild and generous as it certainly was, but also by his eyes and expression, but many other signs as well, which I could more easily discern than describe, was just this—I felt that your restoration was a certainty." In making his case which was pleaded in the forum, Cicero refers to the dictator's *clementia* six times and to his *misericordia* four times, pointing out that Caesar's considerations grew out of wisdom, *sapientia*. At one point he says he was not making his case, as if he was pleading before a jury, but as a prodigal son pleading before his father. He projects what the contrite Ligarius would say, "I have erred; I have acted rashly; I repent; I flee to your mercy; I beg pardon for my fault; I entreat you to pardon me." With words like these, Plutarch tells us (*Cic* 39.7), "Cicero . . . was moving his hearers beyond measure, and his speech, as it proceeded, showed varying pathos and amazing grace, Caesar's face often changed color and it was manifest that all the emotions of his soul were stirred, and at last when the orator touched upon the struggles at Pharsalus, he was so greatly affected that his body shook and from his hand dropped some documents. At any rate he acquitted Ligarius under compulsion." Ligarius showed his gratitude by joining the conspirators who assassinated Caesar! Ligarius seems to be one of the three Ligarii killed during the proscription of the triumvirs in 43. Appian (*BC* 4, 22) reports, "As for brothers, two of the name of Ligarius, being proscribed together, hid themselves in an oven till their slaves found them, when one of them was killed and the other fled; when he learned that his brother had perished he threw himself from the bridge into the Tiber. Some fishermen seized him thinking that he had fallen into the water instead of leaping in. He stoutly resisted rescue and tried to throw himself into the river again; but when he was overcome by the fishermen he exclaimed 'You are not saving me, but ruining yourself by helping one who is proscribed.' Nevertheless they had pity on him and saved him until some soldiers who were guarding the bridge saw him, ran to him, and cut off his head. One of two other brothers threw himself into the river and one of his slaves searched for the body for five days. At last he found it, and as it was still possible to recognize it, he cut off the head for the sake of the reward. The other brother had concealed himself in a dung-heap and another slave betrayed him. The murderers disdained to go into the heap, but thrust their spears into him and dragged him out, and then cut off his head, just as he was, without even washing it. Another one seeing his brother arrested ran up to him, not knowing that he was himself proscribed also, and said, 'Kill me before him.' The centurion, having the proscription list at hand, said, 'Your request is a proper one, for your name comes before his.' And so saying, he killed both of them in due order."

With respect to the *Pro Rege Deiotaro*, the Deiotarus in question was the Chief Tetrarch of the Tolistobogii in Galatia and an ally of Pompey during the war. In making his argument before Caesar, Cicero uses *clementia* four times calling attention to his *sapientia* and *misericordia* as well. He says (38) the king "attributes the whole of the tranquility and quiet of his old age which he enjoys to your [Caesar's] clemency." Earlier he says (8), "O Caius Caesar, first of all by your good faith, and wisdom and firmness, and clemency deliver us from this fear, and prevent our suspecting that there is any ill-temper lurking in you." In these three cases Caesar is shown as a different man from that of his "*memoria tenebat*" days. In his assessment of the cases, the young historian, Aaron Rozeboom, says (p. 89), "It is clear then that *clementia* becomes a point of negotiation of power for Caesar and Cicero alike, the one asserting his political dominance, the other speaking from a position of moral authority."

134... Indeed, a short time later, Cicero would chide Brutus for espousing *clementia* as a restorative measure (*Brut* 2.5.5), "Now, Brutus, you must take into consideration the whole question of the war. I notice that you take pleasure in lenient measures, and think that the most advantageous line to take. It is an admirable sentiment: but it is for other circumstances and other times that a place for clemency generally is and ought to be reserved."

135... Appolonius Molon was a noted teacher of rhetoric. Cicero says in his *Brutus* (312, 316) that he had taken lessons from Molon at Rome during the time Sulla was dictator (c.82) and again in 78 at Molon's school in Rhodes. Valerius Maximus says (2.2.3) that, when Molon came to Rome, he "was the first foreigner that was ever heard in the senate without an interpreter." It is believed that Cicero and Caesar achieved such great oratorical skills because of their study with the master. Plutarch (*Caes* 1.8) says Caesar was not on his way to Rhodes but on his way back to Rome after visiting King Nicomedes of Bithynia.

136... Pirates remained a constant threat to travel on the Mediterranean from the second century until Rome gave Pompey the assignment to get rid of the scourge in 67-66. With an ingenious management strategy Pompey all but eliminated the presence of the pirates in 40 days.

137... Plutarch (*Pomp* 26.6) says the pirates "seized two praetors, Sextilius and Bellinus, in their purple-edged robes, and carried them away, together with their attendants and lictors. They also captured a daughter of Antonius, a man who had celebrated a triumph, as she was going into the country, and exacted a large sum for her." Appian (*Mith* 14.93) says, "And now the pirates contemptuously assailed the coasts of Italy, around Brundisium and Eutruria, and seized women of noble families who were travelling, and also two praetors with their very insignia of office." According to Dio (36.17.3) Publius Clodius Pulcher was seized by the very pirates he was sent to hunt down and had to pay a ransom to be freed. And Cicero (*Man* 33) provides context with, "Need I mention, how Cnidus, and Colophon, and Samos, most noble cities, and others too in countless numbers, were taken by them, when you know that your own harbors, and those harbors too from which you derive, as it were, your very life and breath, were in the power of the pirates? Are you ignorant that the harbor of Caieta, that illustrious harbor, when full of ships, was plundered by the pirates under the very eyes of the praetor? and that from Misenum, the children of the very man who had before that waged war against the pirates in that place, were carried off by the pirates? For why should I complain of the disaster of Ostia, and of that stain and blot on the republic, when almost under your very eyes, that fleet which was under the command of a Roman consul was taken and destroyed by the pirates? O ye immortal gods! could the incredible and godlike virtue of one man in so short a time bring so much light to the republic, that you who had lately been used to see a fleet of the enemy before the mouth of the Tiber, should now hear that there is not one ship belonging to the pirates on this side of the Atlantic?"

138... On his voyage from Rhodes back home, Caesar, as Velleius tells us (43.1-3), "wishing to escape the notice of the pirates . . . took two friends and ten slaves and embarked in a four-oared boat, and in this way crossed the broad expanse of the Adriatic Sea. During the voyage, sighting, as he thought, some pirate vessels, he removed his outer garments, bound a dagger to his thigh, and prepared himself for any event; soon he saw that his eyes had deceived him and that the illusion had been caused by a row of trees in the distance which looked like mast and yards."

139... Caesar's plea won over the Senate. Cicero's brother, Quintus, another praetor designate, now supported Caesar's measure and Decimus Junius Silanus, who had made the case for execution, backed off and said by execution he really meant imprisonment. Then Marcus Porcius Cato got up—Caesar's arch rival, as we have noted earlier—and made an impassioned speech against Caesar's position. Cicero proposed that Caesar's and Cato's positions be put up for a vote—Caesar backing off a bit saying there should be two votes, one on confiscation, the other on the death penalty—and Cato's position prevailed. A riot nearly ensued when people rushed Caesar with drawn swords, the praetor elect having to be led out of the chamber with guards for protection. The five were executed immediately. Three of the ancient historians describe what immediate meant. Sallust (*Cat* 55.2-6) says, "After the Senate supported Cato's recommendation, as I mentioned, the consul thought it best to take precautions for the coming night . . . He asked those men to make necessary preparations for the execution . . . [one of them] Lentulus . . . the executors strangled with a rope. Cethegus, Statilius, Gabinius, and Caeparius were executed in the same way." Appian (*BC* 2.21-22) says, "Cicero immediately, while the Senate was still in session, conducted each of the conspirators from the houses where they were in custody to the prison, without the knowledge of the crowd and saw them put to death. Then he went back to the forum and signified that they were dead." Dio (37.36.3) says, "the conspirators were punished . . . a sacrifice and period of festival over them was decreed."

140... Bringing suit against such prominent citizens might seem to have been a bold move on Caesar's part but as Lily Ross Taylor (1941, p. 119) points out, such a path was "a well-established custom of the young Roman who wished to secure political advancement." Caesar was unsuccessful in both cases. Dolabella had been defended by two giant legal minds, Gaius Aurelius Cotta and Quintus Hortensius; and Antonius escaped punishment by calling upon the tribunes to halt the trial. That is not to say Caesar was not a competent trial lawyer. Quintilian (*Inst* 10.1.114) speaks of his abilities in glowing terms, "As for Gaius Caesar, if he had had leisure to devote himself to the courts, he would have been the one orator who could have been considered a serious rival to Cicero. Such are his force, his penetration and his energy that we realize that he was as vigorous in speech as in his conduct of war. And yet all these qualities are enhanced by a marvelous elegance of language, of which he was an exceptionally jealous student." And Valerius Maximus (8.9.3) says, "The divine Julius, the perfect pillar of both celestial deity and human genius, aptly demonstrated the force of eloquence, saying in his speech against Cn. Dolabella, whom he was prosecuting, that his excellent case had been wrenched from him by the advocacy of C. Cotta. For then the greatest eloquence complained [about the force of eloquence]."

141... Of Saturninus's character, Diodorus Siculus (36.12) says, "Saturninus the tribune was a man of licentious habits. When he was quaestor, he had been put in charge of the transport of all the corn from Ostia to Rome; but owing to his laziness and his debased character, he was removed from this office by the senate, who committed the task to the care of others. But afterwards, when he had desisted from his former licentiousness, and adopted a sober mode of life, he was chosen by the people to be tribune."

142... Marius sought to rid the city of his political enemy, Quintus Caecilius Metellus Numidicus (consul in 109), by forcing him into exile, after he had him expelled from the Senate. Saturninus proposed a law to exile Metellus but, rather than allow a confrontation between his supporters who were ready to take up arms in his behalf, he went into exile voluntarily in 100. Plutarch (*Mar* 28.4-5) says, "It was Metellus, however, whom he [Marius] especially feared, a man who had experienced his ingratitude, and one whose genuine excellence made him the natural enemy of those who tried to insinuate themselves by devious methods into popular favour and sought to control the masses by pleasing them. Accordingly, he schemed to banish Metellus from the city." And to help him achieve this, Plutarch adds, "For this purpose he allied himself with Saturninus and Glaucia, men of the greatest effrontery, who had a rabble of needy and noisy fellows at their beck and call, and with their assistance would introduce laws." Metellus returned in 99, the year after Saturninus was killed.

143... Appian (*BC* 1.28) says, "but Nonius, a man of noble birth, who used much plainness of speech in reference to Apuleius and reproached Glaucia bitterly, was chosen for the office. They, fearing lest he should punish them as tribune, made a rush upon him with a crowd of ruffians just as he was going away from the comitia, pursued him into an inn, and stabbed him. As this murder bore a pitiful and shocking aspect, the adherents of Glaucia came together early the next morning, before the people had assembled, and elected Apuleius tribune." Plutarch (*Mar* 29.1) says, "In this last consulship [100 B.C.] particularly did Marius make himself hated, because he took part with Saturninus in many of his misdeeds. One of these was the murder of Nonius, whom Saturninus slew because he was a rival candidate for the tribuneship." Valeius Maximus's take (9.7.3) is, "For the people compelled Nunnius, the rival of Saturninus, when nine tribunes had been created, and only one vacancy remained for two candidates, to flee to his own house: and then dragging him out from there, they slew him; so that by the slaughter of an honourable citizen, they might make way for that pernicious man to gain power."

144... Furius, described by Valerius Maximus (8.1d.2) as "a man of a lewd life" met an ignominious end. Having refused to allow Metellus Numidicus to return from exile, when his term was up, he was called to account by the new tribune Gaius Canuleius. Appian (*BC* 1.33) says, "The people did not wait for his excuses, but tore Furius to pieces." Dio (*fr* 95.3) says, "Publius Furius, under indictment for the acts he had performed while tribune, was slain by the Romans in the very assembly. He richly deserved to die, to be sure, for he was a seditious person, who after first joining Saturninus and Glaucia had veered about, deserted to the opposing faction, and joined them in attacking his former associates; yet it was not proper for him to perish in just this way. This deed, then, seemed to have a certain justification."

145... Santiago Aguirre delineates the differing narratives of Appian and Plutarch (pp. 74-75) with respect to the deaths of Glaucia and Saturninus and it worth noting his distinctions. He says, "According to Appian, both Glaucia and Saturninus, had already taken refuge on the Capitol with their partisans before Marius brought his troops, since the urban plebs were not at all pleased by the killing of Memmius. [Appian, *BC* 1.32] Plutarch, on the other hand, states that Glaucia and Saturninus were cornered in the Capitol by Marius and his troops. [Plutarch, *Marius* 30.3] In the end, both Appian and Plutarch agree that Glaucia and Saturninus only surrendered for two reasons: Marius had cut off the water supply to the Capitol; and both Glaucia and Saturninus still believed they could trust Marius to protect them. [Appian, *BC* 1.32; Plutarch, *Marius* 30.3] However, while Appian and Plutarch agree that Marius tried to spare these men from the wrath of the people, they each give their own version as to how Saturninus and Glaucia met their end. Whereas in Plutarch's narrative, both Saturninus and Glaucia were slaughtered as they came out of the Capitol, Appian states that Marius had them hidden in the Senate House for protection until they could be tried for their crime. [Plutarch, *Marius* 30.4; Appian, *BC* 1.32] It was here that some men then broke in through the roof of the Senate house and killed Saturninus and Glaucia with roof tiles."

146... Dio (37.27.2) says the Caesars "had not been chosen according to precedent by the people but by the praetor himself, which was not lawful." Information on the two-person process is limited because there are only three cases in which it was used. In the first case, the trial of Publius Hortensius, Livy (1.26) says the *duo viri* were selected by the king. Ulpian (*Digest* 1.13) assumed they were quaestors named by the king after a vote of the people. In the second case, that of Marcus Manlius (384 BC), Livy (6.20) says tribunes prosecuted the case before a *concilium plebis*. It is supposed that the tribunes were elected to act as prosecutors. In the trial of Rabirius, as noted in the text, the praetor appointed the two judges by lot but it does not specify from what body.

147... For a discussion of the *arbor infelix* and related punishments, see Oldfather. Varro (*LL* 5.41) says, "This hill was previously called the Tarpeian, from the Vestal Virgin Tarpeia, who was there killed by the Sabines with their shields and buried; of her name a reminder is left, that even not its cliff is called the Tarpeian Rock." Murderers, traitors, perjurers, and in some cases slaves, were hurled from the stone to their death. There are more than a few examples. In 33 AD Tacitus (*Ann* 6.19) says, "Sextus Marius, the richest man in Spain, was next accused of incest with his daughter, and thrown headlong from the Tarpeian rock." Tacitus

(*Ann* 2.32.3) also says that in 16 AD, when Tiberius feared a plot to overthrow him, the Senate issued decrees to expel astrologers and magicians from Italy. The magician Lucius Pituanius was hurled from the rock. And Dio (57.22.5) says that Tiberius "brought Aelius Saturninus before the senate for trial on the charge of having recited improper versus about him, and upon his conviction caused him to be hurled from the Capitol." This is explained by the expression "*arx tarpeia Capitoli proxima.*"

148... The Janiculum Hill is sometimes referred to as the eighth hill of Rome even though it is the second highest among them. The name was connected with the god Janus. Livy (1.33.6) says, "The Janiculum also was brought into the city's boundaries, not because the space was wanted, but to prevent such a strong position from being occupied by the enemy." A red flag was flown on the hill when the *comitia centuriata* was in session on the Campus Martius. Dio (37.28.1-3) explains the meaning of the raising and lowering of the flag: "In ancient times there were many enemies dwelling near the city, and the Romans, fearing that while they were holding a centuriated assembly by centuries foes might occupy the Janiculum and attack the city, decided that not all should vote at once, but that some men under arms should by turns always guard that position. So they guarded it as a long as the assembly lasted, but when this was about to be adjoined, the flag was pulled down and the guards departed; for no further business could be transacted when the post was not guarded. This practice was observed only in the case of centuriated assemblies, for these were held outside the wall and all who bore arms were obliged to attend them. Even to this day it is done as a matter of form."

149... Saturninus had been declared a traitor. In 98 Sextus Titius was convicted of *maiestas* for having a portrait of Saturninus in his house and for his sentence was exiled. Gaius Appuleius Decianus, a tribune of the plebs in 98 and a relative of Saturninus, was convicted for mouning the traitor in public.

Cicero (*Rab* 24) says, "And Sextus Titius was condemned for having an image of Lucius Saturninus in his house. The Roman knights laid it down by that decision that that man was a worthless citizen, and one who ought not to be allowed to remain in the state, who either by keeping his image sought, to do credit to the death of a man who was seditious to such a degree as to become an enemy to the republic, or who sought by pity to excite the regrets of ignorant men, or who showed his own inclination to imitate such villainy." *Schol: Bob* 95, mentions "the son of Apuleius Decianus, who had recently been condemned. When the elder Decianus was tribune of the plebs, he tried to avenge {the deaths of} Apuleius Saturninus and C. Servilius Glaucia, and was guilty of many wicked and violent actions. Afterwards, he was prosecuted and condemned. Then he went to Pontus and joined to Mithradates. Therefore the orator refers to the family's disgrace, in order to suggest that the son was imitating his father, and was acting in the interests of {his country's} enemies."

150... When a *damnatio memoriae* was put into effect, the target's image might be removed from coins, inscriptions on buildings, even archival documents. Coins might be recalled and melted down; even the house of the "victim" might be razed to delete the person's presence from history. However successful the *damnationes* were, the procedure continued; more than 30 emperors suffered such a fate.

The most striking example can be found in the emperor Caracalla's [Marcus Aurelius Antoninus] (fl. 198-217) attempts to erase his co-emperor brother, Geta [Publius Septimius Geta] (fl. 209-211) from history. First of all, he murdered him; if that wasn't deletion enough, he then sought to delete his brother's image from reliefs, coins, etc. If anyone were to mention Geta's name, they were subject to the death penalty upon conviction.

When the emperor Domitian (fl. 81-96) was assassinated in September 96, Suetonius in his life of the emperor (*Dom* 23.1), says "The senators on the contrary were so overjoyed, that they raced to fill the House, where they did not refrain from assailing the dead emperor with the most insulting and stinging kind of outcries. They even had ladders brought and his shields [votive shields, adorned with the emperor's image] and images torn down before their eyes and dashed upon the ground; finally they passed a decree that his inscriptions should everywhere be erased, and all record of him obliterated." Pliny in his *Panegyricus*

(52.4-5) describes the emotional release people experienced when the *damnatio memoriae* against Domitian was put into effect, "It was our delight to dash those proud faces to the ground, to smite them with the sword and savage them with the axe, as if blood and agony could follow from every blow. Our transports of joy—so long deferred—were unrestrained; all sought a form of vengeance in beholding those bodies mutilated, limbs hacked in pieces, and finally that baleful, fearsome visage cast into fire, to be melted down, so that from such menacing terror something for man's use and enjoyment should rise out of the flames."

151... As mentioned elsewhere, Caesar's election to the office was made possible by Titus Labienus who, as tribune, brought a law before the *comitia* that returned the power of electing the chief pontiff to the people. That right, which was given by the *lex Domitia* in 104, had been taken away by Sulla who dictated that only the College of Pontiffs would have authority in such elections. Labienus' act raised Caesar's chances of winning considerably.

152... Plutarch (*Caes* 7.2) says, "Catulus, who, as the worthier of Caesar's competitors, dreaded more the uncertainty of the issue, sent and tried to induce Caesar to desist from his ambitious project, offering him large sums of money. But Caesar declared that he would carry the contest through even though he had to borrow still larger sums." For Caesar it was an all-or-nothing situation for, as Plutarch (*Caes* 7.3) continues, "The day for the election came, and as Caesar's mother accompanied him to the door in tears, he kissed her and said: 'Mother, today thou shalt see thy son either pontifex maximus or an exile.'"

153... Valerius Maximus (6.9.5) says, "Who does not know how high the authority of Q. Catulus was raised, at that time when there was a crowd of famous men living? In his younger years you will find him to have been guilty of much luxury and idleness. This however did not prevent him from becoming the leading man of his country. He had the honor to have his name emblazoned upon the roof of the Capitol and by his own courage he suppressed a civil war that had been rising up with mighty force." And elsewhere he (8.15.9) says, "Q. Catulus also was, by the opinion of the Rome people, advanced nearly to the stars. For when they continued to place the whole management of affairs in the hands of Pompey alone, he asked them from the rostra in whom they could have any hope, if Pompey were taken away by a sudden blow of fortune; they replied with one voice, 'In you.' That was a remarkable judgment of his reputation, which within the space of two syllables, equalled Catulus to the great Pompey, with all the distinctions that I have related."

154... Sallust (*Hist* 3.48.9) says, Catulus was "a tyrant far crueler than Sulla." Elsewhere, he (*Hist* 3.34ff.) describes the historian and annalist, Gaius Licinius Macer, as a populist who gave a rousing speech to his supporters beginning with, "If you did not realize, fellow citizens, what a difference there is between the rights left you by your forefathers and this slavery imposed upon you by Sulla . . ." In a section on unusual deaths, Valerius Maximus (9.1.2.7) adds, " Equally vehement was the end of C. Licinius Macer, an ex-praetor, the father of Calvus, who was accused of extortion. While the votes were being counted, he went up to a balcony, and saw that M. Cicero, who was in charge of the trial, was removing his *toga praetrexta*. Macer sent a message to him, to say that he died as a defendant, without being convicted; and that therefore his estate could not be confiscated. Having said this, he covered his mouth and throat with his handkerchief, and with his breath blocked, he prevented his punishment by death. When this became known, Cicero forbore to pronounce sentence upon him."

155... Lepidus had already criticized Sulla's regime with a long blistering speech; see Sallust (*Hist* 1.48.1-27). Thus, when it came to the dictator's funeral, sparks flew. Appian (1.105) says, "Immediately dissensions sprang up in the city over his remains, some proposing to bring them in a procession through Italy and exhibit them in the forum and give him a public funeral. Lepidus and his faction opposed this, but Catulus and the Sullan party prevailed. Sulla's body was borne through Italy on a golden litter with royal splendor. Trumpeters and horsemen in great numbers went in advance and a great multitude of armed men followed on foot. His soldiers flocked from all directions under arms to join the procession, and each one was assigned his place in due order as he came, while the crowd of common people that came together was unprecedented, and in front of all were borne the standards and the fasces that he had used while living and ruling."

156... Caesar was taking advantage of precedent set by Catulus who had delivered a *laudatio* in honor of his mother 30 years earlier.

157... Catulus was no novice to insurrections. In 77, during his proconsulship, the Senate assigned him the task of putting down the rebellion of Marcus Aemilius Lepidus, who served as consul with him in 78. Pithily, Orosius (5.22.16-18) sums up the situation, "On the death of Sulla, Lepidus, a supporter of the Marian party, rose up against Catulus, the Sullan leader, and fanned the coals of civil war into flame. Two battles were then fought. Many of the Romans, now exhausted by their very lack of numbers and up to now utterly distracted by the fury of that struggle, were slain. The city of Alba, besieged and suffering terribly from hunger, was saved by the surrender of its wretched survivors. Scipio, the son of Lepidus, was captured there and put to death. Brutus, while fleeing to Cisalpine Gaul with Pompey in pursuit, was killed at Rhegium. Thus, this civil war, like a fire in straw, subsided with the same speed with which it had blazed forth, as much because of the clemency shown by Catulus himself as because of the disgust aroused by the cruelty of the Sullan faction."

158... With respect to the original dedication, Livy (2.8.5-8) says, "The temple of Jupiter on the Capitol had not yet been dedicated, and the consuls drew lots to decide who should dedicate it. The lot fell to Horatius. Publicola set out for the Veientine war. His friends showed unseemly annoyance at the dedication of so illustrious a shrine being assigned to Horatius, and tried every means of preventing it. When all else failed, they tried to alarm the consul, whilst he was actually holding the doorpost during the dedicatory prayer; by a wicked message that his son was dead, and he could not dedicate a temple while death was in his house. As to whether he disbelieved the message, or whether his conduct simply showed extraordinary self-control, there is no definite tradition, and it is not easy to decide from the records. He only allowed the message to interrupt him so far that he gave orders for the body to be burnt; then, with his hand still on the doorpost, he finished the prayer and dedicated the temple." For more on the history of the Temple, see Livy (7.3).

159... Appian (*BC* 1.86) says, "It was at this time that the Capitol was burned. Some attributed this deed to Carbo, others to the consuls, others to somebody sent by Sulla; but of the exact fact there was no evidence, nor am I able now to conjecture what caused the fire."

160...   Plutarch (*Publ* 15.1-2) says, "The second temple was built by Sulla, but Catulus was commissioned to consecrate it, after the death of Sulla. This temple, too, was destroyed during the troublous times of Vitellius, [69 A.D.] and Vespasian began and completely finished the third, with the good fortune that attended him in all his undertakings. He lived to see it completed, and did not live to see it destroyed, as it was soon after; and in dying before his work was destroyed, he was just so much more fortunate than Sulla, who died before his was consecrated. For upon the death of Vespasian the Capitol was burned.[80 AD]" In *in Verrem* (2.4.69), Cicero says, "And in this place I appeal to you, O Quintus Catulus; for I am speaking of your most honorable and most splendid monument. You ought to take upon yourself not only the severity of a judge with respect to this crime, but something like the vehemence of an enemy and an accuser. For, through the kindness of the senate and people of Rome, your honour is connected with that temple. Your name is consecrated at the same time as that temple in the everlasting recollection of men. It is by you that this case is to be encountered; by you, that this labour is to be undergone, in order that the Capitol, as it has been restored more magnificently, may also be adorned more splendidly than it was originally; that then that fire may seem to have been sent from heaven, not to destroy the temple of the great and good Jupiter, but to demand one for him more noble and more magnificent."

161...   Catulus' father, of the same name, fought alongside Marius and then served as consul with him in 102. He was responsible for two buildings that together were known as *Monumenta Catuli*. The first was the Temple of *Fortuna Huisce Diei* (the "Fortune of the Present Day"), the goddess Fortune believed to bring good luck to her believers this very day. It was vowed by Catulus père during the battle of Vercellae, June 30th, 101 BC, and built with the spoils of the defeated Cimbri. The other was the *Porticus Catuli* on the Palatine Hill adjacent to the house of Catulus, also built from the sale of the Cimbrian spoils. It was said to be the equal of the Temple of Honor and Virtue (*Honos Et Virtus, Aedes*) which Marius built from the spoils of the same war. The senate met to vote on the recall of Cicero from exile which took place on August 5, 57 BC. He says, (*Planc* 78), "when the senators themselves, in that resolution of the senate which was passed in the monument of Marius, in which my safety was recommended to all nations." He says in *Div* 1.59 that Marius had appeared to him in a dream and ordered his lictor to conduct him to his monument, where he would find safety.

162... After Caesar's death, the Senate moved to have Catulus' name rubbed out and Caesar's placed in its stead. They (Dio 43.14.6) "decreed that a chariot of his should be placed on the Capitol facing the statue of Jupiter, that his statue in bronze should be mounted upon a likeness of the inhabited world, with an inscription to the effect that he was a demigod, and that his name should be inscribed upon the Capitol in place of that of Catulus on the ground that he had completed this temple after undertaking to call Catulus to account for the building of it."

163... Pliny (*HN* 33.57) says, "At the present day we see ceilings covered with gold even in private houses, but they were first gilded in the Capitol during the censorship of Lucius Memmius (142 BC) after the fall of Carthage. From ceilings the use of gilding passed over also to vaulted roofs and walls, these too being now gilded like pieces of plate, whereas a variety of judgements were passed on Catulus by his contemporaries for having gilded the brass tilings of the Capitol." With respect to changes Catulus (and others) made at the games, Valerius Maximus (2.4.6) says, "As wealth increased, pomp and magnificence was added to the religion of games. To which purpose Q. Catulus, imitating Campanian luxury, was the first to cover the seats of the spectators with an awning. Cn. Pompeius before any other tempered the heat of summer, by bringing little streams to run along channels. Claudius Pulcher was the first to adorn the stage with a variety of colours, when it had previously consisted of unpainted boards. Afterwards C. Antonius covered it with silver, Petreius with gold, Q. Catulus with ivory. The Luculli made it revolve, and P. Lentulus Spinther adorned it with silver ornaments. For the procession, which was previously dressed in Punic cloaks, M. Scaurus introduced a more exquisite kind of garment."

164... Dio (44.14.6) says that when Caesar was declared "a demigod . . . [it was decided that] his name should be inscribed upon the Capitol in place of that of Catulus on the ground that he had completed this temple after undertaking to call Catulus to account for the building of it." Tacitus (*Hist* 3.72.3) says, "The name of Lutatius Catulus, the dedicator, remained among all the vast erections of the Emperors, down to the days of Vitellius."

165... The mention of the Allobroges might seem to come out of nowhere. T. Rice Holmes (*Rom Repub* 1, pp. 259-272) explains their presence in Rome and subsequent involvement in the arrest of those involved in Catiline's insurrectionist scheme in 63. A delegation of Allobroges had come to Rome to complain of the ill-treatment by the Roman governor Lucius Murena and the extortion of Italian usurers in the region. A trader by the name of Umbrenus, who had dealings in Gaul was singled out by Publius Cornelius Lentulus Sura to approach the envoys and say that, if they were to stage an uprising in Gaul and send a contingent of their cavalry to join Catiline's forces, their grievance would get due attention. After the envoys were given more information about the conspiracy and the names of those involved, they became anxious. They contacted their liaison with the government, Quintus Fabius Maximus Sanga, who informed the consul Cicero of the plan. Cicero told Sanga to return to the envoys and inform them to play along and find out who the ringleaders were and to say they would cooperate with them. The envoys told Lentulus, Cethegus, Statilius, and Cassius to put their promises in writing so they would have something to show the leaders of the tribe back home—after all, it was a great and risky undertaking. They did, the envoys informed Cicero, and departed for Gaul. Cicero set up a sting operation during which the envoys were arrested and the letters seized. On the information the envoys offered, the house of Cethegus was searched and a large quantity of weapons was found. He and the other conspirators were arrested and forced to admit their guilt. Lentulus was compelled to abdicate his praetorship and, as it was feared that there might be an attempt to rescue him, he was put to death in the Tullianum on December 5, 63 along with other senatorial supporters of Catiline.

166... Cicero, himself a cousin of Gratidianus, describes the cult-like following Gratidianus enjoyed because he had dealt with an economic crisis in Rome by sponsoring currency reform. In (*Off* 3.80) he says the reform "brought him great honor; in every street statues of him were erected; before these incense and candles burned. In a word, no one ever enjoyed greater popularity with the masses."

167... Diodorus (38.4.2-2) describes the events leading to the senior Catulus' death thusly, "At that time Quintus Lutatius Catulus, who had celebrated a glorious triumph for his victory over the Cimbri, and was greatly esteemed by the *Roman* people, was accused by a tribune of the plebs on a capital offence. Fearing imminent danger from the accusation, he approached Marius, to entreat him to intercede for his deliverance. Marius, who he had been his friend formerly, but through some suspicion he now entertained of him, had become his enemy, merely replied, 'You must die.' Upon this, Catulus perceived that he had no hope of preservation and sought to die without disgrace. He killed himself in a strange and unusual way; for he shut himself up in a newly plastered house, and caused a fire to be kindled, by the smoke of which, and the moist vapours from the lime, he was there stifled to death."

168... University of New England, New South Wales classicist, Bruce Marshall, follows the genealogy of the details of the death, how it happened and where. He says that there is strong evidence from ancient sources that Catiline was the executioner and that that comes from a speech of Cicero's from 64, *in toga candida*, when he was running for consul against Catiline. Sallust (*Hist* 1.44 M) writes, "*Ut in M. Mario, cui fracta prius crura, bracchiaque, et oculi effossi, scilicet ut per singulos artus exspiraret.*" That is, M. Marius died after his arms and legs had been broken and his eyes gouged out, so that he expired through each and every single limb."

169... It seems Caesar did not leave for his appointment until March. Cicero (*Att* 1.13.8) tells Atticus on January 25 "the praetors have not drawn their provinces yet." On March 1 he tells Atticus (1.15.1) "You have heard that that good brother of mine, Quintus, has Asia assigned him as his province." And, even though Caesar left in great haste for his new assignment—Gelzer (p. 61) says "without waiting for the senatorial decree granting money for his governorship"—it is possible he did not reach Corduba, the capital of the province, until late March or early April. His appointment was truncated on the back end as well for, as Cicero reports (*Att* 2.1.9), in June Caesar was back in Rome, having left before the law allowed.

170...   Drumann produced six volumes on Rome's transition from a republic to an empire, *Geschichte Roms in seinem Uebergange von der republikanischen zur monarchischen Verfassung, oder: Pompeius, Caesar, Cicero und ihre Zeitgenossen* which appeared in 1834–44. Volume III is spent mostly on Caesar. His quotation about Caesar bilking Gaul can be found in Walter p. 129.

171...   Plutarch (*Pomp* 13.4-5) says, "But when he [Sulla] learned the truth, and perceived that everybody was sallying forth to welcome Pompey and accompany him home with marks of goodwill, he was eager to outdo them. So he went out and met him, and after giving him the warmest welcome, saluted him in a loud voice as 'Magnus,' or *The Great*, and ordered those who were by to give him this surname. Others, however, say that this title was first given him in Africa by the whole army, but received authority and weight when thus confirmed by Sulla. Pompey himself, however, was last of all to use it, and it was only after a long time, when he was sent as pro-consul to Spain against Sertorius, that he began to subscribe himself in his letters and ordinances 'Pompeius Magnus;' for the name had become familiar and was no longer invidious."

172...   Plutarch (*Pomp* 45.2) gave as the lands Pompey had already conquered as "Pontus, Armenia, Cappadocia, Paphlagonia, Media, Colchis, Iberia, Albania, Syria, Cilicia, Mesopotamia, Phoenicia and Palestine, Judaea, Arabia, and all the power of the pirates by sea and land which had been overthrown. Among these peoples no less than a thousand strongholds had been captured, according to the inscriptions, and cities not much under nine hundred in number, besides eight hundred piratical ships, while thirty-nine cities had been founded."

173...   *Hispania Ulterior* consisted of what are now Andalusia, Portugal, Extremadura, Castilla, León, Galicia, Asturias, Cantabria, and the Basque Country. During the Republic, *Hispania* was comprised of four major towns, each with its own legal jurisdiction (*conventus juridicus*): Gades (Cádiz); Hispalis (Seville); Astiga (Ejica); and Corduba (Cordova). Pliny (*HN* 3.3) says the province consisted of: 175 towns—nine of which were colonies and eight municipal towns, 29 of which possessed old Latin rights; six were free towns; three were federated (*Fœderati civitates* whose inhabitants were called "*foederati*" or "*socii*"); and 120 tributary. What is remarkable as well is that the territory was already well known to him. Ulterior Spain has been assigned to him eight years earlier when he was sent there to serve as quaestor under Antistius Vetus in Corduba. And, we must take a moment to examine what happened in 69 to help make sense of his propraetorian administration.

174... Dio (37.53.1-4) describes the military response of the inhabitants of the Herminian [sic] Mountains, "Meanwhile he learned that the inhabitants of the Herminian Mountains had withdrawn and were intending to ambush him as he returned. So for the time being he withdrew by another road, but later marched against them and, being victorious, pursued them in flight to the ocean. When, however, they abandoned the mainland and crossed over to an island, he stayed where he was, for his supply of boats was not large; but he put together some rafts, by means of which he sent on a part of his army, and lost a number of men. For the man in command of them landed at a breakwater near the island and disembarked the troops, thinking they could cross over on foot, when he was forced off by the returning tide and put out to sea, leaving them in the lurch. All but one of them died bravely defending themselves; Publius Scaevius, the only one to survive, after losing his shield and receiving many wounds, leaped into the water and escaped by swimming. Such was the result of that attempt; later, Caesar sent for boats from Gades, crossed over to the island with his whole army, and reduced the people there without a blow, as they were hard pressed for want of food. Thence sailing along to Brigantium, a city of Callaecia, he alarmed the people, who had never before seen a fleet, by the breakers which his approach to land caused, and subjugated them."

175... Appian (*Hisp* 12.71) says, "guerilla bands made incursions into Lusitania and ravaged it." With respect to their tactics, Strabo (3.3.6) says, the Lusitanians "are given to laying ambush, given to spying out, are quick, nimble, and good at deploying troops." Decimus Junius Brutus was not about to play a cat-and-mouse game with the brigands so he (Appian, *Hisp* 12.71) "turned against the towns thinking that thus he should take vengeance upon them, and at the same time secure a quantity of plunder for his army, and that the robbers would scatter, each to his own place, when their homes were threatened. With this design he began destroying everything that came in his way." It is unclear what Appian means by destroyed, for some towns that had surrendered, revolted again and "These he reduced to subjection again." Gomes et al (2005) indicate that there was considerable destruction during this period.

176...   Silus Italicus in his long poem *Punica*, written about 84 AD, is the only source that points to these tribes joining the Carthaginians. Book 3, lines 344-356 read:

> Rich Gallicia sent her people, men who have knowledge concerning the entrails of beasts, the flight of birds, and the lightnings of heaven; they delight, at one time, to chant the rude songs of their native tongue, at another to stamp the ground in the dance and clash their noisy shields in time to the music. Such is the relaxation and sport of the men, and such their solemn rejoicings. All other labor is done by the women: the men think it unmanly to throw seed into the furrow and turn the soil by pressure of the plough; but the wife of the Gallician is never still and performs every task but that of stern war. These men, and the Lusitanians drawn forth from their distant forests, were led by the young Viriathus —Viriathus, whose name was to win fame from Roman disasters at a later day.

177...   Tacitus (*Ann* 3.74) says it was "a time-honored tribute to generals who, after a successful campaign, were acclaimed by the joyful and spontaneous voice of a conquering army. Several might hold the title simultaneously, nor did it raise them above an equality with their colleagues. It was awarded in a few cases even by Augustus" but apparently not after the formation of the principate in 27 BC.

178... Pliny (*HN* 34. 156-157) speaks of the quality of the lead and tin in the region. He says, "The next topic is the nature of lead, of which there are two kinds, black and white. White lead {tin} is the most valuable; the Greeks applied to it the name *cassiteros*, and there was a legendary story of their going to islands of the Atlantic Ocean to fetch it and importing it in platted vessels made of osiers and covered with stitched hides. It is now known that it is a product of Lusitania and Gallaecia found in the surface-strata of the ground which is sandy and of a black color. It is only detected by its weight, and also tiny pebbles of it occasionally appear, especially in dry beds of torrents. The miners wash this sand and heat the deposit in furnaces. It is also found in the goldmines called '*alutiae*,' through which a stream of water is passed that washes out black pebbles of tin mottled with small white spots, and of the same weight as gold, and consequently they remain with the gold in the bowls in which it is collected, and afterwards are separated in the furnaces, and fused and melted into white lead." The market price of white lead shows that it is worth killing people for, as Pliny continues (*HN* 34.161) "The price of pure white lead without alloy is 80 denarii, and of black lead 7 denarii."

179... It is worth quoting Plutarch (*Pomp* 10.5) again at this point when he says that during Sulla's proscription, Pompey allowed "as many as possible to escape detection, and even helped to send some out of the country." This is an act Caesar could not entertain.

180... Cicero says (*Imper* 33-35), "For why should I complain of the disaster of Ostia, and of that stain and blot on the republic, when almost under your very eyes, that fleet which was under the command of a Roman consul was taken and destroyed by the pirates? O ye immortal gods! could the incredible and godlike virtue of one man in so short a time bring so much light to the republic, that you who had lately been used to see a fleet of the enemy before the mouth of the Tiber, should now hear that there is not one ship belonging to the pirates on this side of the Atlantic? And although you have seen with what rapidity these things were done, still that rapidity ought not to be passed over by me in speaking of them.—For whoever, even if he were only going for the purpose of transacting business or making profit, contrived in so short a time to visit so many places, and to perform such long journeys, with as great celerity as Gnaeus Pompeius has performed his voyage, bearing with him the terrors of war as our general? He, when the weather could hardly be called open for sailing, went to Sicily, explored the coasts of Africa; from thence he came with his fleet to Sardinia, and these three great granaries of the republic he fortified with powerful garrisons and fleets; when, leaving Sardinia, he came to Italy, having secured the two Spains and Cisalpine Gaul with garrisons and ships. Having sent vessels also to the coast of Illyricum, and to every part of Achaia and Greece, he also adorned the two seas of Italy with very large fleets, and very sufficient garrisons; and he himself going in person, added all Cilicia to the dominions of the Roman people, on the forty-ninth day after he set out from Brundusium. Will the pirates who were anywhere to be found, were either taken prisoners and put to death, or else had surrendered themselves voluntarily to the power and authority of this one man."

181... Of course, a goodly number in the administration were dubious about the effectiveness of such a command because seven years earlier the then-praetor Marcus Antonius Creticus had received a smiliar commission—*imperium infinitum*—to clear the Mediterranean but failed miserably. He received the moniker Creticus, seemingly in derision, for his failed effort in attacking Crete for aiding the pirates. Florus (1.42.2-3) says, "Marcus Antonius made the first attack upon the island with such expectation of victory and confidence that he carried more fetters than arms on board his ships. And so he paid the penalty of his rashness; for the enemy cut off most of his ships and hung the bodies of their prisoners from the sails and tackle; and then spreading their sails the Cretans returned in triumph to their harbors." And although Plutarch (*Ant* 1) describes him as "kindly and honest, and particularly a liberal giver," Cicero in his case against Verres (2.3.213) says, "In the middle of his course of injustice and covetousness death overtook Antony, while he was still both doing and planning many things contrary to the safety of the allies many things contrary to the advantage of our provinces." In 100, Antonius' father, also of the same name, received a triumph for achieving some success during his command to rid the sea of the Cilician pirates. Ironically, as Plutarch (*Pomp* 24.6) reveals, his daughter Antonia was kidnapped by pirates from his villa near Misenum and released only after a substantial ransom was paid.

182... Appian (*Hisp* 20.100) describes how Titus Didius, who served as governor of Hispania Citerior from 97 to 93, responded to poverty-stricken Celtiberians who "were living by robbery on account of their poverty. Didius, with the concurrence of the ten legates who were still present, resolved to destroy them. Accordingly, he told their principal men that he would allot the land of Colenda to them because they were poor. Finding them very much pleased with this offer, he told them to communicate it to their people, and to come with their wives and children to the parceling out of the land. When they had done so he ordered his soldiers to vacate their camp, and these people, whom he wanted to ensnare, to go inside, so that he might make a list of their names, the men on one register and the women and children on another, in order to know how much land should be set apart for them. When they had gone inside the ditch and palisade, Didius surrounded them with his army and killed them all, and for this he was honored with a triumph." For this, the powers-that-be in Rome awarded him a triumph. The first thing Gaius Valerius Flaccus, the proconsul who succeeded Didius in the province had to deal with was an uprising of the Celtiberi because of the exceptional cruelty and treachery of Didius. Appian's words (*Hisp* 20. 100) are, "At a later period, the Celtiberians having revolted again, Flaccus was sent against them and slew 20,000. The people of the town of Belgida were eager for revolt, and when their senate hesitated they set fire to the senate house and burned the senators. When Flaccus arrived there he put the authors of this crime to death."

183... For epigraphic information see Reynolds, pp. 970ff.

184... On one visit to Posidonius, when the philosopher was not feeling well, he transcended the pain and gave Pompey an "audience." Cicero describes the situation as (*Tusc* 2.61), "I will tell you what Pompey used to say of him: that when he came to Rhodes, after his departure from Syria, he had a great desire to hear Posidonius, but was informed that he was very ill of a severe fit of the gout; yet he had great inclination to pay a visit to so famous a philosopher. Accordingly, when he had seen him, and paid his compliments, and had spoken with great respect of him, he said he was very sorry that he could not hear him lecture. But indeed you may, replied the other, nor will I suffer any bodily pain to occasion so great a man to visit me in vain. On this Pompey relates that, as he lay on his bed, he disputed with great dignity and fluency on this very subject—That nothing was good but what was honest; and that in his paroxysms he would often say, 'Pain, it is to no purpose, notwithstanding you are troublesome, I will never acknowledge you an evil.' And in general all celebrated and notorious afflictions become endurable by disregarding them." For additional insights into Pompey's relationship with Posidonius, see Morrill, pp. 85-86. Pliny (*HN* 7.12) says, "At the conclusion of the war with Mithridates Gnaeus Pompey when going to enter the abode of the famous professor of philosophy Posidonius forbade his retainer to knock on the door in the customary manner, and the subduer of the East and of the West dipped his standard to the portals of learning."

185... Suburra was a densely-populated section of Rome, inhabited by small traders and people of ill repute. Caesar lived in the family home there until 63 when he was elected *pontifex maximus*. Suetonius (*Div* 46), says, "He lived at first in the Subura in a modest house, but after he became pontifex maximus, in the official residence on the Sacred Way." The district grew up around the property before Caesar's birth. *Suburra* in Italian means "rabble" or "slum." Marcus Terentius Varro in his *De Lingua Latina* (5.48) gives Marcus Junius Gracchanus' description of the origin of "Subbara" [sic]: "Subura is so named because it was at the foot of the old city (*sub urbe*); proof of which may be in the fact that it is under that place which is called the earthwall. But I rather think that from the Succusan district it was called *Succusa*; for even now when abbreviated it is written SVC, with C and not B as third letter. The Succusan district is so named because it *succurrit* 'runs up to' the *Carinae*." The poet Martial lived there and mentions it a number of times in his epigrams. Samuel Ball Platner's 1929 edition of *A Topographical Dictionary of Ancient Rome* (completed and revised by Thomas Ashby) says the district was called "*fervens* (Iuv. XI.51, and schol. frequentissima regio), *clamosa* (Mart. XII.18.2), dirty and wet (*ib.* V.22.59), a resort of harlots (Pers. 5.32; Mart. II.17; VI.66.12; XI.61.3;78.11; Priap. 40.1), of dealers in provisions and delicacies (Iuv. XI.141; Mart. VII.31; X.94.56) and finery (Mart. IX.37), and of tradesmen of various sorts (*praeco*, CIL VI.1953; *crepidarius*, *ib.* 9284; *ferrarius*, 9399; *lanarius*, 9491; *inpilarius*, 33862; *lintearius*, 9526)." Carlo Bonini and Giancarlo De Cataldo have a novel with the title *Suburra* that came out in 2013. A film adaption of the book directed by Stefano Sollima appeared in 2015 which was followed by a Netflix series *Suburra:Blood on Rome* which ran from 2017-2020.

186... The Senate originally consisted of 100 men installed by Romulus. Livy (1.8) says "He created a hundred senators; either because that number was adequate, or because there were only a hundred heads of houses who could be created. In any case they were called the *'Patres'* in virtue of their rank, and their descendants were called 'Patricians.'" He adds (2.1) that, "The senate had been thinned by the murderous cruelty of Tarquin, and [Lucius Junius] Brutus' next care was to strengthen its influence by selecting some of the leading men of equestrian rank to fill the vacancies; by this means he brought it up to the old number of three hundred. The new members were known as *'conscripti,'* the old ones retained their designation of *'patres.'*" By the time of the Republic, Sulla, after murdering many Senators, expanded the number from 300 to close to 600 men who served for life. Augustus reduced the composition of the Senate from 900 to 600. He dismissed many of low birth whom Caesar had appointed. Abbot (pp. 381-382) says, "Augustus also took occasion to exclude many men of low birth, whom Julius Caesar had admitted . . . The conditions of eligibility to membership in the senate included citizenship and free birth, an acceptable reputation, and property rated at 1,000,000 sesterces . . . The emperor could, however, at his discretion grant to men not of senatorial rank, who had the necessary property, the right to wear the *latus clavus*, or broad purple stripe on the tunic. This entitled them to become candidates for a magistracy with the prospect later of entering the senate. Furthermore, citizens with a fortune of 1,000,000 sesterces, who had not held a magistracy, were from time to time admitted to the senate by *adlectio*."

187... In many cases, some of his appointees, as they say, did not pan out. Thus, as Dio says (43.47.4-6), "He released some who were on trial for bribery and were being proved guilty, so that he was charged with bribe-taking himself. This report was strengthened by the fact that he also put up at auction all the public lands, not only the profane, but also the consecrated lots, and sold most of them. Nevertheless, he granted ample gifts to some persons in the form of money or the sale of lands; and in the case of a certain Lucius Basilius, who was praetor, instead of assigning him a province he bestowed a large amount of money upon him, so that Basilius became notorious both on this account as well as because, when insulted during his praetorship by Caesar, he had held out against him. All this suited those citizens who were receiving or even expecting to receive something, since they had no regard for the public weal in comparison with the chance of the moment for their own advancement by such means. But all the rest took it greatly to heart and had much to say about it to each other and also—as many as felt safe in so doing—in outspoken utterances and the publication of anonymous pamphlets."

188... Weinstock clarifies (p. 221) that this empowering, "did not mean that Caesar became a tribune—he was and remained a patrician—or that he received any of the further privileges . . ." Later, after Caesar's murder, Brutus said, "the conspirators had not committed any offense against Caesar's inviolability because it was not granted him freely but extorted from the Senate after his armed entry into Rome and the murder of so many citizens." Appian (*BC* 2.13) says, when Brutus addressed the gathered plebeians whom he and Cassius called to assemble at the Capitol, thusly, "'Have *we* then, or has *he*, done violence to inviolable persons? Or shall Caesar indeed be sacred and inviolable, upon whom we conferred that distinction not of our own free will, but by compulsion, and not until he had invaded his country with arms and killed a great number of our noblest and best citizens, whereas our fathers in a democracy and without compulsion took an oath that the office of tribune should be sacred and inviolable, and declare with maledictions that it should remain so for ever?'"

189... Most of the early literature on Caesar's "fainting spells"—which is how his episodes have been described—attributes them to some form of epilepsy. Suetonius (*Div* 45.1) says, "towards the end he was subject to sudden fainting fits and to nightmare as well. He was twice attacked by the falling sickness [epilepsy] during his campaigns." Plutarch (*Caes* 17.2) says he "suffered from distemper in the head, and was subject to epileptic fits, a trouble which first attacked him, we are told, in Corduba." Appian's take is (*BC* 110), "And now Cæsar, either renouncing his hope, or tired out, and wishing to avoid the plot and accusation, or giving up the city to certain of his enemies, or to cure his bodily ailment of epilepsy and convulsions, which came upon him suddenly and especially when he was inactive, conceived the idea of a long campaign against the Getæ and the Parthians." For years scholars interested in Caesar's life, including medical experts, have been perplexed by the dearth of information the ancients have offered and took it upon themselves to re-examine the case to see if there might be a better or more complete diagnosis of what Caesar periodically suffered from during his life. Some moderns like Hughes reaffirm the epilepsy diagnosis, other analysts have attributed the "episodes" to a brain tumor (cf. Gustavo Gomez et al. and Francois Retief et al.), still others to mild strokes, stress, and Caesar's use of emetics. Cicero reported in several instances (*Deiot* 21 and *Att* 13.52) that Caesar was fond of emetics causing some analysts to conclude that Caesar might have gotten wobbly from a potassium deficiency. We have no idea how often his "attacks" occurred. In a review of the various assessments scholars and medical personnel have offered about the problem, Tim Hamlyn adds to his medical assessment a hardnosed ideological position that essentially says the ailment was another example of Caesar's propaganda tactics. Hamlyn's conclusion is, "An examination of the ancient evidence shows that the illness Caesar suffered in the last couple of years of his life was probably not very serious. It is likely that it was exaggerated at the time by Caesar and his supporters for his own convenience, and some of the information reported in the sources was almost certainly fabricated." Which is a mouthful. He continues, "The abuse of emetics appears to have been the cause Caesar's symptoms, which are consistent with hypokalemia. Chronic hypernatremia from the use of salt water to induce vomiting is also possible. That Caesar's health was not failing is of obvious importance for understanding the need for his assassination. His enemies could not allow Caesar to reinforce his hold on the state. With military victories in the East winning him further fame and popularity and the passage of time entrenching his measures at Rome, Caesar's position of almost god-like power would become unassailable. If he had been at death's door, the prospect of this happening would have been substantially reduced and there would have been great hesitation as to whether the murder needed to be undertaken. Such was not the case, and the desperation of the likes of Cicero and those who urged M. Brutus to emulate his famous namesake was not, it seems, without grounds." Our position here continues to remain: what Caesar suffered from was Post Traumatic Battle Syndrome which in addition to causing dizziness, or what he suffered from in that regard, as well as the nightmares. He had been engaged in slaughter for nearly 15 years non-stop and, at the time of his death, in poor health, he was days away from heading to Parthia to continue warring.

190... Toward the end of July 45, at a festival in his honor, the *Ludi Victoriae Caesaris*, Caesar's statue was carried in a procession among those of the gods of heaven. The statue of the goddess Victoria was in the lead and Caesar's was right behind her. And though he arranged for that position of honor, he rained upon the parade not only of the goddess but his own as well for as Cicero remarks, (*Att* 13.44.1), "The lookers-on were splendid in not applauding even the statue of Victoria because of her bad neighbor."

191... Caesar received the title *Dictator Perpetuus* sometime between January 26, 44 when he was feted with an *ovatio* and February 15, a month before his death. Miriam Pucci Ben Zeev (1996) says that a *senatus consultum* passed on February 9, 44 already calls Caesar "designated Dictator for life." The dictator for life was part of the senatorial decrees bestowing divine honors on the politician.

192... With respect to the senate and other public officials feeling insulted by Caesar not paying due deference to their status, Weinstock (pp. 275-276) offers a different take on the matter and his view is worth nothing in full. He says with respect to the perceived insult, "The following facts are relevant: it was the privilege of the magistrates and of senators to conduct official business seated; a citizen rose when a magistrate came, as did a minor magistrate in the presence of a higher-ranking one; again, men of special merits were honored by rising at their appearance. There is not a single piece of evidence to show that Caesar here committed an offence against tradition or that, as modern scholars maintain, he wanted to demonstrate his new monarchic status. What is quoted in this respect, including the case of the tribune L. Pontius Aquila, is irrelevant. As dictator he was superior to the consuls and could therefore remain seated in their presence; and the senatorial privilege only meant that they were not obliged either to rise in the presence of a magistrate. As to the alleged demonstration of his monarchic status, we have met other and really significant actions and decrees to this effect. At the Lupercalia of 44 when he was officially approached by his fellow consul Antony he remained seated again, and nobody was scandalized on this account."

193... It is worth listening to Appian's full account of the incident (*BC* 2.108): "In this they were disappointed, but some person among those who wished to spread the report of his desire to be king placed a crown of laurel on his statue, bound with a white fillet. The tribunes, Marullus and Caesetius, sought out this person and put him in prison, pretending to gratify Caesar also by this, as he had threatened any who should talk about making him king. Caesar put up with their action, and when some others who met him at the city gates as he was returning from some place greeted him as king, and the people groaned, he said with happy readiness to those who had thus saluted him, 'I am not King, I am Caesar,' as though they had mistaken his name. The attendants of Marullus again found out which man began the shouting and ordered the officers to bring him to trial before his tribunal. Caesar at last put up with it no longer and accused the faction of Marullus before the Senate of artfully conspiring to cast upon him the odium of royalty. He added that they were deserving of death, but that it would be sufficient if they were deprived of their office and expelled from the Senate. Thus, he confirmed the suspicion that he desired the title, and that his tyranny was already complete; for the cause of their punishment was their zeal against the title of king, and, moreover, the office of tribune was sacred and inviolable according to law and the ancient oath. By not even waiting for the expiration of their office he sharpened the public indignation." Nicolaus of Damascus' version (Aug 20.69-70) is, "Something else, such as it was, took place which especially stirred the conspirators against him. There was a golden statue of him which had been erected on the Rostra by vote of the people. A diadem appeared on it, encircling the head, whereupon the Romans became very suspicious, supposing that it was a symbol of servitude. Two of the tribunes, Lucius and Gaius, came up and ordered one of their subordinates to climb up, take it down, and throw it away. When Caesar discovered what had happened, he convened the Senate in the temple of Concordia and arraigned the tribunes asserting that they themselves had secretly placed the diadem on the statue, so that they might have a chance to insult him openly and thus get credit for doing a brave deed by dishonouring the statue, caring nothing either for him or for the Senate. He continued that their action was one which indicated a more serious resolution and plot: if somehow they might slander him to the people as a seeker after unconstitutional power, and thus (themselves stirring up an insurrection) to slay him. After this address, with the concurrence of the Senate he banished them. Accordingly, they went off into exile and other tribunes were appointed in their place. Then the people clamored that he become king and they shouted that there should be no longer any delay in crowning him as such, for Fortune had already crowned him. But Caesar declared that although he would grant the people everything because of their good will toward him, he would never allow this step; and he asked their indulgence for contradicting their wishes in preserving the old form of government, saying that he preferred to hold the office of consul in accordance with the law to being king illegally."

194... Lucius Aurelius Cotta, who served as praetor in 70 (in 65 as consul and censor in 64), passed a law, the *Lex Aurelia*, that no longer allowed senators exclusive right to serve on juries, a monopoly Sulla gave to them when dictator. Cotta's law stipulated that there would be three *decuriae*: one of senators, one of knights, and one of *tribuni aerarii*. The number of tribunes who served seems to have been 70 and they had to meet some level of property ownership. Caesar through his *Lex Judiciaria* took away the right of the tribunes to serve, limiting service to senators and equites. See Velleius (2.32).

195... Valerius Maximus (7.2) says, "The fate of Caesetius, a Roman knight, was not altogether so glorious, but his indulgence towards his son was no less remarkable. When he was commanded by Caesar, now victor over all his foreign and domestic enemies, to disinherit and disown his son, because he, being tribune of the plebs, with his colleague Marullus had maliciously accused Caesar of seeking to become king, he ventured to give him this reply: 'You shall rather take from me, O Caesar, all my sons, than compel me by my own actions to disinherit any one of them.' He had two other sons, young men of high hopes, to whom Caesar had liberally promised great preferment. The father remained safe, through the clemency of the divine princeps. Yet who would not think that he dared with a spirit that was more than human, who would not stoop to him, who had subdued all the world under his command?" Caesar had the pair of tribunes exiled. Nicolaus of Damascus (130.76) notes, "Not long after this, the praetor Cinna [Lucius Cornelius Cinna praetor in 44] propitiated Caesar to the extent of securing a decree which allowed the exiled tribunes to return; though in accordance with the wish of the people they were not to resume their office, but to remain private citizens, yet not excluded from public affairs. Caesar did not prevent their recall, so they returned."

196... Appian (2.113) lists him as among those who conspired against Caesar, and Dio (46.38.3) says he is, "At this time also Pontius Aquila, one of Caesar's slayers." Cicero (*Brut* 1.15.8) says, "In the course of those same days I lavished honors—if you like that word-upon the dead Hirtius, Pansa, and even Aquila." Because of his republican sentiments Cicero (*Phil* 11.14) spoke of him as "*praestantissimus civis*," "that most illustrious citizen Aquila." Münzer (*Col* 36) says, "Of the Caesar murderers known by name, Aquila met the most honorable end."

197... By putting Rufio in charge of the legions in Egypt Caesar defied the tradition of appointing a senator as the commander of an occupying Roman army. The dictator feared that a senator with any aspirations could turn his command along the Nile as a base for countering his measures. Rufio's primary job became one of overseer for Caesar (*BAlex* 33.3-4), "deemed it conducive to the dignity of our empire and to public expediency that, if the rulers remained loyal, they should be protected by our troops: whereas if they proved ungrateful, those same troops could hold them in check."

198... Caesar's prohibition of guilds or voluntary associations was not unique; such groups were outlawed on other occasions and the reason was always the same, that is, they were acting or potentially acting against the public interest, the *res publica*. In 64, for example, the Senate's decree included the words *senatus consulto collegia sublata sunt, quae adversus rem publicam videbantur esse* <constituta>. See Asconius *In senatu Contra L. Pisonem*, editor Albert Curtis Clark (1907). Cotter (1996) provides other instances of the prohibition and the ancient sources documenting their enactment.

199... Dio (43.25.3) says, "since it was by ruling the Gauls for many years in succession that he himself had conceived a greater desire for dominion and had increased the equipment of his force, he limited by law the term of propraetors to one year, and that of proconsuls to two consecutive years, and enacted that no one whatever should be allowed to hold any command for a longer time." See also Cicero (*Phil* 1.19; 24; 3.38; 5.7; and 8.28.

200...   From time to time during his various campaigns, Caesar lost control of his army due to a declared mutiny on the part of the men. The most notable example occurred early in his campaign in Gaul in 58, at Vesontio, when his army refused to face the German force of Ariovistus out of fear. Dio (38.35.2) says they did not want to go against "uncanny ferocious wild beasts" the soldiers offering as a rationale that "they were undertaking a war which was none of their business and had not been decreed, [that it was going on] merely on account of Caesar's personal ambition; and they threatened also to desert him if he did not change his course." Caesar gave the men an oration the great Chrysologus would envy so that, Dio adds (38.47.1), no one raised an objection "even if some thought altogether the opposite." In 47, when Caesar was preparing for a campaign in Africa against the Pompeian army, his troops refused to go. Instead, "they marched to Rome," Stefan Chrissanthos (p. 63) says, "to demand back pay, discharge, and promised bonuses of money and land. Caesar's power and his very survival, were hanging in the balance." Two years earlier in Placentia, Spain, when his army refused to fight, they said it was because his practice of *lenitas* was prolonging the war. Appian (*BC* 2.47) says, "When Caesar heard of this he flew from Massilia to Placentia and coming before the soldiers, who were still in a state of mutiny, addressed them as follows: 'You know what kind of speed I use in everything I undertake. This war is not prolonged by us, but by the enemy, who keep retiring from us. You reaped great advantages from my command in Gaul, and you took an oath to me for the whole of this war and not for a part only; and now you abandon us in the midst of our labors, you revolt against your officers, you propose to give orders to those from whom you are bound to receive orders. Being myself the witness of my liberality to you heretofore I shall now execute the law of our country by decimating the ninth legion, where this mutiny began.' Straightway a cry went up from the whole legion, and the officers threw themselves at Caesar's feet in supplication. Caesar yielded little by little and so far remitted the punishment as to designate 120 only (who seemed to have been the leaders of the revolt), and chose twelve of these by lot to be put to death. One of the twelve proved that he was absent when the conspiracy was formed, and Caesar put to death in his stead the centurion who had accompanied him."

On one level, it is hard to believe that an entire Roman army would refuse to fight for its commander but in the last 50 years of the Republic, Chrissanthos says, there were at least 30 instances of mutinies by armies serving under different generals. Caesar's trusted lieutenant, Titus Labienus, left his commander because he wanted no part in the insurrectionary civil war Caesar was engaged in but there are no solid accounts of the common foot soldier stating he was unwilling to sacrifice his life for the *dignitas* of a king-in-the-making, that is, refusing to fight for ideological reasons. William Messer discusses the mutinies that occurred at different stages of the Republic and how the generals in command, including Caesar, responded to the insubordination. At Placentia, as Dio above mentions, Caesar executed 12 of the ringleaders. The army there said they would not fight because they were exhausted, were not paid properly, and because Caesar, as Dio (41.26.1) says, "did not allow them to plunder the country nor to do all the other things on which their minds were set." Of course, generals were cautious in meting out punishment because it could aggravate the army's grievances. With respect to Dio's version of the speech that Caesar gives at Versontio, Adam Kemezis says in the abstract to his chapter of the book, "Dio's Caesar is a cynical figure whose speech is thoroughly dishonest, but also completely effective, not because it deceives the men, but because it causes them to share the desire for honor that is his driving motivation."

201... Cicero (*Fam* 9.15.2) tells his friend Lucius Papirius Paetus in the fall of 46, "*cum in urbem nostram est infusa peregrinitas, nunc vero etiam bracatis et Transalpinis nationibus, ut nullum veteris leporis vestigium appareat.*" That is, "when provincialism poured like a stream into our city, and now with that of trousered and Transalpine clans ... not a trace of the fine old style of pleasantry [wit] is to be seen."

202... Even after Caesar was dead, Marc Antony continued to remind his fellow citizens of the host of honors afforded the dictator. Suetonius (*Div* 84.2) says, "Antonius caused a herald to recite the decree of the Senate in which it had voted Caesar all divine and human honors at once, and likewise the oath with which they had all pledged themselves to watch over his personal safety." According to Weinstock (p. 351) Cicero was convinced that Marc Antony's speech at the funeral inflamed the populace when he told Antony (*Phil* 2.91), "All that fine panegyric was yours, that commiseration was yours, that exhortation was yours. It was you—you, I say—who hurled those firebrands ... with which your friend himself was nearly burnt ..."

203... Plutarch's record (*Caes* 58.2-3) says, "Therefore, when Maximus the consul died, he appointed Caninius Revilius consul for the one day still remaining of the term of office. To him, as we are told, many were going with congratulations and offers of escort, whereupon Cicero said: 'Let us make haste, or else the man's consulship will have expired.'"

204... Augustus was not happy with the quality of the composition of the senate he inherited from Julius. Suetonius (*Aug* 35.1) says, "Since the number of the senators was swelled by a low-born and ill-assorted rabble (in fact, the senate numbered more than a thousand, some of whom, called by the vulgar Orcivi, were wholly unworthy, and had been admitted after Caesar's death through favor or bribery) he restored it to its former limits and distinction by two enrollments, one according to the choice of the members themselves, each man naming one other, and a second made by Agrippa and himself." Mark Antony kept upping the number of senators as Caesar had done. As mentioned, they were derogatorily referred to as the *Orcini (Orcivi) Senatores*, slaves freed by the grace of Orcus. Mark Antony justified his actions by saying Caesar left a list of nominees he wanted appointed. Dio (52.42ff.) says that in 28 Augustus "purged" the body of those whom Suetonius (*Aug* 35.1) says were appointed "through bribery and corruption." To repeat, Caesar raised the number of senators to 900, Antony upped that number to at least 1000. Augustus approached the Senate and asked those who knew they were unfit to resign; 50 came forth and did so voluntarily. He then added 150 others to that list so that the body was reduced by 19 percent. The rejects did not lose their senatorial perks. As Evans (p. 85) points out, there had been purges in the past. In 115 BC, the Senate had been reduced by 10 percent, in 70 by 13 percent. Though there are no numbers to document the purges during the 80s, Evans says (pp. 85-86) that in 86, "with an already depleted senate following the Social War of 91-89 and the civil unrest of 88 and 87, the senate was further denuded of all supporters of Sulla and of other public officials unwilling to acknowledge the government of Cinna. It is certainly plausible to argue that the lectio of 86 contained, at a conservative estimation, between a third and a half less than the average sized senate of the second century. A purge, in its most modern sense was, therefore, wisely avoided by Octavian in 28. And just as Sulla had diminished the role of the censors when he won sole power in 82, on account of the events in 86, so too did the politician who was soon to become Augustus avoid an office, which had become tarnished in the eyes of his predecessors and contemporaries alike."

205... William Smith in the 1890 edition of his dictionary, offers under the entry *clavus latus* the following, "It was a common usage with many nations of antiquity to adorn a garment by means of stripes of a different color, woven in [p. 1.454] or sewn on the stuff. As instances we may quote the purple stripe down the middle of the robes worn by the priests of the Sun, instituted by Heliogabalus (*Herodian*, 5.5, 9); the broad white stripe down the breast of the purple garment of the Persian leader in the Pompeian mosaic of the battle of Issus; the regulations of the mysteries at Andania, which prescribe that the σημεῖα on the women›s garments are to be not more than half a finger›s breadth (Sauppe, Abhandl. der kgl. Gesellsch., Göttingen, 1860); and among the Romans the female ornament of the patagium. But the Romans made a more characteristic use of these adornments by employing them as badges of office or rank (*ornamenta*), as in the case of the *trabea*, the *toga praetexta*, and the *clavi*."

206... While the Romans sought to assimilate the barbarians into their culture as a source of social control, they in turn were not unaffected by the customs of foreigners; for example, in wearing the trousers the Gauls called *braccae*. Balsdon (1979, p. 221) says, "By Trajan's time many Romans were wearing long shorts which came down to below the knees, as can be seen from representations on his column; while on the arch of Constantine soldiers wear full-length trousers [cf. infra]." There is no evidence that the Greeks ever wore them and the Romans, during the Republic, were still too despising of the barbarian to accede to wearing them. But, during the empire things changed. In 69, for example, when Aulus Caecina Alienus crossed the Swiss Plateau on the orders of Emperor Vitellius at the head of the troops of Upper Germania, Tacitus (*Hist* 2.20) tells us, "His manner of dress the towns and colonies interpreted as a mark of haughtiness, because he addressed civilians wearing a varicoloured cloak and breeches," the latter referring to his *braccae*. And Lampridius, in his life of Severus Alexander (2.40.11) says that Severus "always wore bands on his legs, and he used white trousers [*braccas*], not scarlet ones, as had formerly been the custom." As noted, on Trajan's Column of the Arch of Constantine, soldiers are depicted wearing *braccae*; see https://www.thecollector.com/arch-of-constantine-the-monument-with-many-faces/. It appears that by the end of the fourth century the wearing of such trousers was forbidden in the city as the *Codex Theodosianus* (14.10.2) states, "*Impp. Arcadius et Honorius aa. ad populum. Usum Tzangarum adque Bracarum intra urbem venerabilem nemini liceat usurpare. Si quis autem contra hanc sanctionem venire temptaverit, sententia viri illustris praefecti spoliatum eum omnibus facultatibus tradi in perpetuum exilium praecipimus. Et cetera. Dat. proposita Romae in foro divi Traiani Caesario et Attico conss.*" Etymologically speaking, the Scottish "breeks" and the English "breeches" come from the storied *braccae*.

207... With respect to Caesar's isolation, Balsdon (1958, pp. 87, 88) says, "Of Caesar's arrogance, his unapproachability, at the end of his life, there can be no doubt." He then says one of two things occurred: "One is that in the last months of his life the old Caesar—a generous, compassionate Caesar—had been replaced by a different Caesar, a man drunk with power, a tyrant such as Greek philosophers had described earlier." He then says, "The other possibility is that Caesar was killed not because he changed in any way, but because he did not change. Since 49 he had been in effect, even when he was not holding the title, a military dictator, governing Rome, just as he was directing military operations, from his supreme headquarters, with subordinates in Rome as in the field who acted on his instructions and often, until the instructions came, were afraid to act at all." He adds that, after the Battle of Munda on March 17, 45, "This was the moment for Caesar and for the system to change, the moment for relaxation. But Caesar did not change; nor did the system. Was not this the reason why in the end they killed him?" From the evidence offered in this essay, as the jurors know, Balsdon's either-or amounts to the same thing.

208... Holmes' *Conquest of Gaul* is a magnificent piece of scholarship, a model for every historian especially those tempted to take shortcuts in their narrative. What is remarkable is that Holmes has a 71-page Chapter (pp. 173-244) on whether Caesar was telling the truth about what he did and saw. Holmes felt compelled to refute all prominent critics of Caesar's veracity. Holmes says (p. 143), "I believe that with the two or three exceptions which I have noted, I have refuted them all. But the reader must not run away with the idea that I am not so simple as to regard the *Commentaries* as absolutely true. No history is absolutely true; and Caesar assuredly made mistakes." And then he goes on to say that essentially the biggest mistake Caesar made was failing to dot his "i's" and cross his "t's." Along with the quotation from Montaigne, Holmes doubles-down (pp. 243-244) with the assessment of the *Commentaries* by Duc d'Aumale, a politician, general and noted bibliophile, who wrote in an essay on Caesar's military operations, "We have only sought to establish one thing, which is that, without in any way being a critic of Caesar, and remaining a declared admirer, not only of his great deeds but of the way he recounts them, it was permissible to submit to analysis certain passages of the *Commentaries* and to discuss some of the [Caesar's] assertions when he had an obvious interest in concealing or exaggerating the truth; but we do not believe that this faculty can extend to changing the character of the rigorous interpretation of the text in all that concerns descriptions of places, works, movements ... It cannot be disputed that his stories exude sincerity." Like Montaigne he regales Caesar as, "the most sincere of those who have written their own history."

209... To be fair to Collins, he does list in his essay "Caesar as Political Propagandist" the crimes for which Caesar might be charged in an international court of law.

210... Quintilian in his *Institutio Oratoria* (10.114) waxes eloquent about Caesar's rhetorical prowess, "As for Gaius Caesar, if he had had leisure to devote himself to the courts, he would have been the one orator who could have been considered a serious rival to Cicero. Such are his force, his penetration and his energy that we realise that he was as vigorous in speech as in his conduct of war. And yet all these qualities are enhanced by a marvellous elegance of language, of which he was an exceptionally jealous student."

211... In the same section, Suetonius adds that, "Augustus forbade the publication of [the sayings] in a very brief and frank letter sent to Pompeius Macer, whom he had selected to set his libraries in order." Spaeth (p. 598) suggests that Augustus could have deep-sixed the works of Caesar just mentioned out of jealousy, in that he himself wrote a tragedy that went nowhere. Suetonius (*Aug* 85.2) says, "Though he began a tragedy with much enthusiasm, he destroyed it because his style did not satisfy him, and when some of his friends asked him what in the world had become of Ajax, he answered that 'his Ajax had fallen on his sponge.'"

212... It ought not be forgotten that, when Caesar was captured by pirates as a young man, he serenaded his captors with his verses. Plutarch (*Caes* 2.4.) says that during his captivity, "He also wrote poems and sundry speeches which he read aloud to them, and those who did not admire these he would call to their faces illiterate Barbarians . . . The pirates were delighted at this, and attributed his boldness of speech to a certain simplicity and boyish mirth." And in his life of Terence, Suetonius (5.1) provides six verses Caesar wrote assessing the work of the playwright:

> Tu quoque, tu in summis, o dimidiate Menander,
> Poneris, et merito, puri sermonis amator.
> Lenibus atque utinam scriptis adiuncta foret vis,
> Comica ut aequato virtus polleret honore
> Cum Graecis neve hac despectus parte iaceres!
> Unum hoc maceror ac doleo tibi desse, Terenti.

It reads: "You too, even you, are ranked at the top, o half-Menander, and justly, you lover of language undefiled. But would that they graceful verses had force as well, so that your comic power might have equal honor with that of the Greeks, and you the most mighty not be scorned in this regard and neglected. It hurts and pains me, my Terence, that you lack this one quality."

Right before providing Caesar's lines, Suetonius offers four lines of Cicero's assessment of Terence which also begins with "Tu quoque," leading Spaeth to conclude that the two writers, both of whom were students of the grammarian Marcus Antonius Gnipho, were engaged in a writing exercise for their teacher. They share the same sentiments particularly that Terence lacked a certain "*vis*."

213... The Jesus Seminar was a symposium of biblical scholars and "laypeople," 50 and 100 in number respectively, started by the late New Testament scholar, Robert Funk (1926-2005), in 1985 under the auspices of the Wester Institute located on the campus of Willamette University in Salem, Oregon. For how the seminar worked see Birger A. Person's "The Gospel According to the Jesus Seminar." http://www.veritas-ucsb.org//library/pearson/seminar/home.html

214... Appian (*BC* 2.91) says, "of this [Pontus] battle he wrote to Rome the words, "I came, I saw, I conquered." Plutarch's version (*Caes* 50.3) says Caesar said this to his friends, "In announcing the swiftness and fierceness of this [Pontic] battle to one of his friends at Rome, Amantius, Caesar wrote these words: 'Came, Saw, Conquered.'" University of Gothenburg Swedish historian Ida Östenberg says (2013, p. 818), "All other triumphal *tituli* recorded in literature and art preceded, as we have seen, the captives, spoils or representations on parade and provided descriptive information about names, places, weight, and provenance." The placard is another example of Caesar's hubris helping to shorten his life.

BIBLIOGRAPHY

Abbott, Frank Frost. *A History and Description of Roman Political Institutions.* Boston, MA: Ginn & Company, 1901.

Abbott, Frank Frost. "Titus Labienus." *The Classical Journal* 13 (1917): 4-13.

Aguirre, Santiago. "*Sic Semper Tyrannis*: Tyrannicide and Violence as Political Tools in Republican Rome." MA thesis, California State University Northridge, 2013.

Allen-Hornblower, Emily. "Beasts and Barbarians In Caesar's *Bellum Gallicum* 6.21-8." *The Classical Quarterly* 64 (2014): 682-693.

Altman, William Henry Furness. "Self-Revelation and Concealment in Caesar's *De Bello Gallico*: Cicero, Orgetorix, and the Belgae." *Revista Classica* 28 (2015): 161-176.

André, Jacques. "Densité et repartition de la population en Vénétie romaine." *Annales de Bretagne* 67 (1967): 103-106.

Angel, Natalie. "*Clementia Caesaris*: The Creation and Dissemination of a Reputation." PhD diss., University of Sydney, 2006.

Arnold, William Thomas. *The Roman System of Provincial Administration.* Chicago, IL: Ares Publishers, 1974.

Broadhead, William. "Internal Migration and the Transformation of Republican Italy." PhD diss., University College London, 2002.

Badian, Ernst. *Roman Imperialism in the Late Republic.* Ithaca, NY: Cornell University Press, 1971.

Badian, Ernst. *Foreign Clientelae, 264-70 B.C.* New York, NY: Oxford University Press, 2000.

Baker, Gabriel. *Spare No One: Mass Violence in Roman Warfare*. Lanham, MD: Rowman & Littlefield, 2021.

Balázs, György. "Clementia and divinitas: a study of political thought in the first century B.C." *Oikumene* 5 (1986): 243–327.

Balsdon, John P.V.D. "Consular Provinces under the Late Republic, I: General Considerations." *The Journal of Roman Studies* 29 (1939): 57-73.

Balsdon, John P.V.D. "Consular Provinces under the Late Republic, II: Caesar's Gallic Command." *The Journal of Roman Studies* 29 (1939): 167-183.

Balsdon, John P.V.D. "The Ides of March." *Historia* 7 (1958): 80-94.

Balsdon, John P.V.D. *Romans and Aliens*. Chapel Hill, NC: The University of North Carolina Press, 1979.

Barlow, Jonathan. "Noble Gauls and Their Other in Caesar's Propaganda." In *Julius Caesar as Artful Reporter: The War Commentaries as Political Instruments*, edited by Kathryn Welch and Anton Powell, 139-170. Swansea, UK: The Classical Press of Wales, 2009.

Batstone, William W. and Cynthia Damon. *Caesar's Civil War*. Oxford, UK: Oxford University Press, 2006.

Bauman, Richard A. *Crime and Punishment in Ancient Rome*. London, UK: Routledge, 1996.

Bauman, Richard A. *Human Rights in Ancient Rome*. London, UK: Routledge, 2000.

Beare, Rhona. "The Imperial Oath under Julius Caesar." *Latomus* 38 (1979): 469-473.

Bellemore, Jane. "The Roman Concept of Massacre: Julius Caesar in Gaul." In *Theatres of Violence: Massacre, Mass Killing and Atrocity throughout History*, edited by Philip G Dwyer and Lyndall Ryan, 38-49. New York, NY: Berghahn Books, 2012.

Beness, Jillian Lea. "The Urban Unpopularity of Lucius Appuleius Saturninus." *Antichthon* 25 (1991): 33-62.

Berve, Helmut. "Sertorius." *Hermes* 64 (1929): 199-227.

Best, Jan Gijsbert Pieter and Benjamin H Isaac. "The Helvetians: From Foederati to Stipendiarii." *Talenta* 8-9 (1977): 11-32.

Bloxham, Donald and A. Dirk Moses. *The Oxford Handbook of Genocide Studies*. Oxford, UK: Oxford University Press, 2010.

Bodel, John. "'Caveat emptor': Towards a study of Roman Slave-Traders." *Journal of Roman Archaeology* 18 (2005): 181-195.

Boissier, Gaston. *Tacitus and Other Roman Studies.* New York, NY: G. P. Putnam's Sons, 1906.

Broadhead, William. *Internal Migration and the Transformation of Republican Italy.* PhD diss., University College London, 2002

Broughton, Thomas R. S. *The Magistrates of the Roman Republic*, 3 vols. New York, NY: American Philological Association, 1951-1986.

Broughton, Thomas R. S. "Mistreatment of Foreign Legates and the Fetial Priests: Three Roman Cases." *Phoenix* 41 (1987): 50-62.

Brown, Robert D. "A Civilized Gaul: Caesar's Portrait of Piso Aquitanus (*De Bello Gallico* 4.12.4-6.) *Mnemosyne* 67 (2014): 391-404.

Bryen, Ari Z. "Judging Empire: Courts and Culture in Rome's Eastern Provinces." *Law and History Review* 30 (2012): 771-811.

Burton, Graham. "Proconsuls, Assizes and the Administration of Justice under the Empire." *Journal of Roman Studies* 65 (1975): 92-106.

Buszard, Bradley. "Caesar's Ambition: A Combined Reading of Plutarch's 'Alexander-Caesar and 'Pyrrhus-Marius?'" *Transactions of the American Philological Association* 138 (2008): 185-215.

Carroll, Maureen. "Romans, Germans, and Germania." In *The Landmark Julius Caesar: The Complete Works: Gallic War, Civil War, Alexandrian War, African War, Spanish War*, edited by Kurt A. Raaflaub, 49-51. New York, NY: Pantheon Books, 2017.

Cary, Max. "Rome in the Absence of Pompey." *Cambridge Ancient History* 9 (1932): 475-505.

Champion, Craige. "Romans as Barbaroi: Three Polybian Speeches and the Politics of Cultural Indeterminacy." *Classical Philology* 95 (2000): 425-444.

Chircot, Daniel and Jennifer Edwards. "Making Sense of the Senseless: Understanding Genocide." *Contexts* 2 (2003): 12-19.

Chrissanthos, Stefan G. "Caesar and the Mutiny of 47 B.C." *The Journal of Roman Studies* 91 (2001): 63-75.

Collins, John H. "Propaganda, Ethics, and Psychological Assumptions in Caesar's Writings." PhD diss., Johann Wolfgang Goethe University, 1952.

Collins, John H. "Caesar as Political Propagandist." In *Band 1 Politische Geschichte*, edited by Hildegard Temporini and Wolfgang Haase, 922-966. Berlin, DE: De Gruyter, 2016.

Connerton, Paul. *How societies remember*. Cambridge, UK: Cambridge University Press, 1989.

Cook, Stanley Arthur, Frank Ezra Adcock, and Martin Percival Charlesworth. *The Cambridge Ancient History, Volume 9: The Roman Republic 133 - 44 BC.* Cambridge, UK; Cambridge University Press, 1932.

Corbeill, Anthony. "Anticato." In *The Cambridge Companion to the Writings of Julius Caesar*, edited by Luca Grillo and Christopher B. Krebs, 215-222. Cambridge, UK: Cambridge University Press, 2018.

Cotter, Wendy. "The Collegia and Roman Law: State Restrictions on Voluntary Associations, 64 BCE-200 CE." In *Voluntary Associations in the Graeco-Roman World*, edited by John S. Kloppenborg and Stephen G. Wilson, 74-89. London, UK: Routledge, 1996.

Covino, Ralph. "The Fifth Century, the Decemvirate, and the Quaestorship." in *ASCS 32 Selected Proceedings*, editor Anne Mackay (ascs.org.au/news/ascs32/Author.pdf).

Cunliffe, Barry. *Hengistbury Head*. London, UK: Paul Elek, 1978.

Cunliffe, Barry. "Britain, The Veneti and Beyond." *Oxford Journal of Archaeology* 1 (1982): 39-68.

Cursi, Maria Floriana. "International relations in the ancient world." *Fundamina* 20 (2014): 186-195.

Dando-Collins, Stephen. *Caesar's Legion: The Epic Sage of Julius Caesar's Elite Tenth Legion and the Armies of Rome*. Hoboken, NJ: John Wiley & Sons, Inc., 2002.

Delbrück, Hans. *Warfare in Antiquity: History of the Art of War*. Translated by *Walter J. Renfroe. Lincoln, NE: University of Nebraska Press, 1990.*

Deniaux, Elizabeth. "The Money and Power of Friends and Clients: Successful Aediles in Rome." In *Money and Power in the Roman Republic*, edited by Hans Beck, Martin Jehne, and John Serrati, 178-187. Bruxelles, BE: Éditions Latomus, 2016.

De Sanctis, Gaetano. "Rivoluzione e Reazione N'ell'Età dei Gracchi." *Atene e Roma* 2 (1921): 209-237.

Desjardins, Ernest. *Géographie historique et administragtive de la Gaule romaine.* Paris, FR: Libraire Hachette et Cie, 4 vols, 1876-1893.

De Souza, Philip. *Piracy in the Graeco-Roman World.* Cambridge, UK: Cambridge University Press, 1999.

Deutsch, Monroe E. "Veni, Vidi, Vici." *Philological Quarterly* 4 (1925): 151-156.

Deutsch, Monroe E. "Caesar's Triumphs." *The Classical Weekly* 19 (1926): 101-106.

Deutsch, Monroe E. "'I am Caesar, Not Rex'" *Classical Philology* 23 (1928): 394-398.

DeWitt, Norman J. "The Paradox of Gallo-Roman Relations." *The Classical Journal* 37 (1942): 399-406.

DeWitt, Norman J. "Caesar and the Alexander Legend." *The Classical Weekly* 36 (1942): 51-53.

Dilke, Oswald A. W. "The Literary Output of the Roman Emperors." *Greece & Rome* 4 (1957): 78-97.

Dillon, Sheila and Katherine E. Welch. eds. *Representation of War in Ancient Rome.* New York, NY: Cambridge University Press, 2006.

Dowling, Melissa. *Clemency and Cruelty in the Roman World.* Ann Arbor: University of Michigan Press, 2006.

Drogula, Fred K. *Cato the Younger: Life and Death at the End of the Republic.* Oxford, UK: Oxford University Press, 2019.

Duc d'Aumale, Henri d'Orléans. "Alesia: Étude Sur La Septième Campagne de César En Gaule" *Revue des Deux Mondes* 15 (1858): 64-146.

Dyck, Andrew R. *A Commentary on Cicero, De Officiis.* Ann Arbor: University of Michigan Press, 1996.

Dyson, Stephen L. "Native Revolts in the Roman Empire." *Historia: Zeitschrift Für Alte Geschichte* 20 (1971): 239-274.

Dyson, Stephen L. *The Creation of the Roman Frontier.* Princeton, NJ: Princeton University Press, 1985.

Edmondson, Jonathan. "Public Dress and Social Control in Late Republican and Early Imperial Rome." In *Roman Dress and the Fabrics of Roman Culture*, edited by Jonathan Edmondson and Alison Keith, 21-46. Toronto, CA: University of Toronto Press, 2008.

Ellis, Peter Berresford. *Celt and Roman: The Celts of Italy.* London, UK: Constable and Company, 1998.

Epstein, David F. "Caesar's Personal Enemies on the Ides of March." *Latomus* 46 (1987): 566-570.

Evans, Richard J. "Catiline's Wife." *Acta Classica*, 30 (1987): 69-72.

Evans, Richard J. *Gaius Marius: A Political Biography*. Pretoria, ZA: University of South Africa, 1994.

Evans, Richard J. "The Augustan 'Purge' of the Senate and the Census of 86 BC." *Acta Classica* 40 (1997): 77-86.

Ezov, Amiram. "The 'Missing Dimension' of C. Julius Caesar." *Historia: Zeitschrift für Alte Geschichte* 45 (1996): 64-94.

Fairbank, Keith. "Caesar's Portrait of 'Caesar'" In *The Landmark Julius Caesar: The Complete Works: Gallic War, Civil War, Alexandrian War, African War, Spanish War*, edited by Kurt A. Raaflaub, 214-222. New York, NY: Pantheon Books, 2017.

Fantham, Elaine. "Caesar as Intellectual." In *A Companion to Julius Caesar*, edited by Miriam Griffin, 141-156. Chichester, UK: Wiley-Blackwell, 2009.

Feeney, Denis. *Caesar's Calendar: Ancient Time and the Beginnings of History*. Berkeley, CA: University of California Press, 2008.

Felstiner, William L. F. "Influences of Social Organization on Dispute Processing." 9 *Law and Society Review* 63 (1974): 63-94.

Ferrero, Guglielmo. *The Greatness and Decline of Rome - Vol. II, Julius Caesar*. Translated by Alfred E. Zimmern. New York, NY: G. P. Putnam's Sons, 1909.

Ferris, Iain. "Suffering in Silence." *Journal of Conflict Archaeology* 1 (2005): 67-92.

Ferris, Iain M. *Enemies of Rome: Barbarians Through Roman Eyes*. Stroud, UK: Sutton Publishing, 2000.

Fischer, David Hackett. *Historians' Fallacies: Toward a Logic of Historical Thought*. New York, NY: Harper Torchbooks, 1970.

Flower, Harriet I. "Remembering and Forgetting Temple Destruction: The Destruction of the Temple of Jupiter Optimus Maximus in 83 BC." In *Antiquity in Antiquity: Jewish and Christian Pasts in the Greco-Roman World*, edited by Gregg Gardner and Kevin L. Osterloh, 74-92. Tübingen, DE: Mohr Siebeck, 2008.

Flower, Harriet I. *Roman Republics*. Princeton, NJ: Princeton University Press, 2010.

Fowler, Warde W. "Passing under the Yoke." *The Classical Review* 27 (1913): 48-51.

Fowler, Warde W. "An Unnoticed Trait in the Character of Julius Caesar." *The Classical Review* 30 (1916): 68-71.

Frank, Tenney. *Roman Imperialism*. New York, NY: The MacMillan Company, 1914.

Frears, Rufus J. "The Cult of Virtues and Imperial Ideology." *Aufstieg und Niedergang der römischen Welt* 17 (1980) 827-948.

Frere, Sheppard. *Britannia: A History of Roman Britain*. London, UK: Routledge & Kegan Paul, 1987.

Furger-Gunti, Andres. *Die Helvetier: Kulturgeschichte eines Keltenvolkes*. Zürich, CH: Neue Zürcher Zeitung, 1984.

Galassi, Francesco M. and Hutan Ashrafian. "Has the diagnosis of a stroke been overlooked in the symptoms of Julius Caesar?" *Neurological Sciences* 36 (2015): 1521-1522.

Galliou, Patrick. *L'amorique romaine*. Braspars, FR: Les Bibliophiles de Bretagne, 1984.

Gardner, Jane F. "The 'Gallic Menace' in Caesar's Propaganda." *Greece & Rome* 30 (1983): 181-189.

Gardner, Jane F. "The Dictator." In *A Companion to Julius Caesar*, edited by Miriam Griffin, 57-71. Chichester, UK: Wiley-Blackwell, 2009.

Gelzer, Matthias. *Caesar: Politician and Statesman*. Translated by Peter Needham. Oxford, UK: Oxford University Press, 1968.

Gichon, Mordechai. "Military Intelligence in the Roman Army." In *Labor omnibus unus*, edited by Heinz E. Herzig and Regula Frei-Stolba, 154-170. Historia Einzelschriften Stuttgart, GBP: Franz Steiner Verlag Wiesbaden-GmbH., 1989.

Goldsworthy, Adrian. "'Instinctive genius': The depiction of Caesar the general." In *Julius Caesar as Artful Reporter: The War Commentaries as Political Instruments*, edited by Kathryn Welch and Anton Powell, 193-219. Swansea, UK: The Classical Press of Wales, 2009.

Gomes, Flores, José Manuel and Deolinda Carneiro. *Subtus Montis Terroso* CMPV *Origens do Povoamento* (2005): 74-76.

Gomez, Gustavo, Joshua A. Kotler, and Justin B. Long. "Was Julius Caesar's Epilepsy Due to a Brain Tumor? *Journal of the Florida Medical Association* 82 (1995): 199-201.

Gray-Fow, Michael. "WHAT TO DO WITH CAESARION." *Greece & Rome* 61(2014): 38-67.

Green, Peter. "Caesar and Alexander: Aemulatio, Imitatio, Comparatio" In *Classical Bearings: Interpreting Ancient History and Culture*, edited by Peter Green, 193-209. Berkeley, CA: University of California Press, 1989.

Griffin, Miriam, T. "Clementia after Caesar: From Politics to Philosophy." In *Caesar Against Liberty? Perspectives on his Autocracy*, edited by Francis Cairns and Elaine Fantham, 157-182. Cambridge, UK: Cambridge University Press, 2003.

Griffin, Miriam, T. "Introduction." In *A Companion to Julius Caesar*, edited by Miriam Griffin, 1-8. Chichester, UK: Wiley-Blackwell, 2009.

Grillo, Luca. "The limits and risks of Caesar's leniency." In *The Art of Caesar's Bellum Civile: Literature, Ideology, and Community*, 78-105. Cambridge, UK: Cambridge University Press, 2012.

Grillo, Luca, and Christopher B. Krebs. *The Cambridge Companion to the Writings of Julius Caesar*. Cambridge, UK: Cambridge University Press, 2018.

Griswold, Charles L. and David Konstan. *Ancient Forgiveness: Classical, Judaic, and Christian*. New York, NY: Cambridge University Press, 2012.

Gruen, Erich S. *The Last Generation of the Roman Republic*. Berkeley, CA: University of California Press, 1974.

Gruen, Erich S. "Caesar as a Politician." In *A Companion to Julius Caesar*, edited by Miriam Griffin, 23-36. Chichester, UK: Wiley-Blackwell, 2009.

Gruen, Erich S. "The Legitimacy of Caesar's Wars." In *The Landmark Julius Caesar: The Complete Works: Gallic War, Civil War, Alexandrian War, African War, Spanish War*, edited by Kurt A. Raaflaub, 33-39. New York, NY: Pantheon Books, 2017.

Grummel, William C. "The Consular Elections of 59 B.C." *The Classical Journal* 49 (1954): 351-354.

Hall, Lindsay G. H. "Ratio and Romanitas in Bellum Gallicum." *In Julius Caesar as Artful Reporter: The War Commentaries as Political Instruments*, edited by Kathryn Welch and Anton Powell, 11-43. Swansea, UK: The Classical Press of Wales, 2009.

Hamlyn, Tim. "The Nature of Caesar's Illness." *Latomus* 73 (2014): 360-367.

Hanson, Victor D. *The Western Way of War: Infantry Battle in Classical Greece*. New York, NY: Alfred A. Knopf, 1989.

Hardy, Ernest George. *Some Problems in Roman History: Ten Essays Bearing on the Administrative and Legislative Work of Julius Caesar*. Oxford, UK: The Clarendon Press, 1924.

Harris, William V. *War and Imperialism in Republican Rome, 327-70 B. C.* Oxford, UK: Clarendon Press, 1979.

Hedrick, Charles W. Jr. *History and Silence: Purge and Rehabilitation of Memory in Late Antiquity*. Austin, TX: University of Texas Press, 2000.

Hendrickson, George Lincoln. "The De Analogia of Julius Caesar; Its Occasion, Nature, and Date, with Additional Fragments." *Classical Philology* 1 (1906): 97-120.

Henige, David. "He Came, He Saw, We Counted: The Historiography and Demography of Caesar's Gallic Numbers." *Annales de Démographie Historique* 1 (1998): 215-242.

Herman, Edward S. and Noam Chomsky. *Manufacturing Consent: The Political Economy of* the *Mass Media*. New York, NY: Pantheon Books, 1988.

Hiernard, Jean. "Les Santons, les Helvètes et la Celtique d'Europe centrale." Numismatique, archéologie et histoire, *Aquitania* 16 (1999): 93-125.

HÓgáin, Ó Dáithí. *The Celts: A History*. New York, NY: The Collins Press, 2006.

Holmes, T. Rice. *Caesar's Conquest of Gaul*. London, UK: Macmillan and Co., 1899.

Holmes, T. Rice. *Caesar's Commentaries on the Gallic War*. London, UK: Macmillan and Co., 1908.

Holmes, T. Rice. *The Roman Republic and the Founder of the Empire* Vol 1. London, UK: The Clarendon Press, 1923.

Hruşcă, Iulian-Gabriel. "Humanitas–Clementia and Clementia Caesaris Ancient and Modern Caesar." *European Journal of Science and Theology*, 8 (2012): 263-269.

Hubert, Henri. *The Rise of the Celts*. New York, NY: The Dorset Press, 1988.

Hubert, Henri. *The Greatness and Decline of the Celts*. New York, NY: The Dorset Press, 1988.

Hughes, John R. "Dictator Perpetuus: Julius Caesar—Did he have seizures? If so, what was the etiology?" *Epilepsy & Behavior* 5 (2004): 756-764.

Hunt, Lynn, "Against Presentism." *Perspectives on History.* May 1, 2002 https://www.historians.org/research-and-publications/perspectives-on-history/may-2002/against-presentism

Husband, Richard Wellington. "The Prosecution of Catiline's Associates." *The Classical Journal* 9 (1913): 4-23.

Isaac, Benjamin. *The Invention of Racism in Classical Antiquity.* Princeton, NJ: Princeton University Press, 2004.

Jaffé, Felice C. "Gold deposits in Switzerland." In *Mineral deposits of Europe*, Vol 3 edited by Frederick Weir Dunning and Anthony M. Evans, 41-54. London: UK: Institution of Mining and Metallurgy, 1982.

Jaffé, Felice C. "Gold in Switzerland." *Economic Geology* 84 (1989): 1444–1451.

James, Simon. "Facing the Sword: Confronting the Realities of Martial Violence and Other Mayhem, Present and Past." In *The Archaeology of Violence: Interdisciplinary Approaches*, edited by Sarah Ralph, 98-115. Albany, NY: SUNY Press, 2013.

Jervis, Alexa. "*The* Gallic War *as a Work of Propaganda.*" In *The Landmark Julius Caesar: The Complete Works: Gallic War, Civil War, Alexandrian War, African War, Spanish War*, edited by Kurt A. Raaflaub, 236-240. New York, NY: Pantheon Books, 2017.

Jewell, Evan. "(Re)moving the Masses: Colonisation as Domestic Displacement in the Roman Republic." *Humanities* 8.2 66 (2019): 1-41.

Johnston, Andrew C. "Nostri and 'The Other(s)'" In *The Cambridge Companion to the Writings of Julius Caesar*, edited by Luca Grillo and Christopher B. Krebs, 81-94. Cambridge, UK: Cambridge University Press, 2018.

Jones, Christopher. P. "Cicero's 'Cato.'" *Rheinisches Museum für Philologie.* 113 (1970): 188-196.

Joseph, Timothy. "The Verbs Make the Man: A Reading of Caesar *Gallic War* 1.7 and Civil War 1.1 and 3.2." *The New England Classical Journal* 44.3 (2017): 150-161.

Jullian, Camille. *Histoire de La Gaule 2: La Gaule Indépendante.* Paris, FR: Libraire Hachette, 1908.

Jullian, Camille. *Histoire de La Gaule 3: La Conquête Romaine et Les Premières Invasions Germaniques.* Bruxelles, BE: Culture et civilization, 1920.

Kahn, Arthur D. *The Education of Julius Caesar: A Biography, a Reconstruction.* New York, NY: Knopf Doubleday, 1986.

Katz, Barry R. "The First Fruits of Sulla's March." *L'Antiquité Classique* 44 (1975): 100-125.

Kelsey, Francis W. "The Title of Caesar's Work on the Gallic and Civil Wars." *Transactions and Proceedings of the American Philological Association* 36 (1905): 211-238.

Kemezis, Adam. "Dio, Caesar and the Vesontio Mutineers (38.34–47): A Rhetoric of Lies." In *Cassius Dio: Greek Intellectual and Roman Politician*, edited by Jesper Majbom Madsen and Carsten Hjort Lange, 238–257. Leiden, NL: Brill, 2016.

Kerremans, Bernt. "Metus Gallicus, tumultus Cimbricus?: The Possible Promulgation of a *tumultus* in the Cimbrian War (105-101 BCE)." *Mnemosyne* 69 (2016): 822-841.

Kiernan, Ben. "The First Genocide: Carthage, 146 BC." *Diogenes* 203 (2003): 32-48.

Kloevekorn, Heinrichm. *Die Kämpfe Cäsars Gegen Die Helvetier Im Jahre 58 B. C. Eine Kritik von Cäsars Darstellung in Caesaris de bello gallico* 2-29. Leipzig, DE: Druck von Gustav Schmidt, 1889.

Konstan, David. "Clemency as a Virtue." *Classical Philology* 100 (2007): 337-346.

Kopij, Kamil. "When Did Pompey the Great Engage in His *Imitatio Alexandri*?" *Studies in Ancient Art and Civilization* 21 (2017): 119-141.

Kramer, Herbert G. "Aventicum." *The Classical Journal* 36 (1940): 155-163.

Kraus, Christina S. "*Bellum Gallicum*." In *A Companion to Julius Caesar*, edited by Miriam Griffin, 159-174. Chichester, UK: Wiley-Blackwell, 2009.

Krebs, Christopher B. "Caesar the Historian." In *The Landmark Julius Caesar: The Complete Works: Gallic War, Civil War, Alexandrian War, African War, Spanish War*, edited by Kurt A. Raaflaub, 210-212. New York, NY: Pantheon Books, 2017.

Krebs, Christopher B. "More Than Words: The *Commentarii* in their Propagandistic Context." In *The Cambridge Companion to the Writings of Julius Caesar*, edited by Luca Grillo and Christopher B. Krebs, 29-42. Cambridge, UK: Cambridge University Press, 2018.

Kulikowski, Michael. "Barbarians in Gaul, Usurpers in Britain." *Britannia* 31 (2000): 325-345.

Kulikowski, Michael. "A Very Bad Man." *London Review of Books*. 42, no. 12 (June 2020).

Lanni, Adriaan. "The Laws of War in Ancient Greece." *Law, War, and History* 26 (2008): 469-489.

Latimer, Drew. "Gallic Identity in Caesar's Bellum Gallicum." *New England Classical Journal* 44 (2017): 98-113.

Lavan, Myles. "Devastation: the destruction of populations and human landscapes and the Roman imperial project." In *Reconsidering Roman power: Roman, Greek, Jewish and Christian perceptions and reactions, edited by* Katell Berthelot. http://books.openedition.org/efr/4875. Roma, IT: Publications de l'École française de Rome, 2020.

Leach, John. *Pompey the Great*. London, UK: Croom Helm, 1978.

Lee. K. H. "Caesar's Encounter with the Upisetes and Tencteri." *Greece & Rome* 16 (1969): 100-103.

Lemkin, Raphaël. *Axis Rule in Occupied Europe: Laws of Occupation, Analysis of Government, Proposals for Redress*. Washington, DC: Carnegie Endowment for International Peace, 1944.

Lendon. Jon E. "Julius Caesar, Thinking About Battle and Foreign Relations." *Histos* 9 (2015): 1-28.

Levene, Mark. "Introduction." in *The Massacre in History*, edited by Mark Levene and Penny Roberts, 1-38. Oxford, UK: Berghahn Books, 1999.

Levick, Barbara. "The Veneti revisited: C.E. Stevens and the tradition on Caesar the propagandist." In *Julius Caesar as Artful Reporter: The War Commentaries as Political Instruments, edited by* Kathryn Welch and Anton Powell, 61-83. Swansea, UK: The Classical Press of Wales, 2009.

Lintott, Andrew. "The leges de repetundis and Associate Measures Under the Republic." *Zeitschrift der Savigny-Stiftung für Rechtsgeschichte: Romanistische Abteilung* 98 (1981): 162-212.

Littlewood, R. Joy. "Loyalty and the Lyre: Constructions of *Fides* in Hannibal's Capuan Banquets." In *Flavian Poetry and Its Greek Past, Past*, edited by Antony Augoustakis, 267-285. Boston, MA: Brill, 2014.

Lopez. Davina C. *Apostle to the Conquered: Reimagining Paul's Mission*. Minneapolis, MN: Fortress Press, 2010.

Lot, Ferdinand. *La Gaule. Les fondements ethniques, sociaux et politiques de la nation francaise.* Paris, FR: Librairie Artheme Fayard, 1947.

Lovano, Michael. *The Age of Cinna: Crucible of Late Republican Rome.* Stuttgart, DE: Franz Steiner Verlag, 2002.

Malleson, George B. "Vercingetorix." *Transactions of the Royal Historical Society* 4 (1889): 1-40.

Marincola, John. *Authority* and Tradition in Ancient Historiography. Cambridge, UK: Cambridge University Press, 1997.

Marshall, Bruce. "The Date of Catilina's Marriage to Aurelia Orestilla." *Rivista di Filologia e di Istruzione Classica* 105 (1977): 151-154.

Marshall, Bruce. "Catilina and the Execution of M. Marius Gratidianus." *Classical Quarterly* 35 (1985): 124-133.

Mattern, Susan. *Rome and the Enemy: Imperial Strategy in the Principate.* Berkeley, CA: University of California Press, 1999.

Matthaei, Louise E. "On the Classification of Roman Allies." *The Classical Quarterly* 1 (1907): 182-204.

Matthews, Lydia. "Lydia. Roman Constructions of Fortuna." PhD diss., University of Oxford, 2011.

Mays, Melinda. "Strabo IV 4.1: a reference to Hengistbury Head?" *Antiquity* 55 (1981): 55-57.

McDermott, William C. "In Ligarianam." *Transactions and Proceedings of the American Philological Association* 101 (1970): 317-347.

Meier, Christian. *Caesar: A Biography.* New York, NY: Basic Books, 1982.

Melchior, Aislinn Aja, "Compositions with blood: Violence in late Republican prose." PhD diss., University of Pennsylvania, 2004.

Merlat, Pierre. "Les Vénètes d'Amorique, problèmes d'histoire et d'administration." *Memoires de la Société d'histoire et d'archéologie de Bretagne* 39 (1959): 5-40.

Messer, William S. "Mutiny in the Roman army. The Republic." *Classical Philology* 15 (1920): 158-171.

Mierow, Charles Christopher. "Julius Caesar as a Man of Letters." *The Classical Journal* 41(1946): 353-357.

Mommsen, Theodor. "Schweizer Nachstudien." *Hermes* 16 (1881): 445-494.

Morgan, Llewelyn. "The Autopsy of C. Asinius Pollio." *The Journal of Roman Studies* 90 (2000): 51-69.

Morrell, Kit. "Cato, Caesar, and the Germani." *Antichthon* 49 (2015): 73-93.

Morrell, Kit. *Pompey, Cato, and the Governance of the Roman Empire*. Oxford, UK: Oxford University Press, 2017.

Morstein-Marx, Robert. "Political Graffiti in the Late Roman Republic: 'Hidden Transcripts' and 'Common Knowledge.'" In *Politische Kommunikation und öffentliche Meinung in der antiken Welt* edited by Christina Kuhn, 191-217. Stuttgart, DE: Steiner, 2012.

Morteani, Giukio and Jeremy P. Northover. *Prehistoric Gold in Europe: Mines, Metallurgy and Manufacture*. Dordrecht, NL: Kluwer Academic Publishers, 1996.

Moscovich, Maurice James. The Role of Hostages in Roman Foreign Policy." PhD diss., McMaster University, 1972.

Moscovich, Maurice James. "Obsidibus traditis: Hostages in Caesar's *De bello Gallico*."The *Classical Journal* 75 (1979–80): 122–128.

Murphy, Charles T. "The Use of Speeches in Caesar's Gallic War." *The Classical Journal* 45 (1949): 120-127

Murray, E. W. "Caesar's Fortifications on the Rhone." *The Classical Journal* 4 (1909): 309-320.

Napoleon III. *Histoire de Jules César*, Vol 2, Guerre des Gaules. Paris, FR: Henri Plon, 1866.

North, John A. "The Development of Roman Imperialism." *The Journal of Roman Studies* 71 (1981): 1-9.

Nousek, Debra L. "*The* Gallic War as a Work of Literature." In *The Landmark Julius Caesar: The Complete Works: Gallic War, Civil War, Alexandrian War, African War, Spanish War*, edited by Kurt A Raaflaub, 229-235. New York, NY: Pantheon Books, 2017.

Nousek, Debra L. "Genres and Generic Contaminations: The *Commentarii*." In *The Cambridge Companion to the Writings of Julius Caesar*, edited by Luca Grillo and Christopher B. Krebs, 97-109. Cambridge, UK: Cambridge University Press, 2018.

Odahl, Charles Matson. "The Rise and Fall of the Catilinarian Conspiracy." MA thesis, Fresno State College, 1968.

O'Donnell, James J. *Julius Caesar. The War for Gaul: A New Translation.* Princeton, NJ: Princeton University Press, 2019

Oldfather, William A. "Livy 1.26 and the *Supplicium de More Maiorum.*" *TAPA* 39 (1908): 49-72.

Opperman, Hans. *Probleme und heutiger Stand der Caesarforschung.* In *Caesar*, edited by Detlef Rasmussen, 485-522. Darmstadt, DE: Wissenschaftliche Buchgesellschaft, 1967.

Osgood, Josiah. "Caesar and Nicomedes." *Classical Quarterly* 58 (2008): 687-691.

Ida Östenberg. "VENI VIDI VICI AND CAESAR'S TRIUMPH" *Classical Quarterly* 63 (2013): 813–827.

Otis, Alvah Talbot. "The Helvetian Campaign. Was Caesar Wise or Wilful? An Examination of the Hypothesis of Ferrero Part I." *The Classical Journal* 9 (1914): 241-250.

Otis, Alvah Talbot. "The Helvetian Campaign. Part II." *The Classical Journal* 9 (1914): 292-300.

Paterson, Jeremy. "Caesar the Man." In *A Companion to Julius Caesar*, edited by Miriam Griffin, 126-140. Chichester, UK: Wiley-Blackwell, 2009.

Pezzini, Giuseppe. "Caesar the Linguist: The Debate about the Latin Language." In *The Cambridge Companion to the Writings of Julius Caesar*, edited by Luca Grillo and Christopher B. Krebs, 173-192. Cambridge, UK: Cambridge University Press, 2018.

Potter, Bradley G. "Constructing Caesar: Julius Caesar's Caesar and the Creation of the Myth of Caesar in History and Space." PhD diss., The Ohio State University, 2004.

Powell, Anton. "Julius Caesar and the Presentation of Massacre." *In Julius Caesar as Artful Reporter: The War Commentaries as Political Instruments*, edited by Kathryn Welch and Anton Powell, 111-137. Swansea, UK: The Classical Press of Wales, 2009.

Pucci Ben Zeev, Miriam. "When was the title '*Dictator perpetuus*' given to Caesar?" *L'Antiquité Classique* 65 (1996): 251-253.

Raaflaub, Kurt. *Dignitatis contentio. Studien zur Motivation und politischen Taktik im Bürgerkrieg zwischen Caesar und Pompeius.* Munich, DE: C. H. Beck, 1974.

Raaflaub, Kurt A. "The Roman *Commentarius* and Caesar's Commentaries." In *The Landmark Julius Caesar: The Complete Works: Gallic War, Civil War, Alexandrian War, African War, Spanish War*, edited by Kurt A. Raaflaub, 203-209. New York, NY: Pantheon Books, 2017.

Raaflaub, Kurt A. "The Civil War as a Work of Propaganda." In *The Landmark Julius Caesar: The Complete Works: Gallic War, Civil War, Alexandrian War, African War, Spanish War*, edited by Kurt A. Raaflaub, 246-254. New York, NY: Pantheon Books, 2017.

Raaflaub, Kurt A. ed. The Landmark Julius Caesar: The Complete Works: *Gallic War, Civil War, Alexandrian War, African War, Spanish War.* New York, NY: Pantheon Books, 2017.

Radin, Max. "The International Law of the Gallic Campaigns." *The Classical Journal* 12 (1916): 8-33.

Radin, Max. "The Date of Composition of Caesar's Gallic War." *Classical Philology* 13 (1918): 283-300.

Rambaud, Michel. *De bello Gallico. Secundus tertiusque libri.* Paris, FR: Presses Universitaires de France, 1965.

Rambaud, Michel. *L'art de la déformation historique dans les Commentaires de César.* Paris, FR: Les Belles Lettres, 2011.

Ramsey, John T. "The Proconsular Years: Politics at a Distance." In *A Companion to Julius Caesar*, edited by Miriam Griffin, 37-56. Chichester, UK: Wiley-Blackwell, 2009.

Ranzani, Giacomo Amilcare Mario. "The Rebellion of Dumnorix and the Second Expedition to Britain." *Maia* 70 (2018): 461-476.

Raubitschek, Anthony E. "Epigraphical Notes on Julius Caesar." *The Journal of Roman Studies* 44 (1954): 65-75.

Rawlings, Louis. "Caesar's portrayal of Gauls as warriors." In *Julius Caesar as Artful Reporter: The War Commentaries as Political Instruments*, edited by Kathryn Welch and Anton Powell, 171-192. Swansea, UK: The Classical Press of Wales, 2009.

Rawlings, Louis. "The Roman Conquest of Southern Gaul, 125-121 BC." In *The Encyclopedia of Ancient Battles,* edited by Michael Whitby and Harry Sidebottom, 858-864. Hoboken, NJ: Wiley Blackwell, 2017.

Rawlinson, Canon. "On the Ethnography of the Cimbri." *The Journal of the Anthropological Institute of Great Britain and Ireland* 6 (1877): 150-158.

Retief, Francois P. and Johan F. G. Cilliers. "Julius Caesar (100-44 BC)—Did He Have a Brain Tumour?" *South African Medical Journal* 100 (2010): 26-28.

Reynolds, Joyce. "Cyrenaica, Pompey and Cn. Cornelius Lentulus Marcellinus." *The Journal of Roman Studies* 52 (1962): 97-103.

Rich, John. "The *Fetiales* and Roman International Relations." In *Priests and State in the Roman World*, edited by James H. Richardson and Federico Santangelo, 185-240. Stuttgart, DE: Franz Steiner Verlag, 2011.

Richard, Ernst. *History of German Civilization*. New York, NY: The Macmillan Company, 1913.

Richardson, John S. "The Purpose of the Lex Calpurnia de Repetundis." *The Journal of Roman Studies* 77 (1987): 1-12.

Riggsby, Andrew M. *Caesar in Gaul and Rome: War in Words*. Austin, TX: University of Texas Press, 2006.

Robinson, Joshua John. "Pompey's Organization of the East." MA thesis, University of Central Florida, 2013.

Rosenberger, Veit. "The Gallic Disaster." *The Classical World* 96 (2003): 365-373.

Rosenstein, Nathan. "General and Imperialist." In *A Companion to Julius Caesar*, edited by Miriam Griffin, 85-99. Chichester, UK: Wiley-Blackwell, 2009.

Roymans, Nico. *Ethnic Identity and Imperial Power: The Batavians in the Early Roman Empire*. Amsterdam, NL: Amsterdam University Press, 2004.

Roymans, Nico. "A Roman massacre in the far north. Caesar's annihilation of the Tencteri and Usipetes. in the Dutch river area." In *Conflict archaeology: materialities of collective violence in late prehistoric and early historic Europe*, Themes in Contemporary Archaeology, edited by Manuel Fernández-Götz and Nico Roymans, 167-181. London, UK: Routledge, 2018.

Rozeboom, Aaron. "The Rhetorical Implications of *Clementia* in Cicero's Caesarian Speeches." *McNair Scholars Journal* 11 (2007): 82-90.

Saddington, Dennis Bain. "Roman attitudes to the '*externae gentes*' of the North." *Acta Classica* 4 (2014): 90-102.

Saeger, Robin. *Pompey: A Political Biography*. Berkeley, CA: University of California Press, 1979.

Salmon. Edward T. "Catiline, Crassus, and Caesar." *The American Journal of Philology* 56 (1935): 302-316.

Sands, Percy Cooper. *The Client Princes of the Roman Empire Under the Republic.* New York, NY: Arno Press, 1975.

Sanquer, René. "Amphorae Romaines trouvees à Alet en Saint Malo." *Les Dossiers du Centre Regional Archeologique d'Alet* 6 (1978): 51-56.

Schadee, Hester. "Caesar the Ethnographer." In *The Landmark Julius Caesar: The Complete Works: Gallic War, Civil War, Alexandrian War, African War, Spanish War*, edited by Kurt A. Raaflaub, 223-228. New York, NY: Pantheon Books, 2017.

Sémelin, Jacques and Cynthia Schoch. *Purify and Destroy: The Political Uses of Massacre and Genocide.* New York, NY: Columbia University Press, 2009.

Sheldon, Rose Mary. "Tinker, Tailor, Caesar, Spy: Espionage in Ancient Rome." PhD diss., University of Michigan, 1987.

Sherwin-White, Adrian Nicholas. "Caesar as an Imperialist." *Greece & Rome* 4 (1957): 36-45.

Sherwin-White, Adrian Nicholas. *The Roman Citizenship.* Oxford, UK: Clarendon Press, 1973.

Sinclair, Patrick. "Political declension in Latin grammar and oratory 55 B.C.E.-C.E. 39." *Ramus* 23 (1994): 92-109.

Slonsky, Kristin. "The Manipulation of Fear in Julius Caesar's *Bellum Gallicum*." MA thesis, Dalhousie University, 2008.

Smith Richard E. "The Conspiracy and the Conspirators." *Greece & Rome* 4 (1957): 58-70.

Smith, Richard E. "The Significance of Caesar's Consulship in 59 B. C." *Phoenix* 18 (1964): 303-313.

Smith, William. ed. *Dictionary of Greek and Roman Antiquities.* New York, NY: Harper & Brothers, 1870.

Smith, William, William Wayte, and George E. Marindin, eds., *A Dictionary of Greek and Roman Antiquities.* London: John Murray, 1890.

Spaeth, John W. "Caesar's Friends and Enemies among the Poets." *The Classical Journal* 32 (1937): 541-556.

Spaeth, John William Jr. "Caesar's Poetic Interests." *The Classical Journal* 26 (1931): 598-604.

Sparavigna, Amelia Carolina. "Julius Caesar and the Germans." 10.5281/zenodo.1870892, 2018.

Steel, Catherine. "Friends, Associates, and Wives." In *A Companion to Julius Caesar*, edited by Miriam Griffin, 112-125. Chichester, UK: Wiley-Blackwell, 2009.

Steel, Catherine. "Pompeius, Helvius Mancia and the politics of public debate. In *Community and Communication: Oratory and Politics in Republican Rome, edited by Catherine Steel and* Henriette van der Blom, 151-159. Oxford, UK: Oxford University Press, 2013.

Stevens, Courtenay E. "The *Bellum Gallicum* as a Work of Propaganda." *Latomus*, (1952): 3-18.

Stimson, Jacqueline J. "Killing Romans: Legitimizing Violence in Cicero and Caesar." PhD diss., University of Michigan, 2017.

Stoffel, Le Colonel. *Histoire de Jules César. Guerre Civile*. Vol 2, Paris, FR: Imprimerie Nationale, 1887.

Stoffel, Le Colonel. *Guerre de César Et d'Arioviste Et Premières Opérations de César En l'An 702*. Paris, FR: Imprimerie Nationale, 1890.

Strasburger, Hermann. *Caesars Eintritt in die Geschichte*. Munich, DE: Neuer Filser Verlag, 1938.

Strasburger, Hermann. 'Poseidonios on Problems of the Roman Empire." *The Journal of Roman Studies* 55 (1965): 40-53.

Strauss, Richard. *The Death of Caesar: The Story of History's Most Famous Assassination*. New York, NY: Simon & Schuster, 2015.

Sumner, Graham V. "Roman Policy in Spain before the Hannibalic War." *Harvard Studies in Classical Philology* 72 (1968): 205-246.

Sumner, Graham V. "Notes on Provinciae in Spain (197-133 B. C.)." *Classical Philology* 72 (1977): 126-130.

Sullivan, Dennis, (2017). "STATE AND CHURCH ON THE REMISSION OF SIN: Seneca the Younger v. Pope Francis; Preliminary Notes on a Debate Regarding the Efficacy of Clemency versus Mercy as a Source of Well-Being For Recipients as well as Practitioners. Paper presented at the 54th Annual Institute of The Classical Association of the Empire State, October 27-28 at Union College, Schenectady, NY.

Suolahti, Jaako. *The Roman Censors: A Study on Social Structure*. Annales Academiae Scientiarum Fennicae 117. Helsinki, FI: Suomalainen Tiedakatemia, 1963.

Syme, Ronald. "Helvetian Aristocrats." *Museum Helveticum* 34 (1977): 129-140.

Syme, Ronald. "Caesar as *Pontifex Maximus*." In *Approaching the Roman Revolution: Papers on Republican History*, edited by Federico Santangelo, 186-195. Oxford, UK: Oxford University Press, 2017.

Taylor, Lily Ross. "Caesar's Early Career." *Classical Philology* 36 (April 1941): 113-132.

Taylor, Lily Ross. "The Election of the Pontifex Maximus in the Late Republic." *Classical Philology* 37 (1942): 421-424.

Taylor, Lily Ross. "Caesar and the Roman Nobility." *Transactions of the American Philological Association* 73 (1942): 1-24.

Taylor, Lily Ross. *Party Politics in the Age of Caesar*, Sather Classical Lectures 22. Berkeley and Los Angeles, CA: University of California Press, 1949.

Taylor, Lily Ross. "The Date and the Meaning of the Vettius Affair." *Historia: Zeitschrift Für Alte Geschichte* 1 (1950): 45-51.

Taylor, Lily Ross. "On the Chronology of Caesar's First Consulship." *The American Journal of Philology* 72 (1951): 254-268.

Taylor, Lily Ross. "The Rise of Julius Caesar." *Greece & Rome* 4 (1957): 10-18.

Taylor, Lily Ross. *The Voting Districts of the Roman Republic: The Thirty-five Urban and Rural Tribes*. Papers and Monographs of the American Academy in Rome, 20 Rome, 1960.

Telford, Lynda. *Sulla: A Dictator Reconsidered*. Barnsley, UK: Pen and Sword Books, 2014.

Thijs, Simon. "Hostages of Rome." *Athens Journal of History* 2 (2016): 199-212.

Thompson, Lloyd A. "The Relationship Between Provincial Quaestors and Their Commanders-in-Chief." *Historia* 11 (1962): 339-355.

Thorne, James. "The Chronology of the Campaign against the Helvetii: A Clue to Caesar's Intentions." *Historia: Zeitschrift für Alte Geschichte* 56 (2007): 27-36.

Toch, Hans. *Violent Men: An Inquiry into the Psychology of Violence*. Chicago, IL: Aldine Publishing Company, 1969.

Todd, Alexander K. "Forced Perception: Evaluating the Validity and Applicability of the *Adulescentulus Carnifex* Label in Relation to the Early Career Character of Gnaeus Pompeius Magnus." MA thesis, University of Amsterdam, 2019.

Torigian, Catherine. "The Λόγος of Caesar's *Bellum Gallicum*, especially as revealed in its first five chapters." In *Julius Caesar as Artful Reporter: The War Commentaries as Political Instruments, edited by* Kathryn Welch and Anton Powell, 45-60. Swansea, UK: The Classical Press of Wales, 2009.

Townsend, Gavin B. "C. Oppius on Julius Caesar." *The American Journal of Philology* 108 (1987): 325-342.

Toynbee, Jocelyn M. C. "Portraits of Julius Caesar." *Greece & Rome* 4 (1957): 2-9.

Tranoy, Laurence. "Mediolanum Santonum, Saintes : de la fondation à l'époque julio-claudienne," *Roma. La época de la expansión exterior de Roma. Cartago*, Alicante: Biblioteca Virtual Miguel de Cervantes, 2007.

Treu, Max. "Zur clementia Caesaris." *Museum Helveticum* 5 (1948): 197-217.

Tröster, Manuel. "Roman Hegemony and Non-State Violence: A Fresh Look at Pompey›s Campaign against the Pirates." *Greece and Rome* 56 (2009): 14-33.

Turquin, Pierre. "La Bataille de la Selle (du Sabis) en l'An 57 avant J.-C." *Les Études Classiques* 23/2 (1955): 113-156.

Tyrrell, Robert Velverton and Louis Clause Purser. "Introduction." in *The Correspondence of M. Tullius Cicero*, Vol V. Second ed. Dublin, IE: Hodges, Figgis, & Co, 1915.

Tyrrell, William B. "*Biography* of Titus Labienus, Caesar's Lieutenant in Gaul." PhD diss., Michigan State University, 1970.

Tyrrell, William B. "Labienus' Departure from Caesar in January 49 B.C." *Historia* 21 (1972): 224-240.

Tyrrell, William Blake. "The Trial of C. Rabirius in 63 B.C." *Latomus* 32 (1973): 285-300.

Urch, Erwin J. "Procedure in the Courts of the Roman Provincial Governors." *The Classical Journal* 25 (1929): 93-101.

Vahl, Jessica. "Imperial Representations of *Clementia*: From Augustus to Marcus Aurelius." Master's thesis, McMaster University, 2007.

Valsan, Remus. "Fides, bona fides, and bonus vir." *Journal of Law, Religion and State* 5 (2017): 48-85.

Van Wees, Hans. "*Stasis*, Destroyer of Men." In *Sécurité collective et ordre public dans les sociétés anciennes*, edited by Cédric Brélaz and Pierre Ducrey, 1-48. Genève, CH: Fondation Hardt, 2008.

Van Wees, Hans. "Genocide in the Ancient World." In *The Oxford Handbook of Genocide Studies*, edited by Donald Bloxham and A. Dirk Moses, 239-258. Oxford, UK: Oxford University Press, 2010.

VerSteeg, Russ. "Law and Justice in Caesar's *Gallic Wars*." *Hofstra Law Review* 33 (2004): 571-601.

Walter, Gérard. *Caesar: A Biography*. Translated by Emma Craufurd. New York: Charles Scribner's Sons, 1952.

Ward, Allen M. "Caesar and the Pirates II: The Elusive M. Junius Iuncus and the Year 75/4." *American Journal of Ancient History* 2 (1977): 26-36.

Wardle, David. "Caesar and Religion." In *A Companion to Julius Caesar*, edited by Miriam Griffin, 100-111. Chichester, UK: Wiley-Blackwell, 2009.

Weatherhill, Craig. "The ships of the Veneti: a fresh look at the Iron Age tin ships." *Cornish Archaeology* 24 (1985): 163-169.

Weinstock, Stefan. *Divus Julius*. Oxford, UK: The Clarendon Press, 1971.

Welch, Katherine E. "Introduction." In *Representation of War in Ancient Rome*, edited by Sheila Dillon and Katherine E. Welch, 1-26. New York, NY: Cambridge University Press, 2006.

Welch, Kathryn. "Caesar and his officers in the Gallic War Commentaries." In *Julius Caesar as Artful Reporter: The War Commentaries as Political Instruments*, edited by Kathryn Welch and Anton Powell, 85-110. Swansea, UK: The Classical Press of Wales, 2009.

Welch, Kathryn and Anton Powell. *Julius Caesar as Artful Reporter: The War Commentaries as Political Instruments*. Swansea, UK: The Classical Press of Wales, 2009.

Westermann, William L. *The Slave Systems of Greek and Roman Antiquity*. Philadelphia, PA: The American Philosophical Society, 1955.

Westington, Mars McClelland. "Atrocities in Roman Warfare to 133 B.C." PhD diss., Chicago, IL: University of Chicago Libraries, 1938.

Wickham, Jason Paul. "The Enslavement of War Captives by the Romans to 146 BC." PhD diss., University of Liverpool, 2014.

Wightman, Edith Mary. *Roman Trier and the Treveri*. London, UK: Hart-Davis, 1970.

Wightman, Edith Mary. *Gallia Belgica*. Berkeley, CA: University of California Press, 1985.

Willi, Andreas. "Campaigning for *utilitas*: Style, grammar and philosophy in C. Julius Caesar." In *Colloquial and Literary Latin*, edited by Eleanor Dickey and Anna Chahoud, 229-242. Cambridge, UK: Cambridge University Press, 2010.

Winterbottom, Michael. "Caesar." In *Texts and Transmission*, edited by Leighton Durham Reynolds, 35-36. Oxford, UK: Oxford University Press, 1983.

Wiseman, Timothy Peter. "The publication of *De Bello Gallico*." In *Julius Caesar as Artful Reporter: The War Commentaries as Political Instruments, edited by* Kathryn Welch and Anton Powell, 1-9. Swansea, UK: The Classical Press of Wales, 2009.

Wistrand, Erik. *Caesar and Contemporary Roman Society*. Göteborg, SE: Kungl. Vetenskaps- Och Vitterhets-Samhället. 1979.

Worthington, Ian. "How 'great' was Alexander." In *Alexander the Great: A Reader*, edited by Ian Worthington, 303-318. London, UK: Routledge, 2003.

Zanker, Paul. "The Irritating Statues and Contradictory Portraits of Julius Caesar." In *A Companion to Julius Caesar*, edited by Miriam Griffin, 288-314. Chichester, UK: Wiley-Blackwell, 2009.

Ziolkowski, Adam. "The Plundering of Epirus in 167 B.C: Economic Considerations." *Papers of the British School at Rome 54* (1986): 69-80.

ACKNOWLEDGMENTS

Of course, a work of this sort requires an extraordinary supportive infrastructure. I therefore wish to thank all the gifted scholars who have dedicated their lives to creating enlightening books and articles on Caesar and the Roman Republic. For any word or phrase I have failed to pay them credit for in my references, I offer the sincerest *mea culpa*. I would like to call attention as well to the work of Ms. Molly Davis, the interlibrary loan specialist at the Voorheesville Public Library, Albany County, NY who secured every item in the bibliography not available in my personal library. Then comes James Coyne who offered his services as a tireless copy editor of the work; formerly an award-winning headmaster of a lauded high school in Connecticut, Mr. Coyne was a Latin student of mine 60 years ago. At different junctures in his editing he was assisted by his former classmates at St. Patrick's High School in Newburgh, NY, Albert Pacione and Bob "Tetter" Rogers. Georgia Gray also offered a most discerning eye for every errant "p" and "q" within the manuscript. For her expertise in the design and production of the book, I call attention to the highly creative spirit of Meradith Kill at Troy Book Makers; she is an artist. And it is not possible to pass over the emergency technical support Frank Faber of Delanson, NY offered on more than one occasion to keep the presses rolling on my iMac. Dedicated scholars Terry MacAvery and Ed Sausville—former Latin students of mine at St. Patrick's 59 and 58 years ago respectively—also offered valuable comments on the text. And, finally, esteemed Caesar translator and scholar James O'Donnell at Arizona State University offered welcome insights into the manuscript and, in his own way, has served as a valued bellwether.

DENNIS SULLIVAN is a poet who lives in Voorheesville, New York with his wife Georgia Gray and their feline family: Clare; Catherine (aka Slinky); Stephanie; Juniper; and Fiddler. Dennis has served as the Voorheesville Village Historian for 37 years and in that capacity has written a number of local history texts most prominent of which is *Voorheesville, New York: A Sketch of the Beginnings of a Nineteenth Century Railroad Town*. In 2017 his history of a small Catholic high school in Newburgh, New York, where he taught from 1963-1967, was published: *The Little Engine That Could, and Did: A Memoir and Brief History of The Christian Brothers in Newburgh, New York From Their Arrival in 1866 Until Their Departure in 1969*. It was followed by *Homeward Bound: Sixty-Two Stories from The Enterprise*, a collection of his award-winning column "Field Notes" in the Albany County weekly, *The Altamont Enterprise*. Early on, his well-received *Handbook of Restorative Justice: A Global Perspective*, edited with Larry Tifft, was voted Outstanding Book of 2007 by *Choice* and his *The Punishment of Crime in Colonial New York: The Dutch Experience in Albany During the Seventeenth Century* received the Hendricks Manuscript Award in 1997.